THE
GENERALITY
OF
DEVIANCE

THE
GENERALITY
OF
DEVIANCE

Edited by
Travis Hirschi &
Michael R. Gottfredson

Transaction Publishers
New Brunswick (U.S.A.) and London (U.K.)

Library of Congress Catalog Number: 93-16816
ISBN: 1-56000-116-X
Printed in the United States of America

Library of Congress Cataloging-in-Publication Data
The Generality of deviance / edited by Travis Hirschi, Michael R. Gottfredson.
    p. cm.
  Includes bibliographical references (p.   ) and index.
  ISBN 1-56000-116-X
  1. Deviant behavior. 2. Self-control. I. Hirschi, Travis. II. Gottfredson, Michael R.
HM291.G33   1993
302.5'42—dc20
                                                    93-16816
                                                       CIP

Contents

List of Tables   vii

List of Figures   xi

Acknowledgments   xiii

1. The Generality of Deviance   1
   Travis Hirschi and Michael R. Gottfredson

2. Aggression   23
   Michael R. Gottfredson and Travis Hirschi

3. Family   47
   Travis Hirschi

4. Gender and Crime   71
   Mary Ann Zager

5. Accidents   81
   Marianne Junger

6. Motor Vehicle Accidents   113
   David W. M. Sorensen

7. Driving Under the Influence   131
   George C. Strand, Jr. and Michael S. Garr

8. Drugs and Alcohol   149
   Carolyn Uihlein

9. Rape   159
   Victor Larragoite

10. Versatility   173
    Chester L. Britt

11. Participation and Frequency   193
    Chester L. Britt

12. The Victim-Offender Relationship   215
    Leonore M. J. Simon

13. Unemployment, Marital Discord, and Deviant Behavior:
    The Long-term Correlates of Childhood Misbehavior   235
    John H. Laub and Robert J. Sampson

14. Substantive Positivism and the Idea of Crime   253
        Travis Hirschi and Michael R. Gottfredson

    Contributors   271

    Index   273

List of Tables

Table 2.1. Correlations among Measures of Aggression, Theft, Drug Use, and Exogenous Variables 32

Table 2.2. Laboratory Aggression by Race and Sex 33

Table 2.3. Correlations among Measures of Aggression 37

Table 2.4. Percent with Police or Court Records, by Self-Reported Aggression 38

Table 2.5. Correlates of Aggressive Behavior and Alternative Measures of Low Self-Control 38

Table 3.1. Correlations between Parental Supervision, Mother's Supervision, Number of Siblings, and Various Indicators of Self- Control 56

Table 3.2. Percent of Adolescents Deviant by Parental Makeup of Home 60

Table 3.3. Percent of Adolescents Deviant by Number of Siblings 62

Table 3.4. Percent with Police Record by Parental Makeup of Home and Number of Siblings 63

Table 4.1. Male/Female Prevalence Ratios for Seven Delinquency Items 76

Table 4.2. Coefficients for Logistic Regression Models 78

Table 5.1. Accident Mortality in Europe and North America from Motor Vehicle Accidents, Accidents Caused by Fire, Accidental Drownings, and All Causes, by Age and Sex 100

Table 5.2. Race Mortality Ratios of Children by Age and Sex 101

Table 5.3. Serious Accidents among Delinquents and Nondelinquents 103

Table 5.4. Factors Related to Accidents and to Delinquency among Juveniles 106

Table 6.1. Personality Survey on Group of Taxi Drivers 117

Table 6.2. Social Records of 96 Accident Repeaters and 100 Accident-Free Drivers 118

Table 7.1. Correlation Matrix of Conforming, Drug Use, Risky Driving, and DUI Variables 139

Table 7.2. Hierarchical Multiple Regression Model of DUI
   with Conforming, Drug Use, and Risky Driving Variables   141

Table 8.1. Recency of Marijuana Use, 1982   150

Table 8.2. Correlations of Delinquency and Drug Use
   between and across Waves, National Youth Survey   151

Table 8.3. Correlations of Delinquency across Waves 1–4
   of National Youth Survey   152

Table 8.4. Correlations of Drug Use across Waves 1–4
   of National Youth Survey   152

Table 8.5. Correlations among Individual Drug Variables,
   National Youth Survey, by Wave   154

Table 8.6. Correlations between Delinquency, Drug Use,
   and Independent Variables, by Wave   155

Table 9.1. Average Annual Rate of Completed and Attempted
   Rape, by Selected Characteristics of Female Victims,
   1973–87   169

Table 9.2. Age of Females Victims of Rape with One Victim
   and One Offender, by Age of Offender, 1979–87   171

Table 10.1. Logistic Regression Results by Race and Gender
   for Offenders with One or More Prior Arrests   185

Table 10.2. Interaction Effects by Race and Gender for
   Offenders with One or More Prior Arrests   185

Table 10.3. Latent-Class Model Fits for All Males in the
   Seattle Youth Study   188

Table 10.4. Latent-Class Model Fits for White Males in
   the Seattle Youth Study   188

Table 10.5. Latent-Class Model Fits for Nonwhite Males
   in the Seattle Youth Study   189

Table 11.1. Bail Decisionmaking Study Means, Standard
   Deviations, and Ranges for the Participation and
   Frequency Analyses   198

Table 11.2. Probit and Tobit Estimates With Standard
   Errors for the Bail Decisionmaking Study Participation
   and Frequency Analyses   200

Table 11.3. Seattle Youth Study Means, Standard
   Deviations, and Ranges for the Participation and
   Frequency Analyses   201

Table 11.4. National Youth Survey Means, Standard Deviations, and Ranges for the Participation and Frequency Analyses   202

Table 11.5. Probit and Tobit Estimates with Standard Errors for the Seattle Youth Study Participation and Frequency Analyses   206

Table 11.6. Probit Estimates with Standard Errors for the National Youth Survey Participation Analyses, Waves 1 through 4   207

Table 11.7. Tobit Estimates with Standard Errors for the National Youth Survey Frequency Analyses for One or More Delinquent Acts, Waves 1 through 4   208

Table 11.8. Tobit Estimates with Standard Errors for the National Youth Survey Frequency Analyses for Five or More Delinquent Acts, Waves 1 through 4   209

Table 12.1. Offender Self-Report Questionnaire   218

Table 12.2. Median and Mean Annual Offense Rates   220

Table 12.3. Sample Characteristics: Past Offenses and Behaviors   223

Table 12.4. Number of Offenses/Acts Committed during the Three-Year Period, by Victim-Offender Relationship   224

Table 12.5. Versatility Scale—Number of Crime Types in Which Respondent Is Active   226

Table 12.6. Varimax Rotated Factor Loading of Eleven Offenses on "Violent Offense" and "Property Offense" Factors   227

Table 12.7. Factor Loadings of Eleven Offenses Forced into One Factor, Total Sample   228

Table 12.8. Correlations between Offense Rates for Specific Crimes and Summary Indices   229

Table 13.1. Relationships between Delinquent and Antisocial Behavior in Childhood and Later Adult Crime and Deviance   242

Table 13.2. Relationships between Delinquent and Antisocial Behavior in Childhood and Later Adult Behavior in the Military   243

Table 13.3. Relationships between Delinquent and Antisocial Behavior in Childhood and Later Adult Outcomes Relating to School, Work, and Family   245

List of Figures

Figure 6.1. Age-Specific Accident and Arrest Rates   122

Figure 10.1. Offense-Specific Age Plots, Total, Murder,
and Gambling Offenses   180

Figure 10.2. Offense-Specific Age Plots, Total, Rape, and
Suspicion Offenses   181

Figure 10.3. Offense-Specific Age Plots, Total, Robbery,
and Vagrancy Offenses   181

Figure 10.4. Offense-Specific Age Plots, Total, Assault,
and Conduct Offenses   182

Acknowledgments

The editors gratefully acknowledge the following publishers and publications for permission to use previously published material: University Press of America, Inc., for "Family Structure and Crime," in *When Families Fail . . . The Social Costs*, ed. Bryce J. Christensen (1991), 43–65; Sage Publications, Inc., for "Substantive Positivism and the Idea of Crime," *Rationality and Society* 2 (October 1990):412–28; American Psychological Association, for "A Control Theory Interpretation of Psychological Research on Aggression," in *Aggression and Violence: Social Interactionist Perspectives*, ed. R. B. Felson and J. T. Tedeschi (1993), 47–68.

1

The Generality of Deviance

Travis Hirschi and Michael R. Gottfredson

Theories in criminology are typically tested by examining their ability to provide conceptual and empirical explanations of forms of crime or deviance, but they are not restricted to this role alone. In fact, theories of crime may also act as guides to public policy, as bases for assessment of the functioning of social institutions, and even as sources of insight into the practices of academic disciplines. The more general a theory, the more diverse the topics to which it can be applied. With this thought in mind, the chapters in this volume assess the empirical adequacy and conceptual utility of the theory of self control advanced in our book, *A General Theory of Crime* (Gottfredson and Hirschi 1990). The topics covered are correspondingly diverse, ranging from such concrete forms of deviance as rape, drug use, and accidents to such abstract issues as versatility, aggression, and even "positivism." In all cases the goal is the same: to explore the generality of the theory, its applicability to a variety of questions of interest to criminology.

Although none of the essays is based on data collected with the theory explicitly in mind, each explores the applicability of the theory to a particular institution, conceptual issue, social problem, or form of risky behavior. Collectively, then, the works in this volume are meant to illustrate and even test the generality of the theory, a theory explicitly designed to encompass the full range of criminal, deviant, and reckless behavior.

The theory, simply stated, is this: Criminal acts are a subset of acts in which the actor ignores the long-term negative consequences that flow from the act itself (e.g., the health consequences of drug use), from the social or familial environment (e.g., a spouse's reaction to infidelity), or from the state (e.g., the criminal justice response to robbery). All acts that share this feature, including criminal acts, are therefore likely to be engaged in by individuals unusually sensitive to immediate pleasure and insensitive to long-term consequences. The immediacy of the benefits of crime implies that they are obvious to the actor, that no special skill or learning is required. The property of individuals that explains variation in the likelihood of engaging in such acts we call "self-control." The evidence suggests to us that variation in self-control is established early in life, and that differences between individuals remain reasonably constant over the life course. It also suggests, consistent with the idea of self-control, that individuals will tend to engage in (or avoid) a wide variety of criminal and analogous behaviors—that they will not special-ize in some to the exclusion of others, nor will they "escalate" into more serious or skillful criminal behavior over time.

Both the stability of differences between individuals and the versatility of offenders can be derived from the fact that all such acts follow a predictable path over the life course, peaking in the middle to late teens, and then declining steadily throughout life. If children who offend by whining and pushing and shoving are the adults who offend by robbing and raping, it must be that whining and pushing and shoving are the theoretical equivalents of robbery and rape. If robbery and rape are theoretical equivalents, they should be engaged in by the same people. They *are* engaged in by the same people (putting the lie to the idea that each of them is peculiarly motivated). If deviant acts at different phases of the life course are engaged in differentially by the same individuals, the underlying trait must be extremely stable over time. If the same individuals tend to engage in serious and trivial acts, these acts must satisfy equivalent desires of the actor.

Evidence for a "latent trait" that somehow causes deviant behavior thus comes from two primary sources. The first is the statistical associa-tion among diverse criminal, deviant, or reckless acts. Because these acts are behaviorally heterogeneous, because they occur in a variety of situations, and because they entail different sets of necessary conditions, it seems reasonable to suppose that what they have in common somehow resides in the person committing them. The second is the stability of differences between individuals over time. Because individuals relative-ly likely to commit criminal, deviant, or reckless acts at one point in time are also relatively likely to commit such acts at later points in time, it seems reasonable to ascribe these differences to a persistent underlying trait possessed in different degrees by those whose behavior is being compared.

The standards described are well-known as tests of internal consistency and test-retest reliability (or stability). When applied to measures of crime, they offer compelling evidence that a stable trait of personality underlies much criminal, deviant, and reckless behavior (Greenberg 1991; Rowe, Osgood, and Nicewander 1990; Osgood 1990; Osgood et al. 1988; Olweus 1979; Nagin and Farrington 1992).

If the evidence requires that we grant the existence of reliable differences among individuals in the tendency to commit deviant acts, the evidence it seems to us also requires that we conceptualize this "latent trait" in particular ways. For example, we cannot make it conducive to specialization in some deviant acts rather than others, because that would be contrary to its generality (we cannot easily conceptualize it as "internalization of norms," because that would suggest the possibility of internalizing some norms and not others, an idea also contrary to the finding of generality); we cannot make it akin to aggressiveness, because that would be contrary to its often passive, furtive, or retreatist consequences; we cannot make it a positive force requiring for its satisfaction the commission of clearly criminal acts, because it is not conducive to persistence in a course of action but is instead conducive to momentary satisfaction of transient desires. Reasoning in this way, and from examination of the diverse acts produced by or consistent with this "latent trait," we concluded that it was best seen as *self-control*, the tendency to avoid acts whose long-term costs exceed their momentary advantages.

Natural Sanctions

This conception of the trait underlying criminal, deviant, and reckless behavior solves several problems. A persistent problem in this area is extinction, the tendency of responses created and maintained by sanctions to evaporate in the absence of continued reinforcement. How is self-control maintained when there are no obvious social or legal supports for it? It is not hard to find examples of people who continue to "conform" during very long periods in which their behavior is not observed by other people or subject to the sanctions of the criminal law. In our view, self control is resistant to extinction because its ultimate sources are natural sanctions that by definition do not require continued input from others. Socialization, in this sense, may be seen as a process of educating individuals about the consequences of their behavior. Once they have such knowledge and the habit of acting on it, no further reinforcement is required. In fact in most areas natural sanctions so exceed in strength social or legal sanctions that the latter are not really necessary to explain the conformity of most people. The mystery is, rather, how some people can ignore or misapprehend the automatic consequences of their behavior, both positive and negative, and thus continue to act as though these consequences did not exist.

For example, opportunities to drink are virtually unlimited for all members of the population. Alcohol in one form or another is relatively cheap and is widely available. For many people, normative control is for all intents and purposes absent. They lead essentially private lives, or those around them do not really care about their consumption. The pleasures of alcohol are known and acknowledged by a large majority of the population. Yet self control predicts consumption of alcohol in both public and private settings over the life course. It must be that self-control is maintained by the natural consequences of behavior including but by no means limited to the reactions of others. Consistent with this argument, alcohol consumption also declines with age, suggesting that consumption is governed more by its physiological than by its social consequences.

Self control is highly efficient precisely because it is effective in a variety of settings, many of which lack social or legal surveillance, but few of which lack natural sanctions. People with self control do not risk accidents on lonely mountain roads even though no one is there to see them exceed the speed limit. They do not steal goods belonging to others despite countless opportunities to do so because such actions are inconsistent with prospects for success (prospects that do not allow a record of criminal behavior, but are otherwise independent of social or legal sanctions).

The idea of self control suggests that the origin of all sanctions or norms is to be found in natural sanctions, the rewards and punishments that follow automatically from particular acts or lines of behavior. Many natural sanctions are of course physical or physiological, affecting the health or well-being of the body—producing injury, disease, deterioration, or even death. Excessive use of drugs, interpersonal violence, promiscuous sexual behavior, and theft of all sorts can yield such consequences. As a result, normative and legal systems evolve to draw attention to these consequences (the difficulty we have in saying precisely what these systems are up to suggests that they have many sources and functions). The relation between natural and normative sanctions helps account for the universality of norms governing those behaviors with the most serious consequences, such as interpersonal violence and theft. At the same time, it helps explain society's ambiguous stance toward some norms and their enforcement, such as drug use and sexual promiscuity.

Implications of Self-Control

Our conception of the trait underlying criminal, deviant, and reckless behavior is, we believe, consistent with

- research showing the importance of the family in delinquency causation (Glueck and Glueck 1950; Hirschi 1969; Loeber and Stouthamer-Loeber 1986);
- research showing the importance of opportunities to commit criminal acts (Cohen and Felson 1979);
- research showing a sharp decline in all kinds of criminal, deviant, and reckless behavior with age (Hirschi and Gottfredson 1983).

At the same time, this conceptualization of the trait underlying criminal, deviant, and reckless behavior is *in*consistent with

- the idea of a career criminal, an individual who makes a living from well-planned and executed crimes over an extended period of time, or who at least persists in a definite line of criminal activity;
- the idea of organized crime, or organized delinquent gangs engaged in long-term and highly profitable illegal activities, such as gambling, prostitution, and drug trafficking;
- the idea that the causes of "adolescent delinquency" are different from the causes of "adult crime" (see Trasler 1991:440);
- the idea that the causes of "white-collar" crime are different from the causes of "ordinary" crime;
- the idea that crime is learned, that it must be acquired from other people.

As might be expected from all this, the idea that low self-control underlies the bulk of criminal and deviant acts has not been greeted with enthusiasm by all segments of the criminological community. On the contrary, the theory has attracted a variety of criticisms. According to the critics, the theory

- is too general. It attempts to encompass too broad a range of deviant behavior. Instrumental and expressive crimes have different causes, as do white-collar and street crimes. Purposive criminal acts have little in common with accidents, bad habits, mental illnesses, or school truancy.

- is tautological. If criminal acts are defined as acts in which the long-term negative consequences for the actor outweigh the short-term gains, it is a matter of definition that those committing such acts tend to ignore or discount long-term consequences.

- is based on an erroneous conception of the relation between age and the various behaviors it attempts to explain, and ignores evidence that the causes of the onset of crime differ from the causes of persistence in and desistence from crime.

- ignores important distinctions between the incidence and prevalence of criminal or deviant behavior.

- fails to distinguish among classes of offenders who differ markedly in the level and variety of their deviant behavior.

- suggests erroneously that the penalties of the criminal justice system are ineffective in crime control. The theory also fails to anticipate important differences among offenders in their sensitivity to institutional experiences or sanctions.

- overstates the importance of self-control, regarding it as the sole cause of crime.

- ignores the fact that self-control is not the stable, general trait the theory claims it to be.

It is not a straightforward matter to respond to critiques of a theory. Such critiques have diverse origins. One ostensibly valid source of criticism is the research literature. But published research may be based on samples or data or interpretations of the theory that are inadequate or inappropriate, and response to research-based criticism therefore requires case-by-case examination of specific studies. Another presumably valid source of criticism is the compatibility between the theory and the rules described by experts in theory construction. But there is in fact considerable disagreement about the logical standards that one can legitimately employ in assessing the adequacy of a theory. Presumably, each theory has its own logic and its own basic assumptions. Adequate response to logic-based criticism would therefore require articulation of the philosophy of science underlying the theory and its competitors, a task that should not be undertaken lightly. Finally, there are the textbooks in a field. These books often provide extensive lists of criticisms of particular theories gathered from a variety of sources. But it is entirely possible that such generic lists of criticisms do more harm than good, suggesting as they do that everything is equally open to doubt, that all research and theory in the field is problematic, that the student is therefore free to believe anything he or she wishes to believe without fear of contradiction.

This is not to say, of course, that theories should be immune from criticism. In fact, in our view, the field suffers from lack of rigorous and persistent criticism of its theories, methods, and assumptions, and too readily accepts the view that all theories contain a grain of truth. (For a recent, excellent review of the field from a critical perspective, see Roshier 1989.) In our view, the primary test of a theory is its ability to organize the data in an area relative to the ability of alternative theories to organize the same data. We recognize that many scholars (e.g., Tittle 1991; Akers 1991) prefer to avoid drawing sharp distinctions between theories, or to presenting them in an oppositional mode. But in our view good criticism *must be comparative*, asking how one theory fares relative to its competitors. Our perspective places little value on lists of strengths and weaknesses of theories, and sees little benefit in uncritical "integrations" of competing theories. It requires merely a willingness to abide by the dictates of logic and the results of competent research.

One problem with "criticisms" of theories is that, absent a context of competing theories, they are hard to evaluate. Take the most damning criticism one can allege against a theory (after internal inconsistency): that it is false. The record is reasonably clear that even this criticism will have little impact on the viability of a theory in the absence of a competing theory that claims the same territory.

By the same token, the charge that a theory is "too general" is hard to evaluate absent a context of competing theory. When specified in the statement "robbery is not murder" (or, more telling, in the statement "accidents are not crimes!") this criticism implies that these are such different events that they must have different explanations. But this is tantamount to a critique of the germ theory of disease that asserts that diphtheria is not whooping cough. The theory that diseases are caused by infectious agents is even more general than the germ theory. Is it "too general" because it includes viruses as well as bacteria? Obviously, a general theory is not damaged by the charge of excess generality.

General theories do not assert that the concrete events or states they explain are identical. They assert only that they have something in common. They assert that robbery and murder have something in common that explains the fact that both are likely to be committed by the same people. It would be a legitimate criticism of such theory if the critic were able to show that people who commit robbery are not more likely than nonrobbers to commit murder, but that would only imply that the theory is wrong, not that it is "too general."

Even more curious is the charge that our theory is tautological (Akers 1991). In our view, the charge of tautology is in fact a compliment, an assertion that we followed the path of logic in producing an internally consistent result. Indeed, this is what we set out to do. We started with a conception of crime, and from it attempted to *derive* a conception of the offender. As a result, there should be strict definitional consistency between our image of the actor and our image of the act. What distinguishes our theory from many criminological theories is that we begin with the act, whereas they normally begin with the actor. Theories that start from the causes of crime—for example, economic deprivation— eventually define crime as a response to the causes they invoke. Thus, a theory that sees economic deprivation as the cause of crime will by definition see crime as an attempt to remedy economic deprivation, making the connection between cause and effect tautological.

What makes our theory *peculiarly* vulnerable to complaints about tautology is that we explicitly show the logical connections between our conception of the actor and the act, whereas many theorists leave this task to those interpreting or testing their theory, but again we are not impressed that we are unusual in this regard. One more example: Sutherland's theory of differential association says that offenders have peculiar skills and attitudes toward crime learned from their subcultures. Crime is thus a reflection of those skills and attitudes. In this theory too the connection between the image of the offender and the image of crime (both require particular skills and attitudes) is tautological.

In a comparative framework, the charge of tautology suggests that a theory that is nontautological would be preferable. But what would such a theory look like? It would advance definitions of crime and of criminals that are independent of one another (e.g., crime is a violation of the law; the criminal is a person denied access to legitimate opportunity). Several historically important theories cannot show an empirical connection between their definition of crime and their image of the offender, and must therefore be said to be false (Kornhauser 1978: 180).

Those charging us with tautology do not see the issue in this light. Thus Akers says, it would appear to be tautological to explain the propensity to commit crime by low self-control. They are one and the same, and such assertions about them are true by definition. The assertion means that low self-control causes low self-control. Similarly, since no operational definition of self-control is given, we cannot know that a person has low self-control (stable propensity to commit crime) unless he or she commits crimes or analogous behavior. The statement that low self-control is a cause of crime, then, is also tautological. (1991:204)

It seems to us that here (and elsewhere) Akers's concept of self-control differs fundamentally from our own. We do not see self-control as the propensity to commit crime, or as the motivating force underlying criminal acts. Rather, we see self-control as the barrier that stands between the actor and the obvious momentary benefits crime provides. We explicitly propose that the link between self-control and crime is *not* deterministic, but probabilistic, affected by opportunities and other constraints. If so, the problem with our conception is more likely to be that it is nonfalsifiable than that it merely definitional.

Fortunately for the theory, Akers himself proposes that the problems he identifies can be resolved by operationalizing the concept of self-control. Thus, following the discussion above, he writes: "To avoid the tautology problem, independent indicators of self-control are needed" (1991: 204). The question then becomes, can independent indicators of self-control be identified. With respect to crime, we would propose such items as whining, pushing, and shoving (as a child); smoking and drinking and excessive television watching and accident frequency (as a teenager); difficulties in interpersonal relations, employment instability, automobile accidents, drinking, and smoking (as an adult). None of these acts or behaviors is a crime. They are logically independent of crime. Therefore the relation between them and crime is not a matter of definition, and the theory survives the charge that it is mere tautology and that it is nonfalsifiable.

Clearly, our theory cannot be at once nonfalsifiable, true by definition, and false. We know that many readers find that our description of crime rings true, that it corresponds on the whole to what they have seen and heard. Such readers will not understand that our conception is really radically different from the conceptions implicit in the theories that have dominated the field for many years. If they accuse us of being trite or true by definition, we cannot blame them—but we accept their inevitable conclusion that competing theories must be false.

The attractiveness of a theory that identifies commonalities among apparently disparate events is often counterbalanced by the feeling that too much has been sacrificed on the alter of generality. For theorists the problem is made worse by the modern tendency to divide the world into ever more narrow research problems ("homicide among the elderly female population"), each with its own cadre of experts, with the consequence that application of a general theory will be opposed by specialists in each subarea it was intended to subsume (for a summary of the historical roots of this tendency, see chap. 14).

As stated, the theory applies to acts that provide immediate benefit at the risk of long-term cost to actors who find opportunities for such acts appealing. Because such acts are injurious to long-term individual and collective interests, they are universally resisted, at least at some level. Confusion arises from the obvious fact that groups vary in their reaction to such events, sometimes dealing with them harshly and formally in the criminal law, sometimes dealing with them as medical problems, sometimes as welfare problems, and sometimes appearing to ignore them altogether. From the point of view of the theory, such reactions are aspects of the long-term costs of the behavior, serving to reduce or intensify them, but never eliminating them altogether. To the extent that alterations in social costs affect the development of self control, they can be important in causing variation in the behaviors in question. Thus, for example, tobacco and alcohol use have natural consequences that to some degree limit their use, but variation in alcohol and tobacco use may also be traced to restrictions on availability and to differences in social and legal sanctions from one group to another. These differences do not negate the conclusion that tobacco and alcohol use fall within the purview of the theory; indeed they show that tobacco and alcohol are in the same class as such currently illegal substances as marijuana and cocaine.

A related source of confusion is the idea that some acts encompassed by the theory have not always been socially condemned, or may not be so condemned in the future. Thus, it is said, cigarette smoking was once actually fashionable, and it is possible to imagine a time when the use of marijuana will be promoted as socially and legally accepted behavior. Does the theory apply equally to both substances when they are legal and illegal? Indeed it does. The only requirement of the theory is that at all times those low in self-control are more likely to engage in the behavior than those high in self control. In fact, even when smoking was fashionable in the United States delinquents were much more likely than nondelinquents to smoke (Schoff 1915; Glueck and Glueck 1950; Hirschi 1969). We can therefore assume that when or if marijuana is legalized, the correlation between marijuana use and deviant behavior will remain at current levels.

These facts may suggest that self-control inhibits pursuit of immediate pleasure, whatever its long-term consequences—that is, that high self-control people have no fun even when it is free. We think this interpretation is probably incorrect. Knowledge that smoking has long-term harmful effects did not come into the world with the surgeon general's report in 1964. On the contrary, cigarettes were known as "coffin nails" before the turn of the century. Similarly, it would be unlikely that the deleterious consequences of repeated marijuana use would escape the notice of those concerned with the long term.

The theory thus produces clear expectations about the generality of deviance and the versatility of offenders. This aspect of the theory is particularly amenable to empirical test. Several of the essays in this volume speak directly to the generality question by showing the connections among behaviors engaged in by those with relatively little self control. All speak indirectly to this question by showing the applicability of the theory to acts or behaviors that are not necessarily criminal. The connection between childhood accidents and delinquency is documented by Marianne Junger (chap. 5).

Automobile accidents provide a particularly compelling case for the view that the tendency to ignore long-term costs in one arena predicts a similar tendency in other arenas as well. (It also confirms the view that long-term costs are not restricted to social disapproval or legal penalties.) The paper by David Sorensen (chap. 6) shows that individuals involved in automobile accidents are likely to have the more general characteristics of offenders, that they are likely to be involved in a variety of deviant acts, and that the age and stability effects parallel those reported for crime.

George Strand and Michael Garr (chap. 7) analyze self-report data to show the strong relations among alcohol use, smoking, marijuana use, and risky driving practices. Strand and Garr also show that these diverse measures are similarly related to outside variables such as grade point average and perceived importance of education.

Another criticism of the theory focuses on variation in the versatility of offenders, arguing that the theory predicts that all classes of offenders will be equally diverse. Thus, for example, some claim that the theory of self-control predicts that all offenders should be equally likely to commit all forms of offenses. If "white-collar" offenders are said by the theory to exhibit low self-control, they should be as likely as other offenders to have prior and subsequent records of offending. Two flaws in this argument are readily apparent. First, it ignores the impact of self-control on selection by individuals and by institutions into the occupational structure. When researchers define "white-collar" crime as an activity engaged in by a group highly selected on self-control, they greatly restrict the range of variability on the independent variable. It thus comes as no surprise to find that such offenders will have lower levels of involvement in crime than offenders who have not been so selected. Second, the theory has no difficulty with the idea that "white-collar" offenders are lower on self-control than "white-collar" workers who have not committed criminal offenses in the workplace. In fact, it predicts they will be more likely than their white-collar colleagues to engage in analogous acts such as drinking and smoking and gambling. In brief, the theory actually predicts that (1) to the extent that being a white-collar worker requires a modicum of self-control (as evidenced by education, certification, training, or occupational experience), "white-collar" offenders will be less likely than "unemployed" or "blue-collar" offenders to have records of other criminal activity; (2) that "white-collar" offenders will be more likely than other white collar workers to have records of criminal or analogous activity. It should be obvious that the second prediction cannot be assessed solely by comparing groups of offenders.

Age

In the initial stages of development of the theory, we advanced the thesis that the effect of age on crime and analogous behaviors is invariant across social and cultural conditions, and that it applies to all demographic groups (Hirschi and Gottfredson 1983). Crime increases sharply with age until the mid- to late teens, and then declines rapidly and continuously throughout life. In advancing this view, we cited available statistics from a variety of times and places and tried to show that our conclusions did not depend on method of data collection or definition of crime. This thesis has the property that much follows from it: As mentioned, the stability and versatility effects can be derived from it. It gives new light to efforts to find diverse causes for crimes over the life course. It enables a general theory by showing that diverse acts spread over the life course must have common causes. It has profound consequences for research design, casting doubt on the utility and efficiency of longitudinal research, and showing the advantages of large-scale cross-sectional work focusing on the early years of life. It has equally significant implications for social policy, suggesting the limitations of deterrence, incapacitation, and rehabilitation as crime-control devices. (Deterrence is limited by the short-term orientation of the offender, incapacitation and rehabilitation by the early and sharp decline in crime with age.)

Given the many logically necessary consequences of an invariant age effect, a number of facts can be interpreted as bearing on its validity. Thus, distributions of crime and analogous behaviors by age obviously bear on the question, but so too do studies of the effects of rehabilitation and incapacitation. Evidence of stability of individual differences in deviance over the life course, and evidence of versatility also pertain to the validity of the hypothesis. Research on the organization of criminal activity and the professionalization of offenders is relevant, as is consistency between the findings of longitudinal and cross-sectional studies (i.e., conceptually similar measures are shown to have similar effects at different ages). In short, the consequences of an invariant age effect are so diverse that they are reflected in a large portion of the criminological research literature, a fact that makes a concise summary difficult.

However, one thing is clear: The invariant age effect organizes in a consistent way an enormously diverse body of criminological findings. It tells us why the treatment of offenders is usually unsuccessful, and why experiments involving random arrests show no effects on recidivism. It explains why differences in the delinquency rates of various areas or countries predict parallel differences in their rates of adult crime, and why the principal "finding" of cohort studies is the overwhelming consistency of differences between offenders and nonoffenders over time. Few facts in the behavioral sciences have such power to predict other facts, or to explain so much.

It is against this background that empirical studies of statistical variation among age curves should be evaluated. Some of these studies treat invariance as a statistical issue, to be decided by tests of significance on otherwise uninterpreted data (e.g., Steffensmeier et al. 1989; Farrington 1986). Given the myriad ways that "the data" on crime and criminals might be subdivided, and given the huge samples ordinarily available to such studies, it would be surprising not to find an occasional factoid apparently contrary to the thesis. Such studies work to preserve the theoretical status quo, but are otherwise without scientific import.

Another set of studies treats invariance as a substantive hypothesis to be judged by its ability to account for important facts about crime (e.g., Osgood et al. 1988; Rowe, Osgood, and Nicewander 1990; Greenberg 1991; Loeber and Snyder 1990; Ross and Mirowsky 1987; Sampson and Laub 1990; Haapanen 1990). These studies show, among other things, that firm and explicit acceptance of the fact of an age effect on crime has useful consequences.[1] Although none of the chapters in this book deals primarily with the age question, all of them explore hypotheses that may be derived from the age effect. The long-term consistency in deviance shown by John Laub and Robert Sampson (chap. 13), the crime and drugs connection described by Carolyn Uihlein (chap. 8), and of course the connection between age and motor vehicle accidents described by David Sorensen (chap. 6) are all facts made possible by an invariant age distribution. Although the chapter by Mary Ann Zager (chap. 4) deals with gender differences in criminal acts, it offers a model for analysis of age effects. If our contentions are correct, application of Zager's analysis to age would show that its effects on crime are independent of level of self control.

The Distinction between the Prevalence and Incidence of Criminal, Delinquent, and Risky Acts

As indicated by Chester Britt (chap. 11), a major feature of the criminal career paradigm in criminology is the distinction between the prevalence and incidence of crime (also sometimes called the distinction between participation and frequency). Prevalence (participation) is the proportion of a group engaging in an act, irrespective of the number of times they do so. Incidence is the number of times those who engage in the act do so. In standard measurement theory in the social and behavioral sciences, where traits are conceptualized as continua, this distinction would be treated as a "cutting point" issue whose utility would be determined by subsequent analysis. This wait and see stance is advocated because researchers have learned that a priori categorizations may be misleading or inconsistent with the data, or may unfairly favor one hypothesis over another. Similarly, they avoid premature restriction of the range of variation in their variables because it is easily shown that such restriction typically works to attenuate the correlations among the variables under consideration.

The career paradigm rests on the assumption that such measurement principles are irrelevant to the substantive analysis of crime, where it can be shown that the distinction between participation and frequency is of considerable analytic and policy value (Blumstein, Cohen, and Farrington 1988a, 1988b). Those adopting this paradigm claim important differences between those who engage in criminal behavior only once and those who engage in it many times or not at all. By the same logic, some suggest, there may be important differences between those who engage in n criminal acts and those who engage in $n + 1$ crimes. This model is now sufficiently influential that it organizes theoretical as well as policy analysis. Some suggest that well-known crime theories rest on distinctions such as these, being *either* theories of participation *or* theories of frequency, theories of onset, persistence, or termination, theories that require special measures of crime consistent with their interests. Papers based on these distinctions are now frequently found in the journals of criminology. Some report small differences in coefficients that may simply reflect the analytical procedures employed (e.g., Paternoster and Triplett 1988; Smith, Christy, and Jarjoura 1991); in more sophisticated analyses, others find no differences in result when the distribution of crime is dichotomized as suggested by the career paradigm (Rowe, Osgood, and Nicewander 1990, Greenberg 1991, 1992).

These latter analyses are based on latent trait models, in which an underlying trait is inferred from the covariation of various measures of criminal, delinquent, and risky behavior. As indicated, the results do not depend on how the various indicators are coded. In fact, one of the best measures of "delinquency" is a "frequency" count constructed by adding together "participation" counts for diverse forms of misconduct (Hindelang et al. 1981). Although a general theory has no problem with such a measure (it alone demonstrates the interchangeability of measures of deviance and crime), it is obviously a source of some difficulty for those who argue that the distinction between participation and frequency demands the explicit attention of the field.

Seriousness

The theory of self-control covers common delinquencies (theft and assault), serious crimes (burglary and murder), reckless behaviors (speeding), school and employment difficulties (truancy, tardiness, in-school misbehavior, job instability), promiscuous sexual behavior, drug use, and family violence (spouse abuse or child abuse), all of which have negative long-term consequences. No special motivation for any of these acts is assumed. They all provide immediate, obvious benefits to the actor (as, indeed, do all purposeful acts). They typically entail no certain or meaningful short-term costs. They all, however, involve risk of substantial long-term costs to the actor.

Confusion arises from the obvious fact that criminal and deviant acts appear to differ greatly among themselves in the seriousness of their consequences for victims and offenders. Murder may carry the death penalty; mislabeling oil supplies may cost thousands of motorists at the pump; tardiness may draw only a nasty look from the teacher; truancy may reduce prospects for further schooling and ruin employment opportunities; taking drugs may result in seriously impaired health. From the perspective of society, these acts also differ greatly among themselves in their apparent seriousness. No one other than the offender is obviously seriously hurt by truancy, smoking, or shoplifting; others are, however, severely damaged by homicide, forcible rape, burglary, and child abuse.

This variability *in the consequences for others* produces differences in legal penalties and drives many theorists and researchers to distinguish between serious and trivial acts. (It also leads to distinctions between crimes committed against acquaintances and those committed against strangers, an issue addressed by Leonore Simon in chap. 12.) Such distinctions often result in dissatisfaction with our theory, which focuses on the equivalence of acts in terms of their *consequences for the offender.* It is this equivalence that causes all of them to be avoided by those with high self-control. Because those with low self-control do not attend to long-term costs, *whatever their magnitude*, they have a relatively high probability of engaging in all acts that entail mainly long-term costs. As a result, increasing the long-term penalties of criminal or deviant acts has little effect on the behavior of individuals low on self-control. If the actor does not attend to the consequences of his acts for himself, why should he care about their consequences for others?

Because those little concerned for their own future will be even less concerned for the welfare of others, it seems to us we are on solid ground theoretically when we lump together acts that differ immensely in their consequences for victims.

But given its centrality, let us pursue this issue further. How can child abuse, forcible rape, price-fixing, and employment instability be said to result from the same cause? Questions such as this assume that serious acts must have serious or strong motives, or that they must be highly profitable (otherwise why have greater penalties in the interest of deterrence for their commission?). But the very nature of deviant acts considered serious belies these assumptions.

Perhaps the most generally "serious" crime is homicide. The motives for homicide, however, are not necessarily more serious than the motives for other crimes. Killing someone because they will not give up the money or because they will not shut up is no more profound than bullying one's way to the front of the line or taking an item from a store without paying for it. Indeed, after the act, many homicide offenders cannot explain why they did it, and often report being overcome by a momentary impulse or the influence of alcohol.

Another serious crime that suggests serious motivation is forcible rape. Some argue that such a horrible act can only result from powerful psychological or sociological pressures—from desires to dominate or demean the victim. These analysts see rape as a crime with a unique set of causes incapable of explanation in the same terms as school truancy or smoking marijuana. As Victor Larragoite shows (chap. 9), there are several ways to dispute such accounts of the rapist's motivation. For one, rapists are versatile offenders. Only a small portion of their offenses are sex offenses. For another, rape is quite often committed in concert with other offenses, offenses that have no meaningful connection to this explanation of rape. For still another, rape appears to be heavily situationally dependent, to be conditioned by the availability of victims and appropriate physical circumstances. But most importantly, the consequences of the act to the victim are clearly of no concern to the offender, a person focused exclusively on his own benefits of the moment.

It should be mentioned too that serious crimes do not necessarily differ from nonserious crimes in terms of the effort or difficulty entailed by their commission. Homicide takes only a moment, and usually little or no skill. The same may be said for heroin or cocaine use, robbery, burglary, or auto theft. It may also be said for many so-called white-collar crimes. It takes little effort, skill, or intelligence to claim that a product is something it is not, or to fail fully to report one's income. No deep motive or sustained plan is involved in these crimes, and theories that presume persistent, powerful, or unique motivation for them cannot accommodate all of the evidence.

Some theorists see great intelligence and long-range scheming among upper-class offenders (Braithwaite 1989). Such a view is possible only through an idiosyncratic definition of crime. It is possible to construct a definition predicated on characteristics of criminals that will meet any contingency. Thus, if one wishes, one can speak of the "crimes of the rich and powerful" or the "crimes of the pious and holy." Such exercises trade on the love of the oxymoronic construction that is the hallmark of nonserious social science.

Researchers are constantly admonished, by the criminal justice community, by funding agencies, and by their disciplines, to focus on serious problems. Important public policy can only attend to important public problems. Thus the emphasis on "serious, repetitive, chronic, career" delinquents, on urban street gangs, and the like. Thus the deemphasis on "status offenses," on school problems, on vandalism and graffiti. But evidence that we should not be persuaded by this bias in constructing our dependant variable is readily available: promiscuous sexual behavior is today serious because the potential long-term consequences have changed, not because the motivation to engage in it has changed. Smoking cigarets is today regarded as a serious problem behavior for adolescents, not because the satisfactions of smoking have changed, but because the health risks are now more certain. Those influenced by long-term consequences are, according to our theory, more likely to change their behavior as a result. Those who are not so influenced, are less likely to change. Put in another context: Hitting a spouse with a heavy object rather than with the fist causes homicide and official reaction rather than a beating and no outside notice, radically altering the long-term cost but not affecting the basic cause of the act.

A theory that seems to take seriously trivial acts (truancy, smoking, driving too fast) is disconcerting to many readers. One source of this uneasiness is that most people, researchers and theorists included, have smoked, occasionally drink to excess, and even drive while legally under the influence, and most are nervous about what they perceive as unwarranted state interference in the lives of ordinary citizens. Put another way, they are concerned that equating currently noncriminal acts with serious criminal acts implies something about public policy. (We think it does, but not in the feared direction.) However, lack of concern for long-term consequences includes lack of concern for the consequences imposed by the state, since they are decidedly long term. Therefore, our theory actually asserts that state sanctions are irrelevant to the control of deviant behavior, whether serious of trivial.

All objections to our equation of behaviors differing greatly in serious-ness must face the fact that those who engage in serious acts are more likely to engage in trivial acts, and vice versa, as Chester Britt shows (chap. 10). They must also face the fact that the correlates of serious and trivial acts are for all intents and purposes the same (Hindelang, Hirschi, and Weis 1981:108; Elliott, Huizinga, and Ageton 1985:109–18).

A final objection to the equation of acts differing greatly in seriousness is that it suggests no basis for distinguishing between murderers and truants in the allocation of punishments by the criminal justice system. Our theory indeed denies the utility of punishment in the interests of deterrence or rehabilitation or incapacitation. But it does not require abandonment of distinctions based on harm to the victim or society as a basis for punishment. In our view, punishment chiefly operates to show those with high self-control the wisdom of their course of action—that is, to reward conformity (see Toby 1964). It also provides retribution and as a consequence promotes a sense of justice. Presumably, both of these functions are necessary whatever the crime rate.

Now that the theory has been stated in initial form, it is time to begin to subject it to operationalization and testing. While in our view the theory was at all times developed with the results of research firmly in mind, it is not possible simultaneously to develop and test theories, as the latter process is understood in the social sciences. Tests are, in effect, extrapola-tions from the theory, hypotheses that should be true if the theory itself is true. The chapters in this collection are thus initial contributions to the testing process. As noted, the theory has many implications for the nature of crime and the characteristics of the offender. Many of these implica-tions can be tested in straightforward ways with available data. Others, such as the operationalization of the central concepts of the theory itself, such as self-control, must await original data collected with the theory in mind.

Because none of these chapters is based on data collected with the theory specifically in mind, the tests they propose should be seen as first approximations. That they are consistent with the theory can be explained in several ways: (1) the theory could be true; (2) the theory was constructed with the results of a great deal of research on crime in mind; (3) the authors of the pieces are friendly to the theory. The first two possibilities bode well for the future of the theory; the third possibility may appear to make less than fully compelling the evidence presented. However, all of our authors, we believe, stress the consistency of their work with previous work in the field. The findings presented here do not stand in isolation from the body of research on the causes and correlates of crime, but are properly seen as established facts interpreted in the light of a "new" theory.

Note

1. Critics of our invariance thesis frequently suggest that it is too general, and that we are too "rigid" in our defense of it. Most criminologists would grant that most or much crime conforms to the characteristic distribution, but many are reluctant to agree with us that the invariance is sufficient to preclude a sociological explanation of it. The issue here is whether science is advanced better by emphasizing our ignorance or by suggesting the possibility that we may be in a position to infer some things from what we now know. We accept the latter view, which we do not consider rigid or inflexible.

References

Akers, Ronald L. 1991. "Self-Control as a General Theory of Crime." *Journal of Quantitative Criminology* 7:201-11.

Blumstein, Alfred, Jacqueline Cohen, and David Farrington. 1988a. "Criminal Career Research: Its Value for Criminology." *Criminology* 26:1-35.

_____. 1988b. "Longitudinal and Criminal Career Research: Further Clarifications." *Criminology* 26:57-74.

Braithwaite, John. 1989. *Crime, Shame and Reintegration.* Cambridge: Cambridge University Press.

Cohen, Lawrence, and Marcus Felson. 1979. "Social Change and Crime Rate Trends: A Routine Activity Approach." *American Sociological Review* 44:588-608.

Elliott, Delbert, David Huizinga, and Suzanne S. Ageton. 1985. *Explaining Delinquency and Drug Use.* Beverly Hills, CA: Sage Publications.

Farrington, David. 1986. "Age and Crime." In *Crime and Justice: An Annual Review of Research*, vol. 7, ed. N. Morris and M. Tonry, 189-250. Chicago: University of Chicago Press.

Glueck, Sheldon, and Eleanor Glueck. 1950. *Unraveling Juvenile Delinquency.* Cambridge, MA: Harvard University Press.

Gottfredson, Michael R., and Travis Hirschi. 1990. *A General Theory of Crime.* Stanford, CA: Stanford University Press.

Greenberg, David. 1992. "Comparing Criminal Career Models." *Criminology* 30:141–47.

_____. 1991. "Modeling Criminal Careers." *Criminology* 25:17–46.

Haapanen, Rudy. 1990. *Selective Incapacitation and the Serious Offender.* New York: Springer Verlag.

Hindelang, Michael J., Travis Hirschi, and Joseph G. Weis. 1981. *Measuring Delinquency.* Beverly Hills, CA: Sage Publications.

Hirschi, Travis. 1969. *Causes of Delinquency.* Berkeley: University of California Press.

Hirschi, Travis, and Michael R. Gottfredson. 1983. "Age and the Explanation of Crime." *American Journal of Sociology* 89:552–84.

Loeber, Rolf, and Howard N. Snyder. 1990. "Rate of Offending in Juvenile Careers: Findings of Constancy and Change in Lambda." *Criminology* 28:97–109.

Loeber, Rolf, and Magda Stouthamer-Loeber. 1986. "Family Factors as Correlates and Predictors of Juvenile Conduct Problems and Delinquency." In *Crime and Justice: An Annual Review of Research,* vol. 7, ed. M. Tonry and N. Morris, 29–149. Chicago: University of Chicago Press.

Nagin, Daniel, and David Farrington. 1992. "The Stability of Criminal Potential from Childhood to Adulthood." *Criminology* 30:235–60.

Olweus, Dan. 1979. "Stability of Aggressive Reaction Patterns in Males: A Review." *Psychological Bulletin* 86:852–75.

Osgood, D. Wayne. 1990. "Covariation and Adolescent Problem Behaviors." Paper presented at the meetings of the American Society of Criminology, Baltimore, MD.

Osgood, D. Wayne, Lloyd Johnston, Patrick O'Malley, and Jerald Bachman. 1988. "The Generality of Deviance in Late Adolescence and Early Adulthood." *American Sociological Review* 53:81–93.

Paternoster, Raymond, and Ruth Triplett. 1988. "Disaggregating Self-Reported Delinquency and Its Implications for Theory." *Criminology* 26:591–625.

Roshier, Bob. 1989. *Controlling Crime: The Classical Perspective in Criminology.* Chicago: Lyceum Books.

Ross, Catherine E., and John Mirowsky. 1987. "Normlessness, Powerlessness, and Trouble with the Law." *Criminology* 25:257–78.

Rowe, David, D. Wayne Osgood, and W. Alan Nicewander. 1990. "A Latent Trait Approach to Unifying Criminal Careers." *Criminology* 28:237–70.

Sampson, Robert J., and John H. Laub. 1990. "Stability and Change in Crime and Deviance over the Life Course: The Salience of Adult Social Bonds." *American Sociological Review* 55:609–27.

Schoff, Hannah Kent. 1915. *The Wayward Child.* Indianapolis: Bobbs-Merrill.

Smith, Douglas A., Christy A. Visher, and G. Roger Jarjoura. 1991. "Dimensions of Delinquency: Exploring the Correlates of Participation, Frequency, and Persistence of Delinquent Behavior." *Journal of Research in Crime and Delinquency* 28:6–32.

Steffensmeier, Darrell, Emilie Allan, Miles D. Harer, and Cathy Streifel. 1989. "Age and the Distribution of Crime: Variant or Invariant?" *American Journal of Sociology* 94:803–31.

Tittle, Charles R. 1991. Review of *A General Theory of Crime,* by Michael Gottfredson and Travis Hirschi. *American Journal of Sociology* 96:1609–11.

Toby, Jackson. 1964. "Is Punishment Necessary?" *Journal of Criminal Law, Criminology and Police Science* 55:332–37.

Trasler, Gordon. 1991. Review of *Explaining Criminal Behaviour: Interdisciplinary Approaches*, by Wouter Buikhuisen and Sarnoff A. Mednick. *Contemporary Psychology* 36:440–41.

2

Aggression

Michael R. Gottfredson and Travis Hirschi

Behavior determined by inner drives poses problems for rational choice or social control theories. In everyday life, and in psychology and law, such behavior is taken to be commonplace. In these domains, acts are frequently characterized as compulsive, expressive, passionate, or violent, with the clear intention of contrasting them to acts governed by their consequences, the acts of interest to control theories. While terms denoting strong drives or motives implicitly acknowledge that some behavior may be explicable because it is rational, they at the same time suggest that much important and interesting behavior is beyond the reach of control theories. Nowhere is the challenge to control theory more conspicuous than in the concept of aggression.

In the late 1930s, the frustration-aggression hypothesis emerged as an important theoretical construct in psychology and sociology. In psychology, Dollard et al. (1939) advanced the view that aggression is a consequence of frustration. With important qualifications and modifications, this tradition has flourished in psychology for the intervening fifty years (Berkowitz 1989). At about the same time in sociology, Merton (1938) advanced the view that *crime* is a consequence of the frustration that flows from failure to achieve culturally prescribed goals. With important qualifications and modifications, this version of the frustration-aggression hypothesis, often called "strain theory," has flourished in sociology as well (Cloward and Ohlin 1960; Blau and Blau 1982; Bernard 1990).

Scholarly interest in aggression remains at high levels. Recent studies of this concept include investigations of the television-violence/aggression link (Cook, Kendzierski, and Thomas 1983; Eron 1987), the role of temperature in the causation of aggression (Anderson 1989), studies of the stability of aggression over time (Olweus 1979), and theoretical work designed to explain individual differences in aggression (Berkowitz 1989; Bandura 1973; Buss 1961).

In criminology, the related concepts of violence and serious offending continue to maintain an important position in research and public policy (Widom 1989a; Monahan 1981; Straus, Gelles, and Steinmetz 1980; Gelles 1980). Two recently issued and prominent reviews of the field, one on behalf of the National Academy of Sciences (Blumstein et al. 1986) and the other on behalf of the MacArthur Foundation (Farrington, Ohlin, and Wilson 1986), urge that attention be focused on violent and serious offenses and offenders. A large literature also focuses on family violence or child and spouse abuse, with the underlying theme that these various forms of abuse are tied together through a cycle of aggression (Widom 1989b). And of course the strain model continues to trace such nonviolent offenses as theft and drug use to the frustration of legitimate aspirations or expectations (Wilson and Herrnstein 1985; Elliott, Huizinga, and Ageton 1985).

Much of the popularity of the concept of aggression may be traced to its compatibility with the basic assumptions of the behavioral science disciplines (Hirschi and Gottfredson 1990). These disciplines assume that events are caused by prior states or events, that the actor is at the mercy of forces beyond the immediate situation, over which he has no control, and that the nature of these forces or motives is not immediately evident in the behavior they produce. These assumptions are especially obvious in studies of aggression (whether the theorist's orientation is frustration-aggression (Berkowitz 1989) or learning theory (Bandura 1973)).

Such ideas may be contrasted to a social control model, in which the actor seeks to satisfy general needs and desires while attending to the relative social costs and benefits of alternative lines of action. In sociological control theories (Hirschi 1969; Gottfredson and Hirschi 1990; Heckathorn 1990), individuals differ in the extent to which they attend to short-term as opposed to the long-term or social consequences of their acts. In this view, aggressive or violent acts are merely attempts to pursue some immediate self-interest through the use of force: The robber shoots the clerk to expedite the theft; the bully assaults the playmate to improve his position in the lunch line; the husband kills the wife to end an annoying argument. Such acts may seem irrational, impulsive, or inexplicable—the product of some deep-seated psychological need—even to the actor. After all, it appears to make little sense to risk the death penalty for a few dollars, to risk losing a friend for a momentary advantage, or to lose a wife for the sake of an argument. But this judgment compares the act's immediate benefits with its long-term costs. When immediate benefits are compared with immediate costs, the impression of irrationality is dispelled.

A social control perspective assumes that comparison of immediate benefits with immediate costs governs the behavior of some people in some situations, while comparison of immediate benefits with long-term costs governs the behavior of most people most of the time. Whichever comparison is operative, the ultimate decision is consistent with control principles.

The social control explanation is consistent with the long-established fact that most criminal acts are nonviolent, that the majority involve theft without confrontation between victim and offender. In these acts, too, the offender ignores long-term social costs in favor of the benefits of the moment. Although theft may seem more rational than violence because it produces immediate tangible benefits, social control theory explains the two acts in the same way. The control model is thus consistent with the observation that violence and theft are typically found in the same offender—that is, there is very little tendency to specialize in one of these types of offense to the exclusion of the other (Osgood et al. 1988; Osgood 1990; Rowe, Osgood, and Nicewander 1990).

The psychological aggression model is inconsistent with the versatility of offenders: The frustration-aggression version (Dollard et al. 1939; Berkowitz 1989) predicts behavior consistent with the frustration encountered; the learning version (Bandura 1973) predicts behavior consistent with the role model imitated. Both versions thus tend to be actor behavior-specific, and as such overlook good evidence for a general tendency to engage in or avoid criminal acts.

Similar problems emerge from policy-oriented research on the origins of aggressive behavior. Most such research assumes that particular experiences (e.g., watching violent television programs, reading violent pornography) are causes of particular violent acts. Policies aimed at violence control through content restrictions would be seen in a new light were it established that exposure to such content is itself a product of a latent trait that is consistent with aggressive behavior but that cannot reasonably be called aggressiveness (see e.g., National Institute of Mental Health 1982).

All this would seem to raise sufficient question about the usefulness of the concept of aggression to justify further inquiry. In the analyses that follow, we assess the validity of the concept as it is used in experimental and nonexperimental research in psychology, using social control as the rival concept.

The predictive and convergent validity of aggression in nonexperimental research seems well established (Eron 1987; Olweus 1980). But strong convergent validity is a double-edged sword: It may suggest problems with discriminant validity. In this study we therefore apply the principles of convergent and discriminant validity (Campbell and Fiske 1959) to measures of cognate concepts, aggression, and social control, to determine whether they are separable.

Operational Definitions of Aggression

Studies of aggression in psychology take place in the field and in laboratory settings. In field studies, aggression is measured by interviews, questionnaires, or observation. Operational definitions of the concept typically include such acts as hitting and hurting, pushing and shoving, injuring and irritating (Eron 1987), unprovoked physical aggression (starting a fight), and mildly provoked verbal aggression (e.g., sassing a teacher) (Olweus 1979). But they also often include stealing and vandalism (sometimes referred to as "property aggression"), lying, insulting, auto theft, and robbery (Eron 1987; Milavsky et al. 1982; Tedeschi, Brown III, and Brown, Jr. 1974).

Such behavior can be measured with a high degree of reliability (Eron 1987; Huesmann et al. 1984), and differences among individuals are highly stable over time. Olweus reports that aggression scores and intelligence scores are about equally stable: "The difference between the estimated coefficients would be only .10 for an interval of 10 years (.70

for intelligence and .60 for aggression)" (1979:866). Huesmann et al. show that aggression scores remain reasonably stable over a twenty-two-year period. In fact, they conclude: "What is not arguable is that aggressive behavior, however engendered, once established, remains remarkably stable across time, situation, and even generations within a family" (1984:1133).

Such naturalistic measures of aggression predict criminal behavior. In fact, they predict criminal behavior so well that those studying the stability of aggression over the life course often use standard crime counts (e.g., "criminal justice convictions," "seriousness of criminal acts," "driving while intoxicated") as *measures of aggression* during the later or adult years (Heusmann et al. 1984:1124; Farrington 1978). Given such long-term predictability, short-term predictability would be expected to be excellent: Eron reports that his aggression scale has a "one-month test-retest reliability [of] .91" (1987:436).

Studying infrequent phenomena like aggression (infrequent at least among adults) is difficult in laboratory settings. Investigators interested in aggression cannot sit back and wait for it to occur, but must generate it in sufficient quantities to allow reliable analysis. The problem may be further complicated by the standard practice of relying on university undergraduates, a population with especially low rates of aggression as it is typically measured in natural settings.

A few protocols seem to be standard. Subjects are asked to participate in a learning experiment in which deception is used about the true purpose of the study. The subject works with another subject on the learning task, and the subject's grade, score, or reward is partially dependent on the behavior of the second subject. The second subject is a confederate of the experimenter, instructed to interfere with performance of the task. The subject has the opportunity to punish the confederate (often with electrical shock) for his or her failure to perform adequately. Manipulations involve the setting (e.g., temperature), characteristics of the confederate, level of insult, and the legitimacy of the frustrated expectation (e.g., Gentry 1970; Gaebelein and Taylor 1971; Geen 1968; Baron 1976; Hynan and Grush 1986; Kulik and Brown 1979). These studies more or less consistently demonstrate that subjects can be induced to punish (behave aggressively toward) the confederate, and that the degree of punishment (aggression) varies by setting, characteristics of the confederate, level of insult, and legitimacy of the frustration.

Authors of laboratory studies often suggest that a major purpose in studying aggression is to better understand criminal violence, spouse abuse, civil disorder, or war (e.g., Anderson 1989; Baron 1976; Berkowitz 1989). Both laboratory and field research traditions therefore seek justification for the study of aggression in the real-world problem of criminal behavior. (The connection between aggressive acts in the laboratory and stable aggressive inclinations is thought to be straightforward. Because stable aggression accumulates "over repeated instances of unsatisfied expectation" (Berkowitz 1989:61), aggression observed in the laboratory may be assumed to reflect prior and subsequent states of the individual as well.)

Given the explanatory benefits that derive from equating aggressive acts with aggressive tendencies, the scientific community has not been particularly sensitive to the question of validity.[1] In our view, field research in psychology has been insufficiently sensitive to the problem of discriminant validity between aggression and crime, and laboratory research in psychology has not attended sufficiently to the prior question of convergent validity of its operational indicators with measures of aggression produced by other means.

Convergent Validity and Laboratory Measures of Aggression

In criminal law, as in common usage, the idea of aggression connotes unprovoked, senseless, or unjustifiable violence or threat of violence. The criminal law justifies the use of force under conditions of duress and in defense of self and others. Following similar logic, the *Oxford Dictionary* defines aggression as "an unprovoked attack; the first attack in a quarrel; an assault."

Laboratory research in psychology seems little concerned with these standard definitions of aggression, and not particularly concerned with maintaining consistency of meaning from one experiment to another. If, as Kulik and Brown (1979:183) note, "recent experimental studies of human aggression have generally employed electric shock as the primary, if not sole, measure of aggression," the meaning of this operational definition is not obvious. In fact, Anderson (1989:74) gives as a "partial listing" five types of aggression, several of which would not qualify as aggression as it is generally understood: "predatory, pain elicited, defensive, offensive, and instrumental." Unprovoked electric shock of a colleague would clearly qualify as aggression under common understandings of the concept. But the electric shock administered in the psychology experiment on aggression is not unprovoked. On the contrary, it is carefully orchestrated. The experimenter's confederates insult the subject, fail to collaborate on an assigned task, or frustrate the achievement of some common goal—earning, it could be said, the hostility shown toward them. Nor do subjects hit upon the idea of aggression on their own. On the contrary, they are instructed to administer punishment, typically electric shock, to fellow experimental subjects who have agreed to accept it as punishment for their mistakes, all in the name of some lofty moral or scientific purpose—that is, good reasons are given to support the experimenter's instructions to shock the confederate.

On their face, then, hostile acts in the laboratory are not necessarily aggressive behavior as the term is traditionally defined. We could substitute words like *retribution, reciprocity*, or even *punishment* (and the latter is in fact common in the literature) for aggression, and we could easily justify the behavior as defense, as reasonable response to duress, or as simply following the instructions of a credible authority. (Tedeschi, Gaes, and Rivera [1977] make precisely this point.)

Supporting this interpretation is the fact that physical punishment of confederates has also been used to study obedience to authority. In these studies, the subject is also paid to participate in a scientific experiment devoted to understanding the learning process; is told that the confederate has volunteered to accept the electric shock the subject is instructed to administer; is repeatedly prodded to continue by the scientist in charge; and is told if necessary that his or her actions produce no permanent damage to the confederate (Milgram 1974:19-21).

Commenting on the most famous of these obedience experiments, Milgram says that the subject's shocking behavior has nothing to do with aggression (1974:165-68), and points out that the increase in voltage produced by the experimenter's instructions greatly exceeds the effects obtained from frustration. So, an alternative interpretation of laboratory studies of aggression is that they in fact measure compliance, obedience, or, as it is usually called in survey research, acquiescence (the tendency to agree with whatever the interviewer says). If, in support of scientific progress, subjects find it easier to shock others when they "deserve it," this tendency may reflect nothing more than the fact that it is easier to go along with instructions when they are consistent with the respondent's beliefs about appropriate behavior. On the other hand, these experiments may indeed be relevant to the concept of unprovoked aggression. Provoked and unprovoked aggression may be part of the same underlying construct. Taking the question of the meaning of the behavior provoked in the laboratory as problematic, we undertook to identify analogous behavior in natural settings where its meaning could be clarified.

On its face, the behavior studied in psychological laboratory research on aggression involves punishment of clear violations of rules or normative expectations. It may be that this form of "aggression" reflects tendencies to engage in assaultive or violent behavior outside these contrived settings. If so, such a measure would be said to possess convergent validity. Such a hypothesis seems to us highly implausible. In the absence of empirical evidence, evidence not available in the psychological literature, sociological control theories would predict the reverse—that people unsually sensitive to normative expectations (or the dictates of authorities) would be unlikely to engage in assaultive and violent acts. Available survey research allows a simple test of these competing hypotheses.

The data in table 2.1 are from a large survey much used in the study of delinquency (Hirschi 1969; Jensen and Eve 1976; Matsueda 1982; Matsueda and Heimer 1987) that has not been previously used to study aggression. The results of the survey, administered to junior and senior high school students, have often been shown to parallel results from other large surveys, including national surveys (compare Hirschi [1969], with Dornbusch et al. [1985]; with Elliott, Huizinga, and Ageton [1985], and Hindelang, Hirschi, and Weis [1981]). For present purposes, we construct a measure designed to parallel the common laboratory scenario in which subjects are given the opportunity to punish deviance. In this analogous case, subjects are asked whether they would tell the police after witnessing four deviant or illegal acts, "a 14-year-old drinking in a bar," "a man beating his wife," "someone stealing a coat," and "a man peddling dope." Yes responses to these items are given a value of 1, and summed to form a scale that might in Durkheimian terms be called a measure of "moral outrage," but in laboratory studies is used to measure aggression.[2] Evidence that the scale measures "moral outrage" is provided by its correlations with items measuring ambition (.18), and fatalism (-.17). The more aggressive the subjects' reactions to deviance, the more likely they are to be ambitious and future-oriented.

In contrast, if, as in the psychological laboratory interpretation, punitive responses toward deviant behavior connote aggressiveness, such responses should also connote aggressiveness in natural settings. Therefore, punitive responses toward deviant behavior in natural settings should predict aggressive criminal acts. Other correlations in table 2.1 address this question of construct validity.

Contrary to expectations derived from the psychological interpretation of laboratory studies, the more "aggressive" the subjects, the *less* likely they are to commit delinquent acts, when such acts are measured by commonly used and widely validated self-report methods (for validity evidence, see Hindelang, Hirschi, and Weis 1981; Elliott, Huizinga, and Ageton 1985). These results are not limited to self-report measures of delinquency; they maintain when delinquency is measured by police records (r = -.15). They also hold for general measures of delinquency and measures limited to acts of violence.

We recognize that the correlations in table 2.1 are not large. They are, however, statistically significant *and* in the direction opposite to that expected were the laboratory measure of aggression tapping a more general tendency to aggressive or violent behavior. In this case, convergent validity requires moderate to large *negative* correlations. The correlations observed, although small, are thus greatly different from those required by the pychological hypothesis.

Also contrary to clear expectations from laboratory research, table 2.1 shows that "moral outrage" is negatively related to such forms of deviance as dropping out of school (-.17) and underage smoking and drinking ("drugs") (r= -.18).

Consistent with the findings thus far reported, table 2.1 also shows that this measure of "moral outrage" is *positively* related to verbal aptitude scores and to grade point average, that those with a punitive orientation toward deviation are more rather than less likely to perform well on these tests. Research has consistently shown that intelligence test scores and school grades are negatively correlated with crime, especially crimes of violence (Hirschi and Hindelang 1977; Reichel and Magnusson 1988). All correlations in table 2.1 thus support the conclusion that the reaction of laboratory subjects to provocation represents the opposite of aggression as normally conceived. The greater the parental supervision, the higher the level of "aggression" as measured in the laboratory (r=.18); the more the student likes school, the greater the "laboratory aggression"

TABLE 2.1

Correlations among Measures of Aggression, Theft, Drug Use, and Exogenous Variables, (White Males, Richmond[a])

	Theft	Violence	Drugs	Laboratory
Laboratory aggression	-.23	-.19	-.18	--
Parental supervision	-.27	-.26	-.30	.18
Likes school	-.21	-.24	-.21	.20
Grade point average English#	-.14	-.14	-.28	.11
Verbal aptitude test (DAT)	-.10	-.04*	-.18	.12
Dropout	-.44	-.34	-.48	-.17
Fatalism	.15	.15	.17	-.17
Ambition	-.24	-.19	-.21	.18
Theft	--	.43	.43	-.23
Violence		--	.31	-.19
Official Offenses	.31	.18	.31	-.15

aThe tables in this chapter represent original analyses from the Richmond (California) Youth Project described in Hirschi (1969) and the Seattle Youth Study described in Hindelang, Hirschi, and Weis (1981). The Richmond sample used in this table consists of white males in grades 7-12. Indexes and items in the table are described in the appendix.*Not significant at .01 level. All other correlations significant at .001 level.
(N=1138-1495) #Based on 907 cases due to missing grade point average information.

(r=.20). Again, these correlations are opposite in sign to the results required by the principles of construct validity.

Even the traditional demographic correlates of crime and violence behave incorrectly when "laboratory aggression" is the focus of attention. In table 2.2 we extend the analysis to include a second large survey of adolescents conducted in Seattle. These data were originally collected to provide information on the reliability and validity of self-report measures of violence, crime, and drug use (Hindelang, Hirschi, and Weis 1981). Table 2.2 shows the connection between cooperativeness with authority and race and sex, two well-established correlates of violence. Research consistently shows that boys and members of ethnic minority groups are more likely than girls and whites to commit delinquent acts (see Wilson and Herrnstein 1985). Table 2.2 shows that in two distinct data sets with rather different measures of "laboratory aggression," the groups typically lowest on delinquency are most likely to report offenses to the police. Thus, if we accept the interpretation required by psychological research, we would be forced to conclude that girls are more aggressive than boys, and that whites are more physically aggressive than blacks. Once again, then, the correlates of "laboratory aggression" are opposite in sign from the well-established correlates of crime and delinquency.

TABLE 2.2
Laboratory Aggression by Race and Sex

Percent reporting three or more
(of four) offenses to the police
(Richmond, California[a])

White Girls	White Boys	Black Girls	Black Boys
42	33	20	16
(675)	(1586)	(813)	(1001)

Percent refusing to tell the police
or some other official what they know
about a crime (Seattle, Washington[b])

White Girls	White Boys	Black Girls	Black Boys
11	22	15	31
(272)	(846)	(126)	(368)

[a,b]For details of data collection, see Hirschi (1969), and Hindelang, Hirschi and Weis (1981).

Perhaps to belabor the point, aggression as measured in the laboratory by psychological researchers predicts conformity rather than deviance. The observed connection between "moral outrage" and conformity is, however, consistent with theories of social control.

Psychological researchers will, of course, argue that these survey responses are not aggression as they construe it. In the laboratory subjects are asked to punish violations of norms they observe. In our surveys respondents are asked if they would tell the police were they to observe certain delinquent acts. We would not quarrel with the assertion that the laboratory measure may be a better measure of the underlying construct than is its survey equivalent. We would, however, question the relevance of this fact to a test of construct validity. If we could simulate the laboratory measure more precisely (e.g., by building into the description of the event an obligation to a higher authority), there is reason to believe that the results would be even more strongly contrary to a conception of the responses as reflecting aggression. For that matter, construct validation *requires* the use of different methods, methods that do not share the same strengths or weaknesses.

So, in our view, construct validation turns the meaning of laboratory experiments on aggression on its head. Rather than an aggressive person using unjustified or inappropriate force for personal advantage, we appear to have an individual defending his or her interests in the face of inappropriate or unjustified behavior on the part of the experimenter's confederate. In this interpretation, the "aggressive" subject in the experimental setting actually represents a citizen sensitive to social norms and willing to take steps to defend them. (Or perhaps an agreeable, compliant, individual sensitive to social norms.) The few efforts by laboratory researchers to establish the construct validity of laboratory measures are consistent with these results.[3]

If operational definitions of aggression in the laboratory do not meet ordinary standards of face validity, and have not been subjected to tests of convergent validity, it is possible to understand these deficiencies as stemming from the inherent difficulties in assessing the validity of laboratory definitions. Difficulties of such magnitude should not be present in studies of aggression in natural settings, where behavioral measures of cognate concepts are readily available.

Aggression in Naturalistic or Field Studies

In a well-known study of the stability of aggression (see also Huesmann et al. 1984), Eron defines aggression as

> an act that injures or irritates another person. This definition excludes self-hurt . . . but makes no distinction between accidental and instrumental aggression or between socially acceptable and antisocial aggression. The assumption is that there is a response class, aggression, that can include a variety of behaviors, exhibited in numerous situations, all of which result in injury or irritation to another person. Thus, this category includes both hitting and hurting behaviors, whether or not these behaviors are reinforced by pain cues from the victim or target person. This category also includes *injury to or theft of property.*(1987:435, emphasis added)

This definition excludes nothing found in ordinary sociological defini-tions of crime and delinquency (Hirschi 1969; Wolfgang, Figlio, and Sellin 1972; Elliott, Huizinga, and Ageton 1985). If the *dependent or outcome variable* in studies of aggression is some form of ordinary crime, as measured by self-reports of delinquent activities or by convictions for criminal offenses in a court of law, we cannot simultaneously use *this variable* as a measure of aggression. Put another way, if crime is used as a measure of aggression, aggression cannot be thought of as a cause of crime, contrary to the stated justification of much psychological research (described above).

To illustrate this problem, consider the television-violence-causes-ag-gression-causes-crime issue. In this line of research, it is routinely assumed that aggression may be learned independently of other forms of deviant behavior. For example, Eron comments on a correlation between the frequency of viewing television at age eight and criminal convictions twenty-two years later:

> [W]hat was probably important were the attitudes and behavioral norms inculcated by continued watching of those and similar programs. In this regard, we can consider continued television violence viewing as rehearsal of aggressive sequences. Thus, one who watches more aggressive sequences on television should respond more aggressively when presented with similar or relevant cues. From an information-processing perspective, sociocultural norms, reinforced by continual displays in the broadcast media, play an important role by providing standards and values against which the child can compare his or her own behavior and the behavior of others to judge whether they are appropriate. (Eron 1987:440)

This explanation appears in a different light when it is recalled that television viewing at age eight would (given the operational definition of aggression used in this research) equally well predict theft, motor vehicle accidents, trivial nonviolent offending, drug consumption, and employment instability, behaviors hard to attribute to the number of shootings or fist fights watched on television twenty years previously. In fact, Eron (1987:440) tells us that "aggression at age 8 predicted social failure, psychopathology, aggression, and low educational and occupa-tional success" twenty-two years later. Huesmann et al. (1984:1122) add as "measures of aggressiveness" the number of moving traffic violations, the number of convictions for driving while intoxicated, and number of convictions for criminal acts. However, if psychologists treat aggression as a general concept that includes accidents, theft, withdrawal, lack of ambition, and drug use, they cannot at the same time treat it as a specific concept centered on physical assault. Since it behaves as a general tendency, it seems unlikely that television viewing at age eight was independent of this general tendency at age eight. It therefore seems unlikely that the specific content of television programming viewed at age eight could contribute independently to subsequent levels of "aggression."

Convergent and Discriminant Validity of Field Measures

To put our discussion of the validity of field measures of aggression in context, we use commonly accepted criteria of convergent and discriminant validity (Campbell and Fiske 1959; see also Jackman 1973:332).

1. Valid measures of aggression should be correlated with other measures of aggression produced by the same and by different methods (convergent validity).
2. Measures of aggression can be invalidated by being too strongly correlated to measures of other concepts. Thus, valid measures of aggression will be more strongly correlated to other measures of aggression than to measures of concepts other than aggression produced by the same method (discriminant validity).
3. Valid measures of aggression should not be related to exogenous variables in precisely the same form or pattern as are measures of different concepts (predictors of aggression should not prove to be interchangeable with predictors of concepts distinct from aggression).

Convergent Validity

As reported above, it is established that aggression can be reliably measured, whether one is talking about stability or internal consistency. Table 2.3 shows intercorrelations among such measures of aggression as robbery, assault with weapons, physical assault, and fighting with authorities (teachers and police), in standard self-report delinquency data (Hindelang et al. 1981).

As is evident, the correlations among the measures are all positive, and nearly all are significant at the .001 level. The index of aggressive behavior produced by these twelve items has a split half reliability of .76.

This measure of aggression correlates as expected with measures produced by other methods. Thus table 2.4 shows the relation between

TABLE 2.3

Correlations among Measures of Aggression (White Males, Seattle)

MEASURE	1.	2.	3.	4.	5.	6.	7.	8.	9.	10.	11.	12.
1. Purse snatch	-	09*	16	07**	12	12	15	12	12	15	13	12
2. Armed robbery		-	33	20	34	25	15	19	22	18	31	08*
3. Threaten			-	33	21	16	20	17	16	21	26	10*
4. Strong arm				-	19	15	11	11	13	22	19	07**
5. Carry weapon					-	48	21	18	29	18	25	09*
6. Display weapon						-	24	18	31	20	24	07**
7. Resist arrest							-	19	28	21	14	19
8. Hit teacher								-	20	19	20	21
9. Aggravated assault									-	24	31	10*
10. Picked fight										-	29	11
11. Jumped someone											-	14
12. Hit parent												-

N=833.

*Significant at .01, one tailed test.

**Not significant at .01. Otherwise significant at .001 level.

self reported aggression and police record for delinquency. Among those reporting no violent acts, 39 percent have either police or court records. Among those reporting four or more violent acts, 79 percent have such records. These differences reflect a correlation of .27. (The Seattle study oversampled youth known to have police records. The base rate for delinquency, as shown, is 53 percent, considerably higher than would be found in a general population sample of white juveniles.)

If the validity of concepts is determined by empirical relations between their measures and measures of cognate concepts, the correlation between a reliable measure of aggression and independent measures of criminality would seem to establish at least provisionally the validity of the idea of aggression. The next criterion to consider is the ability to distinguish between measures of aggression and measures of crime.

Discriminant Validity

To examine the discriminant validity of aggression we selected a large set of "nonaggressive" criminal and delinquent acts, acts that connote

stealth, passivity, or retreatism. One group of items within this set
measures theft without the use of force or violence; the other measures
drug use. Both sets of items are conceptually and empirically

TABLE 2.4
Percent with Police or Court Records, by Self-Reported Aggression
(White Males, Seattle)

	Number of Self-Reported Violent Acts					
	None	One	Two	Three	Four+	Total
Official record	39	58	60	69	79	53
	(385)	(193)	(92)	(61)	(103)	(834)

r=.27, gamma=.42, p < .001

homogeneous, as was our measure of aggression. The split half reliability
coefficient for the sixteen theft items is .80, for the ten drug items it is
.87 (for the content of the scales, see the Appendix).

TABLE 2.5
Correlates of Aggressive Behavior and Alternative Measures
of Low Self-Control (White Males, Richmond/Seattle)

	Theft	Violence	Drugs	General
Parental supervision	-.28/-.23	-.23/-.25	-.29/-.30	-.35/-.31
Amorality	.29/.30	.25/.30	.28/.28	.33/.35
Ambition	-.24/-.23	-.18/-.19	-.21/-.29	-.27/-.29
Theft		.43/.48	.42/.56	.89/.88
Violence			.31/.44	.76/.72

For details of data collection, see Hirschi (1969) and Hindelang, Hirschi, and Weis (1981). Ns:
Richmond=1034-1052; Seattle=640. For details of scale construction see Appendix A.

Recalling that the validity of a measure may be called into question if
its correlation with measures of other concepts is too high, there is good
reason to be concerned about the discriminant validity of aggression. The

correlation between the theft and violence indexes is .43 in Richmond and .48 in Seattle; the correlation between drugs and aggression is .31 in Richmond and .44 in Seattle. (Theft is correlated with drugs .42 and .56.) Given the generally moderate correlation among *all* measures of crime and delinquency, these correlations are high enough to question the assumption that aggression is independent of a more general construct encompassing violence, theft, and drug use.

The final test of discriminant validity involves comparison of the explanatory correlates of these potentially overlapping concepts. Can we discriminate between aggression and alternative measures of crime and delinquency on the basis of a set of standard explanatory variables? Table 2.5 presents correlations between violence, theft, and drugs and three indicators of concepts frequently used to explain delinquency, parental supervision, amorality, and ambition (Hindelang, Hirschi, and Weis 1981:129). (Details of index construction are provided in the Appendix.) In all cases, in both data sets, the correlations of the three outside variables and the three dependent variables are indistinguishable. With respect to these independent variables, then, the three measures of "criminality" are interchangeable. Table 2.5 also shows that a composite scale constructed from the three separate measures of criminality produces results identical to those produced by the three taken one at a time. (Similar results are in evidence for a different set of independent variables in table 2.1.) There is thus every reason within these sets of data to treat "aggression" as an idea indistinguishable from the more general idea of criminality. As would be expected from the results of much previous research in sociological criminology, the concept of aggression here fails an explicit test of discriminant validity.

Conclusions and Implications

The results of this study suggest (1) Measures of aggression used in laboratory studies lack convergent validity (are not correlated in the expected direction with other measures of aggression), and seem conceptually and empirically close to the concept of compliance. (2) Measures of aggression in field studies possess good convergent validity and stability, but cannot be discriminated from measures of crime.

From a social control point of view, aggressive or violent acts are explicable as acts that produce immediate benefits and entail long-term social costs for the actor. Such acts are usually defined as criminal by the state and as deviant by society, and are the very acts social control theory is designed to explain (Gottfredson and Hirschi 1990). There are also aggressive or violent acts that produce no immediate benefit to the actor but that are thought to produce long-term social benefits. Such acts are usually conceptualized as conformity, and are therefore also easily explained within a control theory framework.

This chapter argues that psychological laboratory researchers confuse one of these forms of aggression with the other, that they treat conformity as deviance. As a consequence, the results of psychological laboratory research do not threaten the validity of sociological theories of deviance. This research provides no evidence of an individual personality trait or propensity that produces assaultive or violent behavior independent of its social consequences. An additional implication of our interpretation is that sociologists working on violence and aggression should not attempt to incorporate the findings of this laboratory research into their theories.

As noted, violent and assaultive acts that produce immediate benefit at the same time they produce long term social costs are of interest to students of crime and deviance. Indeed, to the extent that aggressive acts share these defining characteristics of most forms of crime and deviance, they will easily fall within the scope of a general control theory. Recently, we have argued that many violent acts can be understood in precisely this way (Gottfredson and Hirschi 1990). For example, upon inspection, much homicide, child abuse, spouse abuse, and violent robbery is undertaken to gain some momentary advantage without regard for long term social consequences. When a husband strikes his wife repeatedly as a way to end an argument; when a father physically assaults a child to end an annoyance of the moment; or, when a robber shoots a clerk because he is nervous about his escape, the advantage of the moment has outweighed considerations of distant costs. Sociological control theorists focus on social forces that produce variability in the extent to which group members are influenced by the long-term costs of their behavior (Hirschi 1969; Kornhauser 1978; Gottfredson and Hirschi 1990; Heckathorn 1990).

This interpretation presupposes strong relationships among forms of crime and deviance. Fortunately, a great deal of research in criminology and sociology is consistent with the assumption that offenders are versatile, that they do not specialize in violent or nonviolent behavior

(Hindelang, Hirschi, and Weis 1981; Osgood et al. 1988: Osgood 1990; Robins 1966; Rojek and Erickson 1982; Rowe, Osgood, and Nicewander 1990; Sampson and Laub 1990, 1993; Wolfgang, Figlio, and Sellin 1972). Such research indeed reveals a latent trait underlying the bulk of criminal, delinquent, and even imprudent behavior (Osgood et al. 1988; Rowe, Osgood, and Nicewander 1990). The manifestations of this general trait, for example, drug use, theft, and employment instability, are often inconsistent with the concept of aggression as used in psychological research (Gottfredson and Hirschi 1990:65–72, 85–120).

Consistent with the finding of a general trait underlying many forms of criminal and deviant behavior, the concept of aggression does not survive an ordinary test of discriminant validity. Aggressive deviant acts share so much in common with nonaggressive deviant acts that individuals prone to commit aggressive criminal acts are prone to commit nonaggressive deviant acts as well. Thus no individual-level trait of aggression is consistent with the results of behavioral research.

Appendix

The Richmond *violence* and *theft* scales were constructed from six four-category items, measuring frequency of involvement in delinquent acts. The two items "Not counting fights you may have had with a brother or sister, have you ever beaten up on anyone or hurt anyone on purpose?" and "Have you ever banged up something that did not belong to you on purpose?" were combined to form the violence measure. The theft scale was composed of three items measuring various amounts of theft, and a single item measuring car theft. The *drug* scale summed responses to questions about smoking and drinking.

The Seattle delinquency indexes were constructed by dichotomizing all items between 0 and 1 or more and summing the results. (Such "ever variety" indexes have been shown to outperform indexes based on raw frequencies of offenses (see Hindelang, Hirschi, and Weis [1981].) Illustrative items include: "Have you ever taken things worth between $10 and $50 from a store without paying for them?" "Have you ever used a club, knife, or gun to get something from someone?" "Have you ever drunk beer or wine?" The items are reproduced in full in Hindelang, Hirschi, and Weis 1981.

In Seattle, the *parental supervision* (table 5) index is based on five items: "When you are away from home, does your Mother (Father) know where you are and who you are with?" "As far as my Mother (Father) is concerned, I am pretty much free to come and go as I please." "I could stay away from home overnight, and no one would ask me where I had been." In Richmond (tables 1 and 5), the supervision index is based on four items assessing parental knowledge of the youth's whereabouts.

In Seattle, the *amorality* index (table 5) is based on four items: "It is alright to get around the law if you can get away with it." "Suckers deserve what they get." "To get ahead, you have to do some things that are not right." "Everybody steals something once in a while." The Richmond index (table 5) is based on the first three items listed above.

In Seattle, the measure of *ambition* (table 5) is based on three items: "How important is getting good grades to you, personally." "I try hard in school." "Whatever I do, I try hard." In Richmond (tables 1 and 5), this index is based on the two "try hard" items and the item, "A person should never stop trying to get ahead."

The measure of *fatalism* in table 1 (Richmond) is based on three items: "What is going to happen to me will happen, no matter what I do." "A person should live for today and let tomorrow take care of itself." "Planning is useless since one's plans hardly ever work out."

Notes

1. The responses of some psychologists to this chapter suggest that they are highly sensitive to the meaning of measures of "aggression." In fact, our ignorance of "what psychologists know" about aggression has more than once been characterized as so colossal that our arguments need not be taken seriously. Fortunately for us, "what psychologists know" about aggression is not itself particularly reliable or stable. Fortunately, too, we are not the first to suggest that much laboratory research on aggression is in fact research on "defensive coercion" compelled by norms of reciprocity (See Tedeschi, Brown III, and Brown, Jr. 1974; Tedeschi, Gaes, and Rivera 1977).
2. In sociological theory, deviant behavior is often defined as a violation of others' expectations (Parsons 1951). In this sense, our operational definition of laboratory aggression is identical to the definition in the original frustration-aggression formulation, where frustration is "an obstacle blocking the attainment on an expected gratification," and aggression is an attempt to inflict injury (Berkowitz 1989:61).
3. Milgram (1974:205) reports little success in his efforts to establish the convergent validity of obedience. In our view, such difficulties should not be taken to show the superiority of "behavioral measures" so much as an all too common lack of attention to the meaning or validity of these measures. For example, Milgram reports that obedient subjects are more authoritarian, but appears unwilling to put much faith in the measure of authoritarianism because it relies on "paper and pencil" responses rather than "actual submission." It seems plausible to assume that the shared variance in the two measures is due to the large acquiescence component in the

measure of authoritarianism. If so, the operative meaning of obedience is something like "agreeableness stemming from diffidence" rather than the more sinister "willingness to punish the weak." Milgram's finding that obedience is correlated with low education (p. 205) is also consistent with our interpretation of his work as dealing with what survey researchers call acquiescence or "yea-saying" (Jackman 1973).

References

Anderson, Craig A. 1989. "Temperature and Aggression: Ubiquitous Effects of Heat on Occurrence of Human Violence." *Psychological Bulletin* 106: 74–96.

Bandura, Albert. 1973. *Aggression: A Social Learning Analysis*. Englewood Cliffs, NJ: Prentice-Hall.

Baron, Robert. 1976. "The Reduction of Human Aggression: A Field Study of the Influence of Incompatible Reactions." *Journal of Applied Social Psychology* 6:260–74.

Berkowitz, Leonard. 1989. "Frustration-Aggression Hypothesis: Examination and Reformulation." *Psychological Bulletin* 106:59–73.

Bernard, Thomas. 1990. "Angry Aggression Among the 'Truly Disadvantaged.'" *Criminology* 28:73–96.

Blau, Judith, and Peter Blau. 1982. "The Cost of Inequality: Metropolitan Structure and Violent Crime." *American Sociological Review* 47: 114–29.

Blumstein, Alfred, Jacqueline Cohen, Jeffrey Roth, and Christy Visher. 1986. *Criminal Careers and "Career Criminals"* Washington, DC: National Academy Press.

Buss, Arnold. 1961. *The Psychology of Aggression*. New York: Wiley.

Campbell, Donald, and Donald Fiske. 1959. "Convergent and Discriminant Validation by the Multitrait-Multimethod Matrix." *Psychological Bulletin* 56:81–105.

Cloward, Richard, and Lloyd Ohlin. 1960. *Delinquency and Opportunity*. New York: Free Press.

Cook, Thomas, Deborah Kendzierski, and Stephen Thomas. 1983. "The Implicit Assumptions of Television Research: An Analysis of the 1982 NIMH Report on Television and Behavior." *Public Opinion Quarterly* 47:161–201.

Dollard, J., L. Doob, N. Miller, O. Mowrer, and R. Sears. 1939. *Frustration and Aggression*. New Haven: Yale University Press.

Dornbusch, Sanford, J. Merrill Carlsmith, Steven Bushwall, Philip Ritter, Herbert Leiderman, Albert Hastorf, and Ruth Gross. 1985. "Single Parents, Extended Households, and the Control of Adolescents." *Child Development* 56:326–41.

Elliott, Delbert, David Huizinga, and Suzanne Ageton. 1985. *Explaining Delinquency and Drug Use*. Beverly Hills, CA: Sage.

Eron, Leonard. 1987. "The Development of Aggressive Behavior from the Perspective of a Developing Behaviorism." *American Psychologist* 42:435–42.

Farrington, David. 1978. "The Family Backgrounds of Aggressive Youth." In *Aggression and Antisocial Behavior in Childhood and Adolescence*, ed. L. Hersov, M. Berger, and D. Shaffer, 73–93. Oxford, England: Pergamon Press.

Farrington, David, Lloyd Ohlin, and James Q. Wilson. 1986. *Understanding and Controlling Crime*. New York: Springer Verlag.

Gaebelein, Jacquelyn, and Stuart Taylor. 1971. "The Effects of Competition and Attack on Physical Aggression." *Psychonomic Science* 24:65–67.

Geen, Russell. 1968. "Effects of Frustration, Attack, and Prior Training in Aggressiveness upon Aggressive Behavior." *Journal of Personality and Social Psychology* 9:316–21.

Gelles, Richard. 1980. "Violence in the Family: A Review of Research in the Seventies." *Journal of Marriage and the Family* 42: 873–85.

Gentry, William. 1970. "Effects of Frustration, Attack, and Prior Aggressive Training on Overt Aggression and Vascular Processes." *Journal of Personality and Social Psychology* 16:718–25.

Gottfredson, Michael, and Travis Hirschi. 1990. *A General Theory of Crime.* Stanford, CA: Stanford University Press.

Heckathorn, Douglas. 1990. "Collective Sanctions and Compliance Norms—A Formal Theory of Group-Mediated Social-Control." *American Sociological Review* 55:366–84.

Hindelang, Michael, Travis Hirschi, and Joseph Weis. 1981. *Measuring Delinquency.* Beverly Hills, CA: Sage.

Hirschi, Travis. 1969. *Causes of Delinquency.* Berkeley: University of California Press.

Hirschi, Travis, and Michael Gottfredson. 1990. "Substantive Positivism and the Idea of Crime." *Rationality and Society* 2:412–28.

Hirschi, Travis, and Michael Hindelang. 1977. "Intelligence and Delinquency: A Revisionist Review." *American Sociological Review* 42:571–87.

Huesmann, L. Rowell, Leonard Eron, Monroe Lefkowitz, and Leopold Walder. 1984. "Stability of Aggression over Time and Generations." *Developmental Psychology* 20:1120–34.

Hynan, D. J., and J. E. Grush. 1986. "Effects of Impulsivity, Depression, Provocation, and Time on Aggressive Behavior." *Journal of Research on Personality* 20:158–71.

Jackman, Mary. 1973. "Education and Prejudice or Education and Response-Set? *American Sociological Review* 38:327–39.

Jensen, Gary, and Raymond Eve. 1976. "Sex Differences in Delinquency: An Examination of Popular Sociological Explanations." *Criminology* 13:427–48.

Kornhauser, Ruth. 1978. *Social Sources of Delinquency.* Chicago: University of Chicago Press.

Kulik, James, and Roger Brown. 1979. "Frustration, Attribution of Blame, and Aggression." *Journal of Experimental Social Psychology* 15:183–94.

Matsueda, Ross. 1982. "Testing Control Theory and Differential Association: A Causal Modeling Approach." *American Sociological Review* 47:489–504.

Matsueda, Ross, and Karen Heimer. 1987. "Race, Family Structure, and Delinquency: A Test of Differential Association and Social Control Theory." *American Sociological Review* 52:826–40.

Merton, Robert. 1938. "Social Structure and 'Anomie.'" *American Sociological Review* 3:672–82.

Milavsky, J., R. Kessler, H. Stipp, and W. Rubens. 1982. *Television and Aggression: The Results of a Panel Study.* New York: Academic Press.

Milgram, Stanley. 1974. *Obedience to Authority: An Experimental View.* New York: Harper & Row.

Monahan, John. 1981. *Predicting Violent Behavior: An Assessment of Clinical Techniques.* Beverly Hills, CA: Sage.

National Institute of Mental Health. 1982. *Television and Behavior: Ten Years of Scientific Progress and Implications for the Eighties.* Rockville, MD: NIMH.

Olweus, Dan. 1979. "Stability of Aggressive Reaction Patterns in Males: A Review." *Psychological Bulletin* 86:852–75.

_____. 1980. "Familial and Temperamental Determinants of Aggressive Behavior in Adolescent Boys: A Causal Analysis." *Developmental Psychology* 16:644–60.

Osgood, D. Wayne. 1990. "Covariation among Adolescent Problem Behaviors." Paper presented at the 1990 meetings of the American Society of Criminology, Baltimore. MD.

Osgood, D. Wayne, Lloyd Johnston, Patrick O'Malley, and Jerald Bachman. 1988. "The Generality of Deviance in Late Adolescence and Early Adulthood." *American Sociological Review* 53:81–93.

Parsons, Talcott. 1951. *The Social System*. New York: The Free Press.

Reichel, Howard, and David Magnusson. 1988. "The Relationship of Intelligence to Registered Criminality: An Exploratory Study." Reports from the Department of Psychology, No. 676, University of Stockholm, Stockholm, Sweden.

Robins, Lee. 1966. *Deviant Children Grown Up*. Baltimore, MD: Williams and Wilkins.

Rojek, Dean, and Maynard Erickson. 1982. "Delinquent Careers: A Test of the Career Escalation Model." *Criminology* 20:5–28.

Rowe, David, D. Wayne Osgood, and W. Alan Nicewander. 1990. "A Latent Trait Approach to Unifying Criminal Careers." *Criminology* 28:237–70.

Sampson, Robert, and John Laub. 1990. "Crime and Deviance over the Life Course: The Salience of Adult Social Bonds." *American Sociological Review* 55:609–27.

_____. 1993. *Crime in the Making: Pathways and Turning Points Through Life*. Cambridge, MA: Harvard University Press.

Straus, Murray, Richard Gelles, and Susan Steinmetz. 1980. *Behind Closed Doors: Violence in the American Family*. Garden City, NY: Anchor Press.

Tedeschi, J. T., R. B. Brown III, and R.C. Brown, Jr. 1974. "A Reinterpretation of Research on Aggression." *Psychological Bulletin* 81:540–63.

Tedeschi, James T., Gerald G. Gaes, and Alba N. Rivera. 1977. "Aggression and the Use of Coercive Power." *Journal of Social Issues* 33:101–25.

Widom, Cathy. 1989a. "The Cycle of Violence." *Science* 244:160–66.

_____. 1989b. "Does Violence Beget Violence? A Critical Examination of the Literature." *Psychological Bulletin* 106:3–28.

Wilson, James Q., and Richard Herrnstein. 1985. *Crime and Human Nature*. New York: Simon and Schuster.

Wolfgang, Marvin, Robert Figlio, and Thorsten Sellin. 1972. *Delinquency in a Birth Cohort*. Chicago: University of Chicago Press.

3

Family

Travis Hirschi

Any influence within or without the family . . . which aids the growing youngster to manage his primitive inclinations . . . is a preventive of delinquency. Per contra, the more the instructive, protective, and supportive social institutions . . . disintegrate and thereby lose their power to socialize . . . , the more will the natural impulses toward selfish, asocial . . . or antisocial expression tend to flow into action. (Sheldon Glueck 1959:126)

It seems reasonable to begin a discussion of family structure and crime with the assumption that the substantial increase in single-parent families in recent years is somehow connected to the high rate of crime and drug abuse in American society. Following the logic of our epigraph, we could go further and suggest that the connection is causal, that any loss of the instructive, protective, or supportive power of the family will eventually show itself in higher rates of deviant behavior. Having said this, we would then have to recognize that the crime rate peaked about ten years ago, moved down for about five years, and is only now approaching 1980 levels. We would also have to recognize that drug use stabilized in the

---

Editors' note: The general theory explicitly assigns to parents or functionally equivalent adults a major role in the development of self-control, but it does not by this deny that familial institutions may affect the likelihood of crime in other ways as well. This chapter looks at the several ways the family may control crime, and how these crime-control functions are affected by the size of the family and the number of parents it contains. Papers yet to be written would apply the theory in similar fashion to the school, the community, the job, and the criminal justice system. We are confident such papers would further illustrate the utility (and essential optimism) of the theory.

This chapter was prepared for a conference sponsored by The Rockford Institute, Rockford, Illinois, and is reprinted from *When Families Fail . . . The Social Costs*, ed. Bryce J. Christensen (Lanham, MD: University Press of American, 1991), 43–65. Reprinted by permission. Copyright 1991 by University Press of America.

first few years of the decade and has actually fallen since 1985. Yet during this decade of stability and even decline in crime and drug use, the two-parent family has continued to take a beating in the statistics.

We are thus warned at the outset that the connection between family structure and crime is probably not as strong as we are sometimes inclined to assume. This warning is reinforced by the conclusion of most research in the area: Structural factors may well be causally connected to crime, but their effects are small, and the mediating or family function-ing variables are so much stronger that it is easy to account for the effects of the structural variables and to find conditions in which they appear to have no effect at all.

Put another way, if we take the direct approach to the question of the connection between family structure and crime, it is virtually assured that we will come eventually to an unsatisfying conclusion. Others have stated it well: "We should expect to find statistical associations with criminality that are partial, easily obscured by other factors, and heavily dependent on the nature of the sample and the measures of criminality" (Wilson and Herrnstein 1985:248; see also Gove and Crutchfield 1982:316).

Given this fact, it seems to me we would be well advised to approach the connection between family structure and crime only after we have satisfied ourselves that we know what to expect to find when we get there—only after we have constructed a theory and spelled out its implications for the role of the family in crime causation. Following this indirect approach, we can at least hope to get beyond the traditional conclusion that all is complex and difficult to a positive conclusion potentially useful to theory and policy.

The indirect approach takes us first to what we wish to explain, in this case crime. Michael Gottfredson and I have published a book (Gottfred-son and Hirschi 1990) that concludes that ineffective child rearing is one of the major causes of crime. In writing this book, we found ourselves returning again and again to four facts. In our view, all argue one way or another for the importance of child rearing, and all are consistent with a particular conception of crime and its causes. Before introducing these facts, let me summarize the conceptual scheme from which we believe they can be derived.

Crime

We begin with the notion, not original to us, that all human acts are attempts to maximize pleasure and minimize pain. From this it follows that crimes are also attempts to increase pleasure and reduce pain. Crimes are distinguished from noncrimes by the fact that they are punished by the state. The state adds painful consequences to some acts in an effort to reduce the frequency of their occurrence. Generally, these are acts whose benefits clearly exceed their costs, at least in the short run, but which have directly painful consequences for others. Put another way, the state is generally interested in reducing the use of force and fraud for private or personal ends. Once attention is called to the common elements in crimes, it is apparent that many noncriminal acts are analogous to them, that many acts not sanctioned by the state also produce immediate gratification at the risk of long-term pain. Obvious examples are alcohol, tobacco, and drug use, truancy from school and work, promiscuous sex, overeating, and rock climbing.[1]

If we turn our attention to the behavior of children, it is not hard to see much of their pushing, shoving, hitting, screaming, and stealing as also analogous to crime—that is, as displaying interest in immediate benefit without concern for the rights of others or for long range costs.

Crimes, then, take little planning, skill, or effort. They and their analogs are available to everyone without training or tutelage. Given that they are governed by the desires of the moment, and are in addition subject to long-term penalties, they may be expected to interfere with the attainment of ends requiring planning, skill, or effort.

Criminals

We assume that the nature of people relatively likely to engage in crimes can be derived from the nature of the acts themselves. Thus, offenders should be oriented to the pleasures of the moment, and little concerned about long-term consequences. They should tend to lack diligence, tenacity, or persistence in a course of action. They should tend to pursue immediate pleasures that are not criminal; they should be more likely to party, to smoke, drink, gamble, and get pregnant before they are married.

We believe the evidence is substantially consistent with these inferences, that a stable, general trait or tendency underlies a broad range of criminal and noncriminal acts. We call this tendency low self-control. Let me summarize this evidence.

Versatility

Much evidence confirms that those committing any given criminal act are likely to commit other criminal acts as well, that tendencies among offenders to specialize in particular crimes are, to put it mildly, weak. As a result, it is misleading to speak of thieves, robbers, rapists, or burglars. In official data, the offender's prior and subsequent offenses are as likely as not to differ from the instant offense, with no apparent trend in sequences of offenses toward greater seriousness, sophistication, or specialization (e.g., Wolfgang, Figlio, and Sellin 1972). Self-report data involving large numbers of delinquent and criminal acts routinely show that responses to all items are positively correlated (Hindelang, Hirschi, and Weis 1981).

The versatility of offenders extends to noncriminal acts analogous to crime. Offenders are more likely to smoke, drink, use drugs (Akers 1992), skip school, and be involved in accidents. In many cases, the correlations between these offenses and criminal acts are as strong as those among criminal acts themselves, suggesting that the distinction between crimes and these particular noncriminal acts is artificial.

Versatility suggests that heinous crimes, trivial peccadillos, and indeed the ordinary self-indulgences of everyday life have the same functions for the individual or are produced by the same causes. Apparently, one feature criminal and deviant acts share is that they are ends in themselves, governed by proximate, direct, and transparent motives.

Immediacy

Most theories assume that the purposes or motives behind crimes are larger than those obvious in the acts themselves, that, for example, the motive behind theft is not goods or money, but success, self-esteem, or the good opinion of others; that the motive behind rape is not sex, but power, control, or hatred of women. Ironically, the search for large or general purposes behind crime leads to the expectation that offenders will favor some offenses to the exclusion of others, that they will tend to become more sophisticated, skillful, or careful over time. In fact, as we have seen, none of these tendencies can be detected in "criminal careers." We are led, then, to the conclusion that criminal and delinquent acts go together because each and all represent one of the myriad ways we can attempt to feel better or hurt less here and now.

If the impulse to a particular criminal or deviant act is fleeting and easily overcome by inconvenience or delay, the general tendency to engage in such acts appears to be made of more resistent material.

Stability

In fact, differences among people in the likelihood that they will commit criminal or analogous acts tend to persist over long periods of time, from childhood to adulthood. Psychologists studying aggression (Olweus 1979), criminologists following children into their teens and "delinquents" into adulthood (Glueck and Glueck 1968; West and Farrington 1977; Shannon 1981), all report that those high on crime or its analogs at early periods are likely to remain more likely to commit such acts after many years have passed (see also Robins 1966).

Age and Crime

Most criminologists agree that crime generally peaks in late adolescence or early adulthood, and then declines rapidly to the end of life. A few years ago, we advanced the idea that this relation is in fact invariant over social and cultural conditions, the idea that age has a direct, or, for all intents and purposes, an unmediated, effect on crime. We believe the evidence also points to similar declines in offenses analogous to crime, in accidents, substance abuse, and illicit sexual activity.

So, we have a trait that is general (has implications for a broad range of behavior) and stable (differences between people are resistent to change), but declines sharply with age. Our trait is also weak in that it allows but does not seem to require deviant behavior. Those high on the tendency to commit criminal and analogous acts quickly lose interest in them as they are made more difficult, time consuming, or painful.

Self-Control

We believe the concept of self control captures the relatively stable tendency to engage in (and avoid) a wide range of criminal, deviant, or reckless acts better than such traditional concepts as criminality, aggression, or conscience. Criminality suggests a specific propensity to crime contrary to the finding that "criminals" can get along quite well without crimes. It also suggests a tendency to specialize in criminal acts, a suggestion contrary to the finding that offenders are as likely to engage in the pursuit of noncriminal as criminal pleasures. Aggression has similar problems. In addition, it is not easily squared with the fact that the bulk of deviant acts are passive, surreptitious, or retreatist (e.g., theft and drug use). With its emphasis on restraint, conscience is closer than criminality to self control. However, it too is more easily applied to sinful, immoral, or illegal acts than to imprudent acts; it has unfortunate connotations of compulsion, if to conformity, and it has not been much developed, even by those inclined to favor it.

The Family and the Facts

What do these facts say about the role of the family or child rearing in crime causation? The fact most obviously relevant to the family is the stability of differences in the likelihood of criminal and deviant behavior over the life course. These stable differences appear to be established as early as ages six to eight. They must therefore be traceable to training in the family, to inherited predispositions, or to some combination of training and predisposition. If the early "onset" of delinquency does not rule out biological inheritance, it devastates theories that ignore the family and assume teenage "desocialization" as a result of exposure to delinquent peer groups or to the American dream of monetary success.

The versatility finding is also significant for the institutional location of explanations of crime. If pushing, shoving, whining, and taking at an early age are equivalent to delinquency in adolescence and crime in adulthood, the family's stake in crime control is obvious, and many of the puzzles of crime research appear in a new light. Crime can be studied well before its "onset," and children can be trained to avoid criminal acts they are at the time incapable of committing.

Immediacy would seem to be the characteristic of criminal acts whose implications for child rearing is most in need of analysis. Under modern conditions of affluence and abundance, the possibilities for immediate satisfaction of transient wants are enormous, and it is often not obvious why these wants should be denied. Put another way, prosperity may reduce the value of self control as it undermines the family's ability to produce it. We will try to return to this issue again in the context of research results.

The age finding indicates that by the time the family is normally done with the child (by the time it is no longer legally responsible), the crime years are rapidly coming to a close anyway. Put another way, if the family is able to keep the child out of trouble during the period it is responsible, the chances of later difficulty are small. Once again, the family does the job of crime control or it is not done at all.

We assume that people can be ranked on a continuum from high to low self-control. At the high end, child rearing institutions and the exigencies of life have somehow built into some people generalized resistence or indifference to the pleasures of the moment. In exchange for their asceticism, these people disproportionately avoid the long term physical, legal, and social costs such pleasures normally entail. At the low end of the self-control continuum, child rearing institutions and the exigencies of life have somehow failed to build into other people the resistence described. In exchange for pleasures of the moment, these people bear disproportionately the long term social, economic, and physical costs such pleasures normally entail.

Our analysis of the costs and benefits of self control suggests that familial institutions, indeed all social institutions, will favor self-control over its absence. We are thus justified in the assumption that low self-control represents the failure of institutions to realize their values, that low self control is evidence that something has gone wrong. We are now perhaps in position to face directly the role of the family in crime prevention. How might the family realize its interest in crime control?

1. *The family may reduce the likelihood of criminal behavior by socializing its children, by teaching them self-control.* If this much is given by previous analysis, the difficult question is how socialization is accomplished or self-control produced. In our view, the best "model" of this process is a statement of the conditions individually necessary and collectively sufficient for socialization to occur. I have previously described this model, derived from the parent training program of the Oregon Social Learning Center (Patterson 1980) and the research of Sheldon and Eleanor Glueck (1950), as containing four elements: caring for the child, monitoring the child's behavior, recognizing deviant behavior when it occurs, and punishing it (Hirschi 1983). Such elementary

training should condition the child to consider the long-range consequences of a wide variety of immediately pleasurable acts.

In the context of the present discussion, and adjusting for criticism of the earlier model, I should more explicitly note that "caring" need not involve parental love, only an adult with sufficient stake in the socialization of the child to do what is necessary to produce it. "Recognizing deviant behavior" should now be replaced with "recognizing evidence of low self-control." While the former term implicitly recognizes that something equivalent to and more general than crime is required to describe the relevant behavior of children, it does not go far enough in recognizing the relevance of many forms of short-sighted behavior that are not necessarily deviant. Finally, something like "correct" should be substituted for "punish." The latter term was justified earlier to highlight the inappropriateness of emphasizing rewards over penalties, but its unsavory connotations remain so strong in the minds of many that it should probably be replaced by a milder term.

Patterson's original parent training model (1980) was much more complex than the model I extracted from it. He now reports no success in attempts to show the importance of such "fine tuning variables" as parent involvement, positive reinforcement, and problem solving: "Although we have put a great deal of time and effort into building these constructs, they do not seem to account for any of the variance in predicting achievement or antisocial behavior other than what we already have in our measures of monitoring and discipline" (Patterson 1989).

In a recent reanalysis of the Gluecks' data, Laub and Sampson (1988) show the primacy of the parent-child variables described by the model (and their ability to account for the family structure variables found to be important by the Gluecks). A recent meta-analysis of the research literature on the family and delinquency (Loeber and Stouthamer-Loeber 1986) reaches similar conclusions. (In all candor, I must say however that it is often hard to know what meaning to attach to the whole body of research in the family-delinquency area. This research tradition has been guided by such diverse concepts, many inadequately defined or measured, that its bearing on some elements of the minimal model of child rearing, especially "recognition" and "discipline," is problematic.)

I continue to believe that a simple model is all the research literature can sustain. For example, when Wilson and Herrnstein summarize the results of research as showing separate etiologies for aggressive children and thieves, they inadvertently run into serious trouble with the facts: "The irritable parent who does not use discipline effectively tends to produce aggressive children; the indifferent and ineffective parent tends to produce larcenous ones. In the first case, the child discovers he can bully his parents; in the second, that he can evade them" (1985:230). Unfortunately for conclusions about the differential effects of child rearing practices, there is no good evidence for the existence of the distinct types allegedly produced by them. As we have seen, aggression and larceny (and drug abuse and truancy) tend to come wrapped together in the same package.

In fact, one way to test our model is to examine its general application to a wide range of acts. Alternative models often suggest specific consequences for specific patterns of child rearing, or complex interactions among family conditions and child rearing practices. Our model suggests, again, that such analyses mistake differences in the form of delinquent acts for differences in their causal content. If we are correct, the child rearing correlates of theft, aggressiveness, drug use, future orientation, achievement orientation, completion of homework, and grade point average (to take only a sample of indicators of self control) should be, for all intents and purposes, the same.

Table 3.1 displays the correlations between parental supervision in the Richmond data (Hirschi 1969) and measures of the variables listed above. In all cases, the correlations are (1) in the predicted direction, and (2) roughly comparable in magnitude, findings consistent with the idea that crime is a species of low self-control, a general trait produced by parental socialization practices.

Let us then move on to another aspect of family child rearing practice.

2. *The family may reduce the likelihood of delinquency by restricting its children's activity, by maintaining actual physical surveillance of them, and by making sure they know their whereabouts when they are out of sight.* Parental supervision should be an important variable in its own right as well as a component variable in a socialization model. Supervision gains its prominence in our scheme through the general youthfulness of offenders and the immediacy of the rewards produced by their delinquent acts. In my first look at this question, I concluded that direct parental control was of little "substantive or theoretical importance" (Hirschi 1969:88). This conclusion stemmed from awareness of the brevity of delinquent acts (a property closely related to the immediacy

of their benefits), and of the freedom enjoyed by most adolescents. But if brevity makes surveillance more difficult, immediacy makes it more profitable. The would-be offender can often do what he wants to do in a hurry, but if he is unable to do so, he is unlikely to persist in the effort. By the same token, adolescents may be relatively free today compared to adolescents in the past, but they remain relatively restricted compared to adults, and there is enough variation among families in this regard to make a difference, at least potentially.

TABLE 3.1
Correlations between Parental Supervision[a], Mother's Supervision, Number of Siblings, and Various Indicators of Self Control

	Parental* Supervision	Mother's** Supervision	Number of Siblings***
Smoking and drinking	-.30	-.27	.12
Self-reported violence	-.25	-.23	.10
Self-reported theft	-.29	-.27	.12
Offenses on police records	-.10	-.14	.15
Finish homework	.22	.20	-.11
Future orientation	.13	.13	-.12
Achievement orientation	.17	.18	.01 (n.s.)
Grade point average--English	.17	.16	-.17

[a]Four items: Does your mother (father) know where you are (whom you are with) when you are away from home. All correlations significant at the .001 level. *Ns range from 1004 to 1187. **N=822. ***Ns range from 1123 to 1547.

3. *The family may reduce the likelihood of delinquency by commanding the love, respect, or dependence of its members.* A self- or social control explanation of crime may focus on the enduring effects of socialization or on the current effects of ties to controlling institutions. In point of fact, the two effects are difficult to separate because those

high on self-control are likely to be well integrated into such institutions. For example, the student high on self-control will do his homework, do well in school, and consequently like school. When attachment to the school predicts nondelinquency, as it does, we cannot know without further analysis whether it does so because of self- or social control.

The same is true for attachment to or respect for parents. These attachments presumably produce conformity in their own right and also make socialization easier. (It is easier for the parent to correct a child who values the parent's opinion.) Our theory suggests that, for persons attached to controlling institutions, conformity carries its own rewards, and its explicit acknowledgment is therefore unnecessary. An alternative model stresses the idea that the power parents command as a result of the child's attachment is reduced if it is not exercised (Wilson and Herrnstein 1985:235). The issue is then whether the child's attitude toward the parents is important irrespective of its connection to their ability to reinforce the child's behavior.

4. *The family may reduce crime by guarding the home: by protecting it from potential thieves, vandals, and burglars.* Criminological theory traditionally focused on offenders rather than on offenses, and assumed that offenders were powerfully motivated to commit their crimes, especially "serious" crimes. Once the focus shifted to criminal events it became evident that offenders were not all that skillful, all that motivated, or all that dangerous. In fact, it soon became plain that familial institutions may play a role in crime control beyond watching their own members, that they can do much by merely protecting their own property. Further, it became clear that to do so effectively they need not brandish weapons or cower behind locked doors. The mere presence of a family member in the house or on the property is enough to deter the typical offender interested in burglary or theft. As a result, a major predictor of the burglary rate in an area is the proportion of homes occupied during the day, a proportion clearly affected by family structure (Cohen and Felson 1979).

5. *The family may reduce delinquency by protecting its members, by deterring potential fornicators, assaulters, molesters, and rapists.* Deterring potential burglars is one thing, deterring those interested in sex with or revenge on family members is another. Lone woman and women only families are at unusual risk from male predators, both inside and outside the home. (And children in families with stepparents, especially step-

fathers, also run unusual risks of sexual and physical abuse.) The situation described by Judith Blake in Jamaica must exist at least in attenuated form in many households whose defense can enlist no adult males:

> One of the most important and effective ways of protecting young girls from sexual exploitation is for male relatives to be ready and able to retaliate if such exploitation occurs. Whether this condition prevails depends heavily on the organization of the family. . . . Among lower-class Jamaicans, however, a father is as likely as not to be absent from the family picture. Brothers may be merely half-brothers, or living elsewhere. . . . The sexual exploitation of young girls therefore both results from family disorganization and contributes to it. Men are provided with a far wider range of sexual partners than they would be if girls were protected. Thus, there are fewer pressures on the man to form a permanent liaison. Moreover, once a woman has a child or two, her disirability can always be weighted by men against that of the childless young girl. Thus, because young girls are in many ways unprotected from male advances, older women are unprotected from the competition of young girls. (Blake 1961:89, quoted by Hartley 1975:67)

6. *Finally, the family may reduce delinquency by acting as an advocate for the child, as a probation or parole agency willing to guarantee the good conduct of its members.* At all levels of the criminal justice system, community or family ties are taken into account in processing decisions. The individual with no family to vouch for him is likely to penetrate the system further than the person whose family is willing to take responsibility for his conduct. It is sometimes said, in fact, that the criminal justice system tends to avoid intervention whenever it has an excuse for doing so. An extended, stable family obviously concerned for the offender's welfare makes a very good excuse indeed.

Now we are ready to turn to family structure and its implications for crime. Let us go directly to what appears to be the major structural trend of the modern age—the increasing prevalence of the mother only family.

The Single-Parent or Mother-Only Family

Our socialization model suggests that, all else being equal, one parent may be enough. Earlier, I argued that "all else is rarely equal" (Hirschi 1983:62), emphasizing the limits on the single parent's ability to monitor the child and punish deviant behavior. The present analysis suggests even further difficulties for the single parent. She is likely to be less able to restrict her children's activity, less able to protect them from predators, less able to guard the house in which they live, and less able to guarantee their good conduct to the school and the criminal justice system. All of this would make her appear less effective than the two-parent family even if it said little or nothing about the actual behavior of her children.

Clearly, we are again in danger of building an argument contrary to observed differences between single- and double-parent families, differences that can rarely be characterized as large. Before proceeding further, we should examine the differences between single-parent and double-parent families on measures of delinquency available to us, and compare these differences with those produced by comparable research (table 3.2).

To my mind, the similarities in table 3.2 between the results of the Richmond Youth Study (Hirschi 1969) and those reported by Dornbusch et al. (1985) for the National Health Examination Survey are remarkable, given the fact that the first is a local and the second a national sample. Both tend to show differences of the same magnitude between the single-parent and double-parent family. These differences are in the expected direction. They are, however, small, at least compared to those observed for the family functioning variables such as supervision, and are, in some cases, too small to reach significance, even with the large samples involved.

The data in table 3.2 would seem to confirm the view that family structure is especially important for forms of deviance that involve the reaction of other institutions (the police and the school). Thus, in the Richmond data, the self-report delinquency scale, made up of theft, fighting, and vandalism items, is unrelated to the parental makeup of the home, as is a combination measure of smoking and drinking. At the same time, the official measures of delinquency, and items measuring difficulty with the school, show differences favoring the two-parent family. All of which suggests that the effects on crime of the parental makeup of the family may be explained through examination of its role as advocate for the child. Apparently, the mother alone is especially handicapped in dealing with other institutions responsible for the child's conduct (Fenwick 1982). Dornbusch et al. (1985) report that youth in mother only households are slightly more likely than youth in two-parent households to be allowed to make their own decisions, but that this difference does not account for the observed effect of family structure. The difference in decision-making power in the Richmond data is even smaller, and given the smaller sample size does not reach statistical significance. Perhaps more significant is the finding that only about one in ten white males reports being free to make his own decisions, whatever the parental makeup of the family. The figure for black males suggests even greater parental control, with about one in fifteen (6.6 percent) saying that decisions are made by them rather than jointly with their mothers or by their mothers alone.

Table 3.2
Percent of Adolescents Deviant by Parental Makeup of Home[a]

	Two Natural Parents	Natural Mother
% police record (Richmond, white males)	23.4 (1113)	30.5 (226) (.01)
% law contact (Dornbusch, all males)	26 (2744)	36 (382) (.01)
% truant--self-report (Richmond, white males)	14.9 (1078)	19.7 (218) (.01)
% truant--school records (Dornbusch, all males)	1 (2501)	6 (318) (.001)
% reporting delinquent acts (Richmond, white males)	60.7 (1083)	61.2 (219) (n.s.)
% suspended--self-report (Richmond, white males)	19.6 (1080)	27.2 (217) (.05)
% school discipline (Dornbusch, all males)	35 (2303)	47 (291) (.001)
% smoke (Richmond, black males*)	29.4 (384)	34.5 (182) (.10)
% smoke regularly (Dornbusch, all males)	15 (2760)	20 (385) (.001)

[a]Dornbusch et al. 1985, and Richmond Youth Project data (Hirschi 1969). N's are in parentheses.
*White males not significant.

As expected, however, the child from the single-parent family is, according to his own reports, less well supervised than the child from the two-parent family—by both his mother and father. There is, then, at least in the eyes of the child, no tendency for the mother to compensate for the absence of her husband by increasing her own supervision. Whereas 59 percent of children in two parent families report that their mothers always know where they are and whom they are with, the comparable figure for children in mother only families is 51 percent. (For the father, these figures are 51 percent and 39 percent, indicating that mother's knowledge of the child's whereabouts under unfavorable conditions is still as good as father's under favorable conditions.)

A related fact seems worth mentioning. When asked what would be the worst thing about being caught stealing, children from two-parent families are significantly more likely than children from mother-only families to mention the reaction of parents (52 percent vs. 41 percent [.001]) (see also Steinberg 1987). If crime may be prevented by a moment's hesitation, a second parent in the child's active social network may make the difference between crime and noncrime.

The single-parent family is consistently shown to be economically disadvantaged compared to the double-parent family (Garfinkel and McLanahan 1986:12–15), a fact that would at one time have been taken to have considerable significance for crime. Our analysis grants only a minor and uncertain role to the economic status of the family in crime causation. Such neglect is justified on several grounds: (1) Research has for many years found little or no relation between family socioeconomic status and delinquency; (2) our theoretical perspective sees crime as noneconomic activity, as leading to economic disaster rather than to economic success; (3) it explicitly denies that offenders are driven to crime by need, deprivation, or poverty. In fact, the theory is inclined in the other direction, tending to see poverty as teaching people to forego current pleasure in the hope of long-term reward (Durkheim 1951). (In this connection, several studies report a positive relation between spending money and drug use in juvenile populations.)

Finally, the finding that membership in mother-only families has a negative effect on intelligence test scores (Garfinkel and McLanahan 1986:28) is certainly relevant. In a range of studies, these scores have been shown to be negatively related to delinquency. In the Richmond data, the family structure, IQ test, delinquency correlations are consistent with previous research. Children from single-parent families have lower Differential Aptitude Test verbal reasoning scores ($r=.08$ [.01]), and children scoring low on this test are more likely to be delinquent ($r=-.20$ [.001]). A major correlate of these test scores is orientation toward time, with low scorers being much more likely to be oriented to the present than to the future. This orientation is, itself, a species of delinquency (see table 3.1).

In sum, the single-parent family appears to have a small impact on crime through its effects on supervision and academic achievement. The child of the single parent is more likely to have a here-and-now orientation to life, and seems slightly more likely to have trouble interacting with adults. The latter problem shows itself in measures of deviant behavior based on the reactions of adults to the behavior of the child, where the effects of family structure are more evident than for deviant acts reported by the child alone. All of these statements, it should be recalled, are based on small, if statistically significant, differences.

Size of Family

I once characterized "size of family" as "an empiricist's dream" (Hirschi 1969:239). It is not hard to see why. Size of family is consistently positively related to delinquency and consistently resists statistical explanation. The third column of table 3.1 shows that size of family, operationalized as number of siblings, predicts a variety of indicators of self control. Table 3.3 shows that the effects of number of siblings are stronger than the effects of the parental structure of the home when attention is restricted to those measures of deviant behavior previously shown to be affected by parental structure.

TABLE 3.3
Percent of Adolescents Deviant by Number of Siblings
(White Males, Richmond Youth Project)

	Number of Siblings						
	0	1	2	3	4	5+	r
% police record	14	22	23	28	31	43	.17
% truant	37	32	31	36	37	52	.09
% self report del.	57	70	68	72	69	78	.11
% suspended	20	18	22	23	25	35	.11
% smoke	20	20	21	25	32	35	.12
Numbers	97- 100	380- 396	403- 419	269- 283	143- 157	178- 192	

This finding leads to interest in the joint effects on delinquency of parental structure and number of siblings. These effects are shown in table 3.4, using police record as the measure of crime because it is predicted best by both structural factors.

TABLE 3.4
Percent with Police Record by Parental Makeup of Home and Number
of Siblings (White Males, Richmond Youth Project)

	Parental Makeup of Home	
Number of Siblings	Two Natural Parents	Natural Mother Only
0	12 (68)	18 (17) (n.s.)
1	19 (300)	32 (47) (.01)
2	21 (314)	21 (34) (n.s.)
3	25 (197)	32 (44) (n.s.)
4	31 (113)	19 (21) (n.s.)
5 or more	36 (105)	38 (55) (n.s.)
Totals*	23 (1113)	30 (226) (.01)

*Totals are from table 3.2.

A reasonable interpretation of table 3.4 might be that "number of siblings" more or less accounts for the effect on delinquency of the parental makeup of the home. In the Richmond data, single-parent families tend to be larger than two-parent families (25 percent of the former as opposed to 10 percent of the latter have six or more children), and for that reason appear to be more conducive to delinquency.

As far as I can now determine, single-parent families are in fact often larger than intact or double-parent families—that is, this phenomenon does not appear to be unique to the Richmond data (see Blake 1985; Glueck and Glueck 1950:120). If so, the family size effect provides a potentially important alternative interpretation of the finding of differences in delinquency associated with the parental makeup of the home.

Given the magnitude of the family size effect on delinquency, it deserves an attempt at systematic explanation. Let me, then, briefly assess the relevance of size to each of the devices available to the family for delinquency prevention.

Socialization/Self Control

It is easy to find reasons to believe that large families may experience greater difficulties than small families in teaching self-control. The greater the number of children in the family, the greater the "dilution" of material and cultural resources (Blake 1989:10–12). Parents with many children have less time, energy, and money to devote to each of them. Children in large families are likely to spend more time with other children and less time with adults, a situation not conducive to intellectual growth or general maturity.

Whatever one may think of these assertions, the fact is that children from large families score lower on intelligence tests (especially those tests that emphasize vocabulary or verbal ability), get poorer grades in school, expect to obtain less education, and actually complete fewer years of schooling than children from small families (Blake 1989). The Richmond data confirm these findings.[2] They also confirm that all of these consequences of large family size are important correlates of delinquency.

We may thus conclude that an important reason large families are less effective than small families in controlling the delinquency potential of their children is that they are less effective in fostering verbal ability and academic success. Put in these terms, these findings seem to reflect the importance of the child-dominated intellectual atmosphere of the large family rather than its restricted material resources. In any event, because family size continues to affect delinquency when verbal ability, school grades, and educational expectations are controlled by statistical adjustment, this cannot be the whole story.[3]

Supervision

The idea that parents in large families have greater difficulty supervising their children seems to follow directly from the idea that such parents have less time and energy to devote to them. In fact, however, direct supervision is so much more efficient with large than with small numbers that it is not hard to imagine parents in large families doing more rather than less of it. Indirect supervision, keeping track of children who are out of sight, may well be a different matter, but here too the effects of size are not obvious.

In the Richmond study, children from very large families (six or more children) are less likely to report that their parents always know where they are and whom they are with, and children from large families also report spending less time talking with their parents, but these differences are small, and do not really begin to account for the effect of family size on delinquency. For that matter, there is reason to believe that even the small supervision differences may be partially misleading. As we have seen, children from large families tend to score low on tests of verbal ability. Children with limited verbal ability are less likely to enjoy school. They are therefore more likely to truant and take up with the wrong crowd. As a result, they are more likely to report that on occasion their parents do not know where they are or whom they are with. The large family may thus cause "poor supervision" through its effect on verbal ability. Along the same lines, the standard supervision hypothesis does not really square with the fact that number of children living at home is *less* predictive of delinquency than the total number of children in the family.

Attachment to Parents

Children from large families are slightly more likely to report having felt unwanted by their parents (r=.10 [.001]), but differences on such items as "do you share your thoughts and feelings with your parents?" and "would you like to be the kind of person your mother is?" do not reach statistical significance, even with the large sample available. Once again, then, although the data are consistent with the thrust of our explanatory scheme, they do not allow us to conclude that the family size effect has been fully explained.[4]

As of now, then, it seems that, in addition to its effects on deviant behavior through verbal ability, supervision, and attachment, number of children in the family has an effect on deviant behavior unexplained by the variables available to our analysis. We are thus free to speculate about other reasons for the relation between family size and crime.

Recall that our self-control theory explicitly applies to all ages, to children, adolescents, and adults. It does not assume that adults are fully socialized or that children are universally unsocialized. On the contrary, it assumes that differences in self-control appear early and continue to manifest themselves throughout life. Recall, too, that the theory is inherently skeptical of the ability of institutions to affect behavior, especially when these institutions are organized and managed by people inclined to neglect the long-term interests of the institution whenever they conflict with their own short-term or immediate interests.

So, our theory suggests that size of family predicts deviant behavior in the children because it is itself an indicator of parental self-control. ("When my father got me, his mind was not on me" —A. E. Housman.) This suggestion does not seem particularly far-fetched when the children are born to unmarried women. After all, premarital pregnancy is probably as good a measure of delinquency among girls as we are likely to find. But if family size accounts for differences in delinquency between one-parent and two-parent families, it must affect delinquency within such families as well (see table 3.4). No one would suggest that bearing children within marriage is itself deviant behavior. However, behavior analogous to crime is clearly involved in the process, and we should perhaps therefore not be surprised to find that such behavior by parents predicts theoretically equivalent behavior in their children.

This hypothesis should be fairly easy to test. Size of family should have little or no effect when direct measures of parental self-control (e.g., criminal record) are taken into account. This hypothesis also has reasonably direct policy implications. It appears that we should worry less about strengthening the family to prevent crime and more about training people in self-control to strengthen the family.

Discussion

This chapter began with the idea that family structure has a small and variable effect on crime, an effect that is easily accounted for by measures of family functioning or process. It ends on a rather different note, arguing that family size has a robust effect on delinquency that is not accounted for by its effects on supervision or attitudes toward parents. I should have known better than to fall for the idea that the consequences of such hard facts as number of parents and number of children depend on their meaning or interpretation. This idea may be resilient and plausible, but it is also a snare and a delusion. The number of parents and siblings does make a difference. In terms of deviant behavior, it is better to have two of one and few of the other.

This chapter also began with the idea that the current trend in marital stability is unfavorable with respect to crime. It should end by noting a perhaps more important trend in family structure that is grounds for considerable optimism about the crime problem. According to Judith Blake (1989:285), "Children in the United States are just beginning, on a large scale, to accrue some of the advantages of being brought up in small families. . . . [T]hese children should be the most fortunate and favored of any in our history. Even if . . . there is some deterioration in family stability and a corresponding rise is single parenthood, the decline in family size will offer compensation."

Notes

1. Modern states are ambivalent about many of these acts. On the one hand, they are inclined to condemn them to prevent individuals from doing harm to themselves. On the other hand, they are inclined to do what they can to make their natural consequences less dangerous or painful. In this context, some advocates of drug legalization argue that the least expensive and most consistent policy is to let nature take its course—that is, let the health consequences of drugs control their use.

2. In the sample of white males in grades seven to twelve represented in tables 3.1–3.4, number of children is correlated -.14 with Differential Aptitude Test (DAT) verbal scores, -.09 with DAT space relations scores, -.16 with grade point average in English, and -.20 with educational expectations (based on 1,275 or more cases). These correlations are in most cases smaller among students in the eleventh and twelveth grades (and correspondingly larger among students in grades seven to ten), a finding consistent with the idea that samples of college students are inadequate for assessing the effects of family size on academic ability. These correlations are also maintained among Catholic, non-Catholic, single-parent, and two-parent families. In my view, these results cast further doubt on research and speculation to the effect that family size does not matter among profamily religious groups (see also Blake 1989:103).

3. Such analysis shows that, of these variables, grade point average in English is the strongest predictor of delinquency. It shows, too, that educational expectations have no effect on delinquency when ability and performance are taken into account. In other words, educational expectations do not help explain the effect of family size on delinquency.

4. In the interest of closure, it should be mentioned that the large family may be better able than the small family to guard the home and protect its members from predators. To the extent this is true, the reduction in crime from a trend toward small families would be smaller than previous analysis suggests. Finally, important differences between large and small families in the effectiveness of their intervention with the criminal justice system are not apparent in the data. For example, large family size predicts smoking about as well as it predicts suspension from school.

References

Akers, Ronald L. 1992. *Drugs, Alcohol, and Society*. Belmont, CA: Wadsworth.

Blake, Judith. 1961. *Family Structure in Jamaica*. Glencoe, IL: Free Press.

_____. 1985. "Number of Siblings and Educational Mobility." *American Sociological Review* 50:84-94.

_____. 1989. *Family Size and Achievement*. Berkeley: University of California Press.

Cohen, Lawrence, and Marcus Felson. 1979. "Social Change and Crime Rate Trends: A Routine Activity Approach." *American Sociological Review* 44:588-608.

Dornbusch, S., J. Carlsmith, S. Bushwall, P. Ritter, H. Leiderman, A. Hastorf, and R. Gross. 1985. "Single Parents, Extended Households, and the Control of Adolescents." *Child Development* 56:326-41.

Durkheim, Emile. 1951. *Suicide*. Glencoe, IL: Free Press.

Fenwick, Charles R. 1982. "Juvenile Court Intake Decision Making: The Importance of Family Affiliation." *Journal of Criminal Justice* 10:443-53.

Garfinkel, Irwin, and Sara S. McLanahan. 1986. *Single Mothers and Their Children: A New American Dilemma*. Washington, DC: The Urban Institute Press.

Glueck, Sheldon, ed. 1959. *The Problem of Delinquency*. Boston: Houghton Mifflin.

Glueck, Sheldon, and Eleanor Glueck. 1950. *Unraveling Juvenile Delinquency*. Cambridge: Harvard University Press.

_____. 1968. *Delinquents and Nondelinquents in Perspective*. Cambridge: Harvard University Press.

Gottfredson, Michael, and Travis Hirschi. 1990. *A General Theory of Crime*. Stanford: Stanford University Press.

Gove, Walter, and Robert Crutchfield. 1982. "The Family and Juvenile Delinquency." *The Sociological Quarterly* 23:301-19.

Hartley, Shirley Foster. 1975. *Illegitimacy*. Berkeley: University of California Press.

Hindelang, Michael, Travis Hirschi, and Joseph Weis. 1981. *Measuring Delinquency*. Beverly Hills, CA: Sage Publications.

Hirschi, Travis. 1969. *Causes of Delinquency*. Berkeley: University of California Press.

_____. 1983. "Crime and the Family." In *Crime and Public Policy*, ed. James Q. Wilson, 53-68. San Francisco: Institute for Contemporary Studies Press.

Laub, John, and Robert Sampson. 1988. "Unraveling Families and Delinquency: A Reanalysis of the Gluecks' Data." *Criminology* 26:355-80.

Loeber, Rolf, and Magda Stouthamer-Loeber. 1986. "Family Factors as Correlates and Predictors of Juvenile Conduct Problems and Delinquency." In *Crime and Justice: An Annual Review of Research*, vol. 7, ed. by M. Tonry and N. Morris, 29-149. Chicago: University of Chicago Press.

Olweus, Dan. 1979. "Stability of Aggressive Reaction Patterns in Males: A Review." *Psychological Bulletin* 86:852-875.

Patterson, Gerald. 1980. "Children Who Steal." In *Understanding Crime*, ed. T. Hirschi and M. Gottfredson, 73-90. Beverly Hills, CA: Sage Publications.

_____. 1989. Personal communication.

Robins, Lee. 1966. *Deviant Children Grown Up*. Baltimore: Williams & Wilkins.

Shannon, Lyle. 1981. "Assessing the Relationship of Adult Criminal Careers to Juvenile Careers." Final Report. Washington, D.C.: National Institute for Juvenile Justice and Delinquency Prevention.

Steinberg, Laurence. 1987. "Single Parents, Stepparents, and the Susceptibility of Adolescents to Antisocial Peer Pressure." *Child Development* 58:269-75.

West, Donald, and David Farrington. 1977. *The Delinquent Way of Life*. London: Heinemann.

Wilson, James Q., and Richard Herrnstein. 1985. *Crime and Human Nature*. New York: Simon and Schuster.

Wolfgang, Marvin, Robert Figlio, and Thorsten Sellin. 1972. *Delinquency in a Birth Cohort*. Chicago: University of Chicago Press.

4

Gender and Crime

Mary Ann Zager

Few topics have so intrigued contemporary criminology as the differences in rates and patterns of delinquency for males and females. The source of this interest is not hard to find. Male-female differences in rates of involvement in deviant activities are very large (Barton and Figueira-McDonough 1985, Cernkovich and Giordano 1979; Hindelang 1971). Although these differences appear to be smaller in developed than in underdeveloped countries, and have declined in recent decades within the United States, they remain sizable (see e.g., Jensen and Rojek 1992: 94). If male-female differences in rates of deviant behavior are on the whole large, they are also highly variable, with male/female ratios sometimes approaching 1:1 for such offenses as running away, smoking, and shoplifting, and being as high as 12:1 for such offenses as burglary, robbery, and homicide (Canter 1982; Hindelang, Hirschi, and Weis 1981).

In this chapter, I apply the central concepts of the general theory of crime, opportunity and self-control (Gottfredson and Hirschi 1990), to *variation from offense to offense in gender differences*. The hope is that frank recognition of such variation will lead to better understanding of the gender effect on crime and deviance, as well as further refinement of the theory.

The Theory

According to Gottfredson and Hirschi (1990), *self-control* is a major component of all delinquent acts, accounting for the tendency of those committing one act to commit other acts as well. Deviant, criminal, and

71

reckless acts all entail long-term negative consequences. Persons low on self-control fail to consider the long-term consequences of their behavior, and thus commit all of these behaviors more frequently than persons attuned to future outcomes.

Low self-control does not require crime or deviance. Persons low on self-control are not driven, but are simply unrestrained. They may act on *opportunities* to commit criminal or reckless acts, but they do not as a rule initiate these acts in the face of obstacles. In this conception, then, opportunities are a necessary condition for reckless or deviant behavior.

Self-control and opportunity are not independent. Persons low on self-control may avoid restrictive conditions or situations, while persons high on self-control may act in ways that limit their own opportunities for delinquency or crime.

This theory implies that all crime differences are a function of differences in opportunity and/or self-control. Therefore, these differences must explain gender differences in crime as well. Gottfredson and Hirschi (1990: chap. 6) confront this issue, but do not take it to a definitive conclusion. They suggest only that both self-control and opportunity may be responsible for gender differences, but do not further specify the nature of these relationships.

How might gender differences be approached in the context of this theory? It is important to consider both self-control and opportunity differences in some systematic way. As a concept, there seems to be nothing about self-control that would make it particularly problematic when applied to gender differences. Presumably one's level of self-control may be assessed irrespective of gender. This does not preclude the possibility that the median level of self-control may be different for males and females. (In fact, given what we know about differences in rates of offending, we would expect females generally to have higher self-control than males.)

Gottfredson and Hirschi suggest several indicators of low self-control, the most obvious of which are the acts low self-control is said to explain—that is, deviant, criminal, delinquent, or reckless behaviors. This list includes behaviors said to be analogous to criminal acts, drug use, overeating, bungee jumping, and downhill skiing. Attitudinal measures of self-control are also in principle abundantly available. These include measures of impulsivity, preference for simple tasks, risk taking, lack of concern for the victim, and short-sightedness (Gottfredson and Hirschi 1990: 89).

Measuring opportunity is more problematic, especially in the context of the gender question. Gottfredson and Hirschi assert, for example, that "the opportunities for women to commit assault or homicide are equivalent to those available to men. In fact, women spend much more time in unsupervised interaction with children, and the amount of time they spend in contact with other people is as large or larger than that of men" (1990: 147). All of this suggests that, other things being equal, females should have higher rates of violent crime than males. And of course it is precisely with respect to violent offenses that the male/female crime ratios are the highest (Canter 1982; Hindelang 1971).

The Gottfredson/Hirschi discussion thus leaves the impression that gender differences must be primarily self-control differences (i.e., differences in criminality), or that there is a direct and unexplained gender effect analogous to the effect they ascribe to age.[1]

I think it would perhaps be more profitable to explore the possibility that gender is an opportunity variable, a variable that influences the likelihood that a specific act will occur, irrespective of level of self control or "objective" opportunity.

This objective element of opportunity shows itself in differential frequencies of offenses, from homicide at one extreme to exceeding the speed limit at the other. This range is presumably determined by a complex web of causal elements. While it is difficult to disentangle this web, it is clear that gender may have an effect on rates of specific crimes over and above the action of "objective" opportunity.

This conceptualization of the problem leads to straightforward analysis. Rather than be concerned with explanation of *the* gender difference, I will attempt to illustrate gender effects for a variety of specific offenses. (Put in the terms used at one point by Gottfredson and Hirschi [see, e.g., Hirschi and Gottfredson 1986], this leads to conceptualization of gender as a "crime" variable, a variable that by definition should have an effect on individual crimes separate from the effect of self-control.)

The obvious place to begin such an analysis is to examine behaviors differing in male/female prevalence ratios. Where these ratios are low, the gender effect should of course be low or inconsequential. As these ratios grow larger, the specific effect of gender should increase. In fact, there is some reason to believe that gender may be responsible for all of the differences in prevalence rates. (An alternative hypothesis might be that these high-ratio crimes, being generally more serious, require lower levels of self-control. The theory of self-control appears to suggest, however, that crime seriousness and self-control are independent concepts.)

The analytic model of choice, then, would include measures of gender, self-control, and opportunity (specific offenses). I would hypothesize that the direct effect of gender will be stronger in models using offenses with high male/female ratios. That is, gender differences in such offenses are not accounted for by differences in self-control. Among offenses with low male/female ratios, direct gender effects will be minimal, with self-control tending to account for the initially small differences. Following Gottfredson and Hirschi's theory, self-control should be a consistent element of these equations, regardless of offense. As suggested above, it should in principle account for a more or less fixed portion of initial gender differences. At the low end of the range of male/female ratios, self-control should account for significantly more of the difference than it accounts for at the high end of this range. In the analysis of a specific offense, objective opportunity is held constant. By definition, those offenses with little objective opportunity (those with low frequencies of occurrence and high male/female ratios) are more difficult to explain than offenses that are more easily committed.

Before determining which offenses are appropriate for this analysis, let me introduce the data set to be analyzed.

The Data

The National Youth Survey (Wave I) is used to examine the gender effect on delinquency.[2] This is a nationwide study conducted in 1977 on a sample of 1725 subjects who were eleven to seventeen years old at the time of the survey. While the representative nature of this sample ensures fewer female delinquents than would be optimal, its size allows comparison of male and female rates on specific offenses. This survey includes self-reports on a wide range of attitudes and behaviors (for details, see Elliott, Huizinga, and Ageton 1985).

Measures

After inspection of Elliott, Huizinga, and Ageton's delinquency scale, items with low, medium, and high male/female prevalence ratios were selected (see Canter 1982). Ratios are shown in table 4.1. Low-ratio items are running away from home and truancy. Medium-ratio items are throwing objects, minor theft, and sexual intercourse. High-ratio items are stealing something worth more than fifty dollars and breaking and entering (for wording of items, see the Appendix).

Self-control is measured in two ways. The behavioral index is composed of six self-report delinquency items, including alcohol use, marijuana use, making obscene phone calls, avoiding payment, strong-arming students, and joyriding (these are described in the Appendix). The attitudinal index is composed of ten items, including measures of honesty, short-sightedness, and concern for victims (see the Appendix for a complete description of all ten items). Each attitudinal item is dichotomized; individual items are coded so that higher values represent lower self-control.

Analysis

Logistic regression was used to model the relations between gender, self-control, and specific offenses.[3] In each model, the effects of two indexes of self-control, one behavioral and one attitudinal, and gender were assessed. The coefficients show (1) the effects of gender on the probability of committing the offense in question, keeping self-control constant; (2) the separate effects of the two self-control measures, keeping gender constant; (3) where appropriate, the combined effects of self-control[4] (these coefficients are displayed in table 4.2). Better or more complete measures of self-control would presumably reduce to some extent the gender effect. However, interaction effects of gender and self control did not contribute to the models, and there is every reason to believe that gender effects similar to those shown would survive analysis utilizing more precise measures of self-control.

Results

Initial logistic models were fitted with an interaction between gender and self-control, as well as the variables listed in the final models (table 4.2). These interactions were not significant in any case, indicating that for this data set, the final models were appropriate within the framework of this question. Although the "thrown objects" model was significantly different from a saturated model, all other models were not different from a perfect predictive model (at the .40 level). Each model was significantly better than the intercept only model (at the .01 level).

TABLE 4.1
Male/Female Prevalence Ratios for Seven Delinquency Items

Item	M/F Ratio	N*
Truancy	1.18	549
Run away	1.21	109
Throw objects	1.63	809
Stolen $5 or less	1.71	309
Sexual intercourse	2.35	246
Breaking and entering	3.25	76
Stolen more than $50	4.44	44

*Number of subjects engaging in the behavior. The total number of valid cases is 1712.

In only one model (Run away) was the attitudinal index of self-control nonsignificant. In all other models both indexes of self-control were significant, and therefore composite self-control coefficients are appropriate. These coefficients (ranging from .46 to .93) indicate that a small change in self-control attitudes or behaviors greatly increases the probability (through an increase in the log odds of the dependent variable's occurrence) that the individual will have engaged in the act in question (recall that the dependent variable is dichotomous). It should perhaps come as no surprise that the self-control coefficients are large. After all, the behavioral measure includes a variety of delinquent acts, and the attitudinal measure reflects the respondent's view that these acts are morally acceptable. (The theory of self-control is of course built on the interchangeability of delinquent acts.) But what is important here is that we have an opportunity to examine the effects of gender above and beyond the effects of self-control. The results are as expected. With the exception of the large theft item (stolen more than $50), gender is generally more significant with those behaviors with high male/female ratios.[5] In fact, models of three delinquent behaviors (truancy, run away, and small theft) show that the effect of gender is not significant, and three (thrown objects, sexual intercourse, and breaking and entering) show that the gender effect is highly significant. The sexual intercourse result reflects the greater prevalence of sexual activity among males. Obviously a measure of the incidence of sexual activity would have different results (Hindelang, Hirschi, and Weis 1981). The thrown objects item is, interestingly enough, almost a pure example of gender-specific behavior, and therefore illustrates one meaning of the concept of opportunity. With the self-control component removed, breaking and entering, especially the former, simply reflect activities that are more common among males, which is again precisely what is meant by an opportunity difference.

Conclusion

The gender question poses peculiar problems for delinquency theory and research. While the differences in crime and delinquency rates for males and females are firmly established, the sources or meaning of these differences are not fully understood. In this chapter I have attempted to take a different tack toward the gender question, treating it as a challenge to the theory of self-control. This theory offers only two concepts, self-control and opportunity, that might be used to explain gender differences. If self-control were the only concept explaining gender differences, the gender effect would be constant from offense to offense. The much-reported variation across offenses in the effect of gender inspired the present chapter, and eventually necessitated equating gender and opportunity. The results, it seems to me, justify the assumption that gender is best seen as an opportunity variable. This conceptualization has the advantage that it explains gender differences without invoking any notion that males and females are differentially motivated, or differentially constrained by consideration of long-term consequences of their acts.

Appendix
Descriptions of Index Items from the National Youth Survey

7 Delinquency Items

1] Run away from home
2] Skipped class without an excuse
3] Thrown objects (such as rocks, snowballs, or bottles) at cars or people
4] Stolen (or tried to steal) things worth $5 or less
5] Had sexual intercourse with a person of the opposite sex other than your wife/husband
6] Stolen (or tried to steal) something worth more than $50

TABLE 4.2
Coefficients for Logistic Regression Models

Dependent Variable	Constant	Self-Control (Attitudinal)	Self-Control (Behavioral)	Gender	SC
Truancy	-4.9851 (.0000)	0.1964 (.0000)	0.7345 (.0000)	-0.1141 (.3526)	.9309
Run away	-4.4990 (.0000)	0.0714 (.2627)	0.2306 (.0000)	-0.0004 (.9987)	
Thrown objects	-2.0432 (.0000)	0.1463 (.0000)	0.3094 (.0000)	0.7880 (.0000)	.4557
Stolen $5 or less	-5.1568 (.0000)	0.3794 (.0000)	0.4718 (.0000)	0.3152 (.0349)	.8512
Sexual intercourse	-4.6975 (.0000)	0.1743 (.0001)	0.3641 (.0000)	0.7654 (.0000)	.5384
Breaking and entering	-7.2382 (.0000)	0.3698 (.0000)	0.4192 (.0000)	0.8617 (.0088)	.7890
Stolen more than $50	-8.6068 (.0000)	0.5809 (.0000)	0.3464 (.0000)	1.3584 (.0135)	.9273

Estimated coefficients
(Significance Level)
SC is the combined effect for behavioral and attitudinal indexes

7] Broken into a building or vehicle (or tried to break in) to steal something or just to look around

All delinquency items measured over a one-year period

6 Behavioral Measures of Self Control

1] Alcoholic beverage use
2] Marijuana/hashish use
3] Made obscene telephone calls, such as such as calling someone and saying dirty things
4] Avoided paying for such things as movies, bus or subway rides, and food
5] Used force (strong-arm methods) to get money or things from other students
6] Taken a vehicle for a ride (drive) without the owner's permission

All behaviors measured for a one-year period.

Attitudinal Measures of Self-Control

1] It's important to be honest with your parents, even if they become upset or you get punished.

2] To stay out of trouble, it is sometimes necessary to lie to teachers.

3] At school it is sometimes necessary to play dirty in order to win.

4] You can make it in school without having to cheat on exams/tests.

5] It may be necessary to break some of your parent's rules in order to keep some of your friends.

For items 1–5, respondents were asked to rank agreement on a 5-point Likert scale. Respondents were assigned a score of 0 (indicating higher self control) if they strongly disagreed or disagreed with items 2,3,5 (others were assigned a score of 1); they were assigned a score of 0 if they strongly agreed or agreed with items 1,4 (others were assigned a score of 1).

6] Purposely damage or destroy property that does not belong to him/her

7] Steal something worth less than $5

8] Hit or threaten to hit someone without any reason

9] Break into a vehicle or building to steal something

10] Steal something worth more than $50

For items 6–10, respondents were asked how wrong it is for someone their age to engage in each behavior. For each item, respondents were assigned a score of 0 if they felt it was wrong or very wrong to engage in each behavior, 1 otherwise. All ten items are positively correlated at the .01 level or better. Correlations range in magnitude from .07 to .48.

I would like to thank Travis Hirschi for help in formulating the problem addressed in this paper, and Delbert Elliott for the National Youth Survey data on which my analysis is based.

Notes

1. While the age effect varies systematically across time but is constant across behaviors, the gender effect varies across behaviors.
2. The first wave was used to ensure the appropriateness of the use of status offenses as delinquency.
3. This is the regression model most appropriate for analysis of a dichotomous dependent variable. See Aldrich and Nelson (1984) and Hanushek and Jackson (1977) for further discussion of these models.
4. When both the attitudinal and behavioral indexes of self-control are significant, it is appropriate to add the coefficients to assess the combined effect. For run away, the attitudinal measure of self-control is not significant.
5. Because only 44 of 1712 subjects had stolen more than $50 in the year prior to the survey, the large negative coefficient of the intercept compensates for any gender effect. Essentially, one would predict that everyone would refrain from this behavior regardless of gender.

References

Aldrich, John H., and Forrest D. Nelson. 1984. *Linear Probability, Logit, and Probit Models*. Quantitative Applications in the Social Sciences, no. 45. Beverly Hills, CA: Sage Publications.

Barton, William, and Josefina Figueira-McDonough. 1985. "Attachments, Gender, and Delinquency." *Deviant Behavior* 6:119-44.

Canter, Rachelle J. 1982. "Sex Differences in Self-Report Delinquency." *Criminology* 20:373-93.

Cernkovich, Stephen, and Peggy C. Giordano. 1979. "Delinquency, Opportunity, and Gender." *Criminology* 70:145-51.

Elliott, Delbert S., David Huizinga, and Suzanne S. Ageton. 1985. *Explaining Delinquency and Drug Use*. Beverly Hills, CA: Sage Publications.

Gottfredson, Michael, and Travis Hirschi. 1990. *A General Theory of Crime*. Stanford: Stanford University Press.

Hanushek, Eric A., and John E. Jackson. 1977. *Statistical Methods for Social Scientists*. Orlando, FL: Academic Press.

Hindelang, Michael J. 1971. "Age, Sex, and the Versatility of Delinquent Involvements." *Social Problems* 18:522-35.

Hindelang, Michael J., Travis Hirschi, and Joseph G. Weis. 1981. *Measuring Delinquency*. Beverly Hills, CA: Sage Publications.

Hirschi, Travis, and Michael Gottfredson. 1986. "The Distinction between Crime and Criminality." In *Critique and Explanation*, ed. T. Hartnagel and R. Silverman, 55-69. New Brunswick, NJ: Transaction Publishers.

Jensen, Gary F., and Dean Rojek. 1992. *Delinquency and Youth Crime*. Prospect Heights, IL: Waveland Press.

5

Accidents

Marianne Junger

Problem behavior can be defined as "behavior that is socially defined as a problem, a source of concern, or as undesired by the norms of conventional society . . . and its occurrence usually elicits some kind of social control response" (Jessor and Jessor 1977:33). Problem behavior consists, among other things, of drug use, criminal behavior, heavy alcohol use, and dangerous driving. There is an increased interest, in recent years, in the relation between various types of problem behavior. A growing body of research supports the view that diverse forms of deviant behavior are positively related to each other. It has been argued that there exists a general factor of deviance/problem behavior that underlies a large number of problem behaviors, that the different forms of problem behavior may form a "syndrome." The concept of a syndrome implies that all forms of problem behavior are the result of the same causal factor(s). This view has been presented by, among others, Jessor and Jessor (1977), Robins and Wish (1977), Osgood et al. (1988) and by Gottfredson and Hirschi (1990).

In several studies Jessor and his colleagues supported the existence of a syndrome of problem behavior with empirical data (Jessor and Jessor 1977; Donovan and Jessor 1985; Donovan, Jessor, and Costa 1988). They examined the relations between a number of problem behaviors (smoking, problem drinking, frequent marijuana/hashish use, use of other illicit drugs, general deviant behavior). In four samples it appeared that a one-factor model fit the data. This single factor could be labeled the "problem behavior" factor. These findings show that generally, people involved in one type of problem behavior are more likely to be involved in other types of problem behavior. This one-dimensional model of problem behavior holds across sex and across samples differing in educational level, socioeconomic status (SES), and ethnic background.

Robins and Wish (1977) analyzed data on black male cohort (N=223) born between 1930 and 1934 and who attended a St. Louis elementary school. They gathered data on thirteen types of problematic and deviant behavior engaged in by members of the sample before age eighteen: elementary school academic problems, truancy, dropping out of school, juvenile offenses, precocious use of alcohol (first drink before fifteen), precocious sexual experiences (intercourse before fifteen), marijuana use, barbiturate use, amphetamine use, opiate use, leaving parental home, marriage, and alcohol problems. They found that all types of deviant behaviors are statistically related and that the most frequently mentioned types of behavior were those started at an early age. The strongest correlations were found between those behaviors that started at the same age or that were conceptually related. Correlations between the diverse types of deviant behavior drop or are reduced when controlling for previous deviance. The authors suggest that these relations may occur because all types of deviance result from one cause. Therefore, they suggest that perhaps a general theory of deviance is needed, a theory that would treat deviance as part of normal growth and development.

Farrington also noted that convicted delinquents are heavily involved in other types of problem behavior. In comparison with nondelinquent boys, delinquent boys (at age eighteen) tend to drink more beer, become drunk more often, start smoking at an earlier age, use more illicit drugs, and are more likely to have had sexual intercourse, especially with a variety of girls (1989:6). Apparently, in Farrington's data various forms of problematic behavior do occur relatively often among the same individuals.

Osgood et al. (1988) presented results from a longitudinal study of high school students eighteen to twenty-two years of age on diverse forms of problem behavior, using confirmatory factor analysis. Problem behavior included criminal behavior (limited to illegal behavior directed at victims), heavy alcohol use, marijuana use, use of other illicit drugs, and dangerous driving. Their analysis supports again the view that there is a general tendency toward deviance. As was the case in the studies mentioned previously, a single latent factor could explain all the cross-sectional and longitudinal relations among the various types of problem behavior, but there remained a portion of variance unexplained by the latent factor. Osgood et al. (1988) conclude that problem behavior is largely a part of a general tendency toward deviance but also, in part, a unique phenomenon. The authors found very little support for the idea that the various forms of problem behavior are causally related to one another.

As did Jessor and his colleagues, Osgood (1990) concludes that there is no reason to believe that these relations are influenced by sex or race. Overall, there appears to be sound empirical support for the fact that many forms of deviant behavior are interrelated. Persons involved in one type of problem behavior are more likely to be involved in other types as well.

This chapter focuses on the question whether, among children and juveniles, there is a relation between two specific forms of problem behavior: crime and accidents. At first glance it seems difficult to imagine a positive relation between the occurrence of accidents and involvement in crime. Although there are several definitions, most authors would agree that a crime is "any act committed in violation of a law that prohibits it and authorizes punishment for its commission" (Wilson and Herrnstein 1985). Crime is generally intentional behavior.[1] Especially in the case of juvenile delinquency most crimes—such as theft, assault, vandalism, or sexual crimes—consist of intentional behavior.

Accidents, on the contrary, are by definition unintentional, "an un-premeditated event resulting in recognizable damage" (Marcusson and Oehmisch 1977:57). There are many types of accidents that may involve children: motor vehicle accidents, other transport accidents, accidental poisonings, accidental falls, accidents caused by fire, accidental drown-ings, accidents caused by fire-arm missiles, accidents mainly of an industrial type, accidents caused by machinery, and accidents caused by hot substances (Marcusson and Oehmisch 1977). In most industrialized nations all types of accidents taken together make up about 40 percent of the deaths among boys and 30 percent of the deaths among girls (Marcusson and Oehmisch 1977, reporting on the age range one to fourteen). The most common type of accidents involving children are traffic accidents, followed by drownings. In the United States injuries are the cause of 40.5 percent of all deaths among children aged one to four. This percentage increases with age and is 59 percent at age fifteen to nineteen.[2] Of course, the growing importance of accidents as a cause of death compared to other causes is partly due to the declining significance of diseases.

Not all children have the same likelihood of getting involved in an accident. Several studies have looked at the distribution of accidents among children. They all conclude that the distribution of accidents is not a random process and that some children are more at risk than others (Beautrais, Fergusson, and Shannon 1982, Langley, Silva, and Williams 1987a). For example, a Belgian study followed infants carefully from birth over the period of one year (Willemijns and Corbisier 1961).[3] Information was assembled on 4,294 children. It was found that 56 percent of the children were not injured during the first year of their life, 31 percent had one or two accidents, 10 percent three to five accidents, and 3 percent more than five accidents. It also appeared that 7 percent of the children had 26 percent of the total number of accidents.

Fuller (1947) conducted a study among sixty-one children of twenty-two to fifty-five months, who were observed in a nursery school. She found that 50 percent of the injuries to boys treated at the health unit involved only 27 percent of the boys. Similarly, 50 percent of the injuries to girls involved only 14 percent of the girls. It seems warranted to conclude that some children are more at risk for getting involved in an accident.[4]

The fact that children differ in the likelihood of getting involved in accidents and the possible link of accident involvement to other forms of deviant behavior led to the subject of this chapter, which will try to discover whether accidents are related to other forms of problem behavior. To answer this question, two paths can be followed: One path is to determine, at the individual level, whether or not the two types of behavior occur relatively often among the same individuals. Children involved in accidents should be involved in other problem behavior more often than children who are not involved in accidents. Or, put the other way around: delinquents should have higher rates of involvement in accidents than nondelinquents. Another path is to find out whether the factors that predict juvenile delinquency are predictors of accident liability among young children. Following this line of reasoning the questions to be addressed in this chapter are:

1. What are the personal and social correlates of involvement in accidents among young children?
2. Are these correlates the same as the correlates of criminal behavior?

3. Is involvement in accidents related to involvement in other forms of
    problem behavior among children?

The first section of the chapter discusses the method it follows. It also
comments on the literature on accidents. The second section introduces
some of the factors relating to the occurrence of accidents among
children. It also asks whether the correlates of involvement in accidents
are similar to the factors related to involvement in crime. The third
section discusses the relation between accident liability and other problem behavior. The chapter ends with a summary of the main results. In
addition some implications for criminological theory are suggested.

Method

The information presented in this chapter is based on a review of the
literature on factors relating to accidents among children. Although there
is a large amount of material on this subject, we attempted to include all
the available material. The literature was traced at the libraries of the
Dutch Institute of Preventive Medicine and the Dutch Institute for the
Scientific Study of Traffic Safety.[5] Some studies could not be traced, and
others have been excluded from this review. Those excluded are based
on very small samples or use projective techniques to describe the
children. As their findings are more likely to be biased, it was felt their
results should not be used.[6]

Besides the information on accidents, information on correlates of
delinquency was assembled. This information comes, to a large extent,
from some of the major reviews of the criminological literature, namely
those of Rutter and Giller (1983), Wilson and Herrnstein (1985), Loeber
and Stouthamer-Loeber (1986), and Gottfredson and Hirschi (1990).

The age range of the studies in both fields—accidents among children
and juvenile delinquency—does not entirely overlap. Most of the studies
looking at accidents among children studied small children, up to age six.
Some studies also looked at older children, up to a maximum of fifteen
years old. Research on delinquency usually focused on older children,
generally from ten to twenty years old. This means that there is some,
but not total, overlap in the age ranges. (All studies on accidents cited in
this article are described in an appendix available from the author.)

Studies of accidents—just as of any other subject—sometimes confront specific methodological problems. For example, some research is

retrospective; it relies on information from the mothers, after the accident has occurred. An "after-effect" could bias the answers by mothers of accident victims. The mothers might describe their child as troublesome or overactive because they want to explain why the accident happened.

However, Bijur and Stewart-Brown (1986) presented some reasons against the view that many results in the literature might be biased.

First, medical records (as an "objective measure") on injuries are more strongly related to (for example) aggressive behavior of the child than to mothers reports on injury (when both are being reported by the mother).

Second, it is plausible that the estimation of the relation between aggression and accidents is a conservative one: mothers do not remember all accidents/injuries.

Third, there is evidence that parents of antisocial children tend to deny the child's aggressive behavior and are reluctant to complete interviews. This probably leads to an underestimation instead of an overestimation of the relation between aggressive behavior and accidents. It should also be mentioned that several studies use the Rutter child behavior scale. This includes many questions on specific forms of behavior that are not influenced too much by ideas of parents or teachers about the children and thus leave less room for personal interpretations.

Fourth, information on a variable such as parental supervision is often self-reported. However, it is unlikely that the relation between parental supervision and accidents will be overstated as a result of a social desirability bias. Parents are more likely to overstate the amount of supervision they provide than to understate it. The findings of Routledge, Repetto-Wright, and Howarth (1974) underscore this point. The authors mention that mothers underreport the amount of traffic their children are exposed to.

Finally, there are some prospective and longitudinal studies that corroborate the findings presented in other research (Wadsworth et al. 1983; Matheny 1986; Langley, Silva, and Williams 1987a; Nyman 1987). For example, Nyman (1987) studied the characteristics of a cohort of 1,855 babies, born in Helsinki during 1975-76 (six to eight months old). Later on, he checked whether these children were hospitalized during the first five years of their life.

Covariates of Accidents and Crime among Children

Many factors may be related to the occurrence of accidents. Taking the individual and the family as the units of analysis[7], this chapter examines those factors that are possible correlates of both crime and accidents (a summary of the results in provided in tabular form at the end of the chapter (table 5.4)).

The Influence of the Environment and Family Factors

Health problems/psychiatric problems in the family. Several studies found that psychiatric disorders of the mother, tensions, or other personal problems are related to the occurrence of accidents among children. For example, Brown and Davidson (1978) mention that during the time that the mother was psychiatrically disturbed, her child (age one to fifteen) had a relatively high risk of becoming involved in an accident (21 percent). After her recovery the risk of her child seemed to decrease to the level of children whose mothers did not have psychiatric problems (5 percent).

Brown and Davidson (1987) found that poor health of the mother is related to a high accident rate among children under sixteen. Similarly, Backett and Johnston (1959) found that mothers in accident families were more often ill. In addition, serious illness in the family also correlated with a higher risk of accidents among children five to fourteen.

Matheny (1986) conducted an interesting study among 116 young children (51 males and 65 females, age one to three) for which information was available from interviews with mothers and from observations of the children themselves and of their homes. It appeared that the mothers of children without accidents tend to be relatively active (tending to participate and be actively engaged in the world), vigorous (liking physical activities and energetic occupations), and stable (steady in mood, not easily overwhelmed) in comparison with mothers of accident children. A low accident rate was also associated with relatively more maternal involvement with the child.

Larson and Pless (1988) established that mothers who smoked, were unemployed, and were single had children with a higher injury liability than mothers who did not smoke, were employed, and were married. Overall they conclude that it is not so much general or chronic family disadvantage but factors indicative of personal stress that are important risk factors (see also Emerick, Foster, and Campbell 1986).

In the field of juvenile delinquency, the Gluecks (1950) also looked at health and psychiatric problems in the family.[8] On the mother's side, they found relatively more mental retardation, emotional disturbance, drunkenness, and criminality in the families of delinquents than in the families of nondelinquent boys. On the father's side, they found more emotional disturbance and criminality in the families of delinquents. The differences were larger when considering the parents themselves. Both the fathers and the mothers of delinquent boys were more burdened by serious physical complaints, mental retardation, emotional disturbances, drunkenness, and criminality in comparison with the parents of nondelinquent boys.

In their review of the literature, Loeber and Stouthamer-Loeber (1986) found that a mother's depression was a strong predictor of later antisocial behavior of her children. Werner's study (1987) is worth mentioning. The research describes the results of a comprehensive longitudinal study of a group of deprived Hawaiian children. Werner followed a birth cohort from 1954 from the mother's pregnancy until the child was eighteen (N=698). Her findings show that sources of stress in the family predict delinquency. The sources of stress she mentions include the illness of the parents or the child, parental mental illness, absence of one of the parents, and placement of the child in a foster home. Stressful events had a cumulative effect on later delinquency.

In their review of the literature, Rutter and Giller (1983) also concluded that problems of parents (excessive drinking, poor work record, reliance on social welfare, criminal record, personality problems) all relate to juvenile crime (see also Wilson and Herrnstein 1985; Gottfredson and Hirschi 1990).

Education of mother. Several studies establish a relation between educational level of the mother and the likelihood that her child will become involved in an accident. A low educational level is related to a higher accident liability (Matheny 1986; Beautrais, Fergusson, and Shannon 1982; Emerick, Foster, and Campbell 1986; Wicklund, Moss, and Frost 1984). This association is usually a relatively strong one. For example, Pless, Verreault, and Tennia (1989) found that when the mother had more than a twelfth-grade education, her children under fifteen has 50 percent fewer accidents. Only one study (Larson and Pless 1988) did not find a relation between educational level and accident liability for children at age four. Van Rijn et al. (1987) studied all children treated for burns (N=101) in Amsterdam (The Netherlands) and compared them with a sample of control children representative of the population of the same age in Amsterdam (N=192). They also found a relation between parent's educational level and the risk of burn injuries. The parents of children with burn injuries had more often not gone beyond primary school.

In their research on juvenile delinquency, the Gluecks (1950) noted that parents of delinquents had less formal education than the parents of nondelinquents, although the difference was not large. Larzelere and Patterson (1990) also established that socioeconomic status, measured by educational level of parents and occupation, was related to delinquency, but that this effect was mediated by parental management skills (N=180). Similarly, Werner (1987) found, among her group of deprived Hawaiian children, that education of the mother reduced the risk of delinquency among her children.

Age of mother. In accident families the mother was more often relatively young (Read et al. 1963; Beautrais, Fergusson, and Shannon 1982; Wadsworth et al. 1983; Emerick, Foster, and Campbell 1986; Wicklund, Moss, and Frost 1984). Stewart-Brown et al. (1986) analyzed information on accidents requiring medical attention among 13,134 children from two birth cohorts in the UK (at age five). They found that maternal age was the most important predictor for the occurrence of accidents among children. Children of young mothers were involved relatively often in accidents.

In their review of the criminological literature, Rutter and Giller (1983) mention that children of teenage mothers are more at risk of developing delinquency. (It should be noted that the age of mother is likely to be related to educational level, younger mothers having less education.)

Working mothers. Some studies mention that in accident families, the mother was more often working (Read et al. 1963). However, other authors mention that a mother's employment was related to a lower accident rate (Alwash and McCarthy 1988; Pless, Perreault, and Tennia 1989). Alwash and McCarthy (1988) suggest that mothers who work make arrangements for their children. Consequently, these children are better looked after than when the mother does not work. In studies on crime the relation between mothers' employment and delinquency has been studied relatively often, generally with inconsistent results (Wilson and Herrnstein 1985). The Gluecks (1950) found that delinquent boys came more often from families where mothers worked. But this effect of mothers' working was completely accounted for by the quality of the supervision provided by the mother. Other studies did not find a relation between mother's employment and crime (Junger-Tas and Junger 1984).

Marital tensions. Marital tensions are associated with a higher risk of children getting involved in accidents (Brown and Davidson 1987). Read et al. (1963) mention that accident families are characterized by more disruption of family life than control families.

Many criminological studies find that marital problems are related positively, and relatively strongly, to juvenile delinquency (Glueck and Glueck 1950; Rutter and Giller 1983; Wilson and Herrnstein 1985). Loeber and Stouthamer-Loeber (1986) conclude from their literature review that marital discord has a stronger relationship to delinquency and aggression than parental absence.

Mobility rate. A high mobility rate was associated positively, and relatively strongly, with accident rates in the birth cohorts studied by Stewart-Brown et al. (1986), Beautrais, Fergusson, and Shannon (1982), and Wadsworth et al. (1983). A high mobility rate is also related to criminal behavior (see for example, Rutter and Giller 1983; Werner 1987; Laub and Sampson 1988; Braithwaite 1989).

Family type. Family type is associated with accident liability. Several studies found that having both natural parents is associated with a lower rate than having only one parent or living with a stepfamily. For example, Larson and Pless (1988) report that single mothers had children with a higher accident liability. In another study, the same relation between family type and accident liability was found. This relation disappeared after controlling for other factors, such as maternal age (Stewart-Brown et al. 1986).

In research on crime there is usually an association, in the expected direction, between family type and crime. The Gluecks (1950) found that delinquents were less often living with both parents. Although reviews of the literature present sometimes mixed results, many studies establish a relation between family structure and crime; children of incomplete families being more at risk of developing delinquent behavior (see Rutter and Giller 1983; Wilson and Herrnstein 1985; Mak 1990, 1991).

Home environment. Matheny (1986) looked at the home environment of toddlers one to three years old. He concluded that low accident rates are associated with an adequate home environment (availability of indoor play space, possibilities for social and physical development), less noise and confusion, cleanliness and lack of disorder.

Not many studies have actually looked inside the homes of delinquents. The Gluecks (1950) however, did so. They found that the homes of delinquents were considered neat and clean in 49 percent of the cases, while among nondelinquents this figure was 66 percent. Among delinquents the "physical adequacy" of the home was described as good in 11 percent of the cases, whereas 27 percent of the homes of nondelinquents were described in this way. Thus, the homes of delinquent boys seem to be less well-kept than the homes of nondelinquent boys.

Socialization practices. Studying children ten to fifteen years of age in Oriental families, Kurokawa (1967) found that traditional mothers, who were less permissive and who reasoned a lot with their children, had a lower risk of having their children involved in accidents than mothers who were very permissive, took an egalitarian role, encouraged masculinity, or yelled a lot at their children. In families where parents engage in many preventive behaviors (like using automobile seat restraints), there is a relatively low accident rate among the children (Pless, Perreault, and Tennia 1989).

Among the various aspects of socialization, much attention has been given to the quality of supervision. Larson and Pless (1988) followed a birth cohort (N=918) for four years. They found that parental supervision (measured by looking at the restrictions and cautions given to the child) was strongly related to accident rates. In another study Pless, Perreault, and Tennia (1989) looked at 200 children with pedestrian or bicycle injuries (with a score of 2 or more on the Maximum Abbreviated Injury Scale) and compared them with two groups of controls).[9] The authors looked at the restrictions and cautions given by parents to the child and divided supervision into three categories. The accident rate in the low supervision category was 150 percent higher than the accident rate in the high supervision category. Several additional studies show that adequate socialization and supervision protect children from accidents (Read et al. 1963; Sharples et al. 1990; Matheny 1986).

Virtually all research on crime and family factors finds that parental socialization is strongly related to delinquent behavior among children. All studies report that children coming from families characterized by relatively strong supervision, affection, communication between parents and children, and where discord and family violence are absent are relatively unlikely to become delinquent. Empirical studies found relatively strong relations between family factors and delinquency (see for example Riley and Shaw 1985; Rosen 1985; LaGrange and White 1985; Patterson and Dishion 1985; Laybourn 1986; Wilson 1987; Patterson

1980, 1986; Cernkovitch and Giordano 1987; Wiatrowski and Anderson 1987; Werner 1987; Van Voorhis et al. 1988; Laub and Sampson 1988; Braithwaite 1989; Mak 1990, 1991; Farrington et al. 1990b; Junger 1988, 1990). Recent reviews of the literature include Rutter and Giller (1983), Wilson and Herrnstein (1985), Snyder and Patterson (1987), and Loeber and Stouthamer-Loeber (1986).

For example, the Gluecks (1950) found that provisions for recreation in the home were better in families of nondelinquent boys than in families of delinquent boys and supervision by the parents was found to be a strong predictor of delinquency. Among delinquents the supervision of the mother was suitable in 7 percent of the cases compared to 65 percent among nondelinquents (Glueck and Glueck 1950). It can be safely concluded that there is a relatively strong association between the quality of supervision and crime in the criminological literature.

Adverse life events. In the literature several authors combine variables, some of which were discussed earlier, under the heading of "adverse life events" such as divorce or financial problems. They report that adverse life events increase the likelihood of accidents: 31 percent of the mothers with accident-children experienced an adverse life event during the six weeks preceding the accident. This was twice the expected rate of 15 percent (p.< 01, Brown and Davidson 1987). According to these authors, these higher accident rates show that adverse life events affect the behavior of the mother and of the child. The mother provides less supervision and the child is more restless and vulnerable to accidents.

In an earlier study, Brown and Davidson (1978) reported similar results: adverse life events seem to increase the likelihood of accidents: 31% of the mothers experienced a life event during six weeks preceding the accident (expected: 15%, p.< 01). There they suggest that this relation explains the class difference in accidents because adverse events occur more frequently among working class families. They mention that difficulties in the home (such as poor health, shortage of money, marital tensions) are related to higher accident rates, independently of the mother's psychiatric condition. Among women without psychiatric problems, 35 percent of the women with at least one difficulty experienced child accidents versus 18 percent of women without such difficulties.

Beautrais, Fergusson, and Shannon (1982) also assessed the relation between adverse life events and injury liability in a birth cohort of four-year-old children. In their study a relatively high level of stress (and of adverse life events) is related to higher accident rates.

Pless, Verreault, and Tennia (1989), however, report that family stress (deaths, divorce, problems at work or school, financial problems) was related only weakly to the occurrence of accidents. Worse, the relation was in the opposite direction from that expected: a low level of stress was related to more accidents among the children. However, in the Pless, Verreault, and Tennia study, the control children and the accident children were matched by SES. In contrast, Beautrais, Fergusson, and Shannon (1982) studied a birth cohort in a small town and Brown and Davidson (1987) studied a random sample of 458 women (age eighteen to sixty five) living in a former inner-London borough. If stress is associated with SES, the matching procedure could lead to less variation in SES in the samples of Pless, Verreault, and Tennia, which might explain the unexpected association they find between family stress and accidents.

In the criminological literature, adverse life events are found to be related to juvenile delinquency. In families of delinquent boys, more fathers are unemployed, there are higher divorce rates, and there are more contacts with different social agencies than in families of nondelinquent boys (Glueck and Glueck 1950:169-71). All this suggests strongly that levels of stress must be higher in families of delinquents than in families of nondelinquents. The literature on crime indeed indicates that families of juvenile delinquents suffer from a higher proportion of adverse life events than families of nondelinquents (see Rutter and Giller 1983; Wilson and Herrnstein 1985; Gottfredson and Hirschi 1990). As was mentioned before, Werner (1987) found stress to be a predictor of delinquency (for example, illness of the parents or the child, absence of one of the parents, placement of the child in foster care).

Causal interpretations of the environment and of family factors. Like Matheny (1986) many authors give the quality of supervision a central place in the causation of children's accidents. In many cases they suggest that the correlates of accidents among children mentioned above (health problems, psychiatric problems, education of mother, age of mother, employment of mother, marital tensions, mobility rate, family type, home environment) relate to or directly affect the mother's capacity to supervise her child, which in turn influences the accident liability (Brown and Davidson 1987).

Similarly, many authors stress that several correlates of delinquency are probably not directly related to delinquency (see Rutter and Giller 1983; Wilson and Herrnstein 1985; Gottfredson and Hirschi, 1990), but operate instead through such family functioning variables as supervision. Laub and Sampson (1988) reanalyzed the data assembled by the Gluecks (1950) using more sophisticated techniques to perform new analyses of the Glueck's data. They conclude that the effect of mother's employment, of household crowding, economic dependence, and parental criminality/drunkenness on crime was mediated by family processes. There is much evidence, then, that the intermediate variable between family disruption (one-parent families) and crime is family functioning. As a result, when a deviant parent leaves the family, problem behavior sometimes decreases instead of increasing (Rutter and Giller 1983).

The Influence of Individual Level Variables

The evidence suggests a relation between psychological problems of the child and accident liability. For example, Manheimer and Mellinger (1967) found that 25 percent of the high accident liability group had been referred for psychological counseling and guidance, compared to only 10 percent of the low accident liability group. In the same study, the accident children were described relatively often as lacking self-control, measured by impulsivity, frustration tolerance, mood variability, and as having psychosomatic problems. It also appeared that boys had more problems that were described as psychosomatic (such as broken out skin, upset stomach).

Fuller (1947) asked head teachers to rate children from twenty two to fifty five months of age on several personality traits.[10] She found that accident children were described much more often than the other children as being exceptionally strong, daredevils, easily aroused, as showing extreme reactions (hysterical), as being impulsive, rude, insulting, insolent, overactive, and as bold or insensitive to social feelings.

Matheny (1986:171) found that individual characteristics of toddlers aged one to three were related to injury liability. Toddlers who were relatively tractable, who were in a positive mood, attentive, approachable, and generally manageable in the laboratory setting were less likely to sustain accidents. However, after controlling for the characteristics of the mother and the home, this relation between individual characteristics and injuries disappeared. (Characteristics of the mother and the home were substantially related to injury liability, producing a multiple correlation of .57.) In his prospective study of a Helsinki birth cohort, Nyman (1987) found that children having accidents are more often described by their mothers (or guardian) as having a negative mood, negative first reactions, and a higher activity level than nonaccident children. Among the accident children, 31 percent were described as having a "difficult" temperament, compared to 15 cent among the nonaccident children. The criminological literature has also studied individual factors related to juvenile crime. The Gluecks (1950) mention that delinquent boys are more often restless, impulsive, extroverted, aggressive, destructive, hostile, resentful, and nonsubmissive to authority than nondelinquents. In her study of Hawaiian children, Werner (1987) found that constitutional factors of the child, such as temperament and health, are related to delinquency. Wilson and Herrnstein (1985) and Rutter and Giller (1983) also concluded that these individual factors correlate with delinquency.

Finally, it is worth mentioning that hyperactivity is related to accident liability as well as to juvenile crime. Langley. Silva, and Williams (1983) mention that hyperactivity is strongly associated with a higher accident liability (see also Manheimer and Mellinger 1967; Bijur and Stewart-Brown 1986). Hyperactivity was also found to be related to crime in several studies (Rutter and Giller 1983; Wilson and Herrnstein 1985; Farrington et al. 1990a).

The relation between hyperactivity and crime might be spurious as it has been found that hyperactivity is related to conduct problems. Farrington, Loeber, and van Kammen (1990a) tried, therefore, to disentangle the effect of both variables on crime. They analyzed the data collected in the Cambridge Study in Delinquent Development, a prospective longitudinal survey of 411 lower class white males. They had information on conduct problems and hyperactivity in combination with impulsivity and attention deficit (HIA). The boys showing hyperactivity, impulsivity, and attention deficit or conduct problems at age eight and at age ten were coded as positive. These researchers concluded that both conduct problems and HIA were independent predictors of later juvenile convictions (ages ten to seventeen) but that conduct problems were a stronger predictor than HIA. There was no interaction effect. Results from self-report measures of delinquency support this result. The authors suggest that HIA may be associated with cognitive handicaps and that HIA, criminal parents, and juvenile convictions may be part of the same causal or developmental sequence.

Of course, the individual characteristics of the child and the characteristics of socialization by parents may be interrelated. This has been mentioned within the framework of delinquency by Werner (1987). In her study of Hawaiian children, Werner argues in favor of a "transactional model" of human development that takes into account the bi-directionality of child-caregiver effects. The child has characteristics that make him easy or difficult to manage, while parents react more or less adequately to the characteristics and/or difficulties of their child (Werner 1987). This assessment leads to the question whether the individual factors are still related to crime, after controlling for socialization practices. Gottfredson and Hirschi (1990) argue, as does Matheny (1986) for accident liability, that socialization is the real causal factor. Rutter and Giller (1983) also argue that individual factors are probably related only indirectly to crime.

Social Disadvantage

There is no consistency in the results looking at the relation between social class or social disadvantage and accident liability (Langley 1984). Several authors established a relation between social disadvantage[11] and accidents (Backett and Johnston 1959; Read et al. 1963; Manheimer and Mellinger 1967; Stewart-Brown et al. 1986; Alwash and McCarthy 1988). For example, Read et al. (1963) found that in accident families the fathers were more often unskilled workers, there were more persons per bedroom, there was a lower income, fewer families owned their home, financial security was lower, more health and welfare services were used, and there was a relatively high mobility level in comparison with nonaccident families.

However, other studies found no relation between SES/social disadvantage and the occurrence of accidents (Dershewitz 1978; Langley, Silva, and Williams 1987a; Nyman 1987; Van Rijn et al. 1987; Larson and Pless 1988). Wadsworth et al. (1983) found only a very small association between social disadvantage and accidents among children. In some studies the relation between SES and accidents disappears after control for characteristics of the mother and the home—psychiatric disorders, marital tensions, and poor health (see Matheny 1986; Brown and Davidson 1978).

U.S. statistics also seem to disagree with the social disadvantage thesis. From 1974 to 1984 there was an increase in adverse socioeconomic conditions: the number of single-parent families grew from 10 percent to 15 percent among whites, and from 38 percent to 58 percent among blacks. In the same period the number of families below the poverty level increased from 13 percent to 18 percent among whites, and from 40 percent to 51 percent among blacks. During these same years, however, the accident mortality rates among children in the United States from all causes decreased from 25.5 in 1970 to 15.4 in 1984 (Fingerhut et al. 1988, see also Wicklund et al. 1984). "Had mortality increased during this period, it is likely that these same socio-economic changes would have been pointed to as contributing factor" according to Fingerhut, Moss, and Frost (1988:405).

Research on crime has also looked very often at the relation between social disadvantage and crime. Deprivation has been found to be related to delinquent behavior in several American and English studies. Poverty, poor housing, unemployment are usually associated with a relatively high involvement in crime. For example, the Gluecks (1950) found that the home of delinquents was more often crowded, that sanitary provisions were worse, that the home was often considered as less good, that the economic condition of the family was worse, that fewer people in the family had a paid job, in comparison with nondelinquents. This difference between delinquent and nondelinquent boys is remarkable because the Gluecks matched the delinquent boys with control boys on age, intelligence, nationality, and residence in an underprivileged neighborhood. The Gluecks argue that probably these factors are not just indicators of SES but also in part the consequence (instead of the cause) of the behavior and way of living of the parents (for example, poor social skills). Consequently, the Gluecks claimed that these factors did not have a direct effect on crime, but considered that they would have an influence only through other variables among which child rearing methods are probably very important. This interpretation of the data was later confirmed through secondary analyses by Laub and Sampson (1988), who as mentioned above, concluded that the effect of mother's employment, of household crowding, economic dependence, and parental criminality/drunkenness on crime was mediated by family processes. Other authors have arrived at similar conclusions: although poverty and poor housing are associated with delinquency in many studies, it is unclear if the direction is causal (Rutter and Giller 1983; Snyder and Patterson 1987; Wilson and Herrnstein 1985; Werner 1987; Gottfredson and Hirschi 1990; Larzelere and Patterson 1990).

Like the Gluecks, other authors mention that to some extent social disadvantage (for example, unemployment) is the consequence of the same set of causes as criminal behavior (see Rutter and Giller 1983; Wilson and Herrnstein 1985; Gottfredson and Hirschi 1990). For example, Rutter and Giller mention that criminal or psychopathic parents are more likely to experience poverty and poor living conditions because of their frequent periods of unemployment and their difficulties in managing their affairs adequately (1983:185). They conclude that "the question of whether poverty and poor housing also have a direct impact on the children which predisposes to delinquency remains unresolved" (1983:185).

Sociodemographic Variables

Sex. Almost every study looking at the relation between sex and accidents finds that boys are much more at risk than girls. In the United States sex differences begin before age one with a risk for boys of 36.3 per 100,000 population and for girls of 29.2 per 100,000 population. These differences increase with age up to 96.7 per 100,000 for boys and 26.1 per 100,000 population for girls (see Rivara and Mueller 1987). In many studies it is found that the accident risk for boys is twice that for girls (Backett and Johnston 1959; Read et al. 1963; Manheimer and Mellinger 1967; Routledge, Repetto-Wright, and Howarth 1974; Brown and Davidson 1978; Beautrais, Fergusson, and Shannon 1982; Langley, Silva, and Williams 1987a; Pless, Verreault, and Tennia 1989).

Marcusson and Oehmisch (1977) analyzed statistics of fifty countries for the period 1950 to 1971. They conclude that sex differences are usually larger for children aged five to fourteen than for children aged one to four. The sex ratio also differs according to type of accident: in Europe and in North America the sex-ratio is relatively large for drownings (sex ratio boys/girls, 4.3 and 3.7 for children five to fourteen) but is smaller for traffic accidents (sex ratio boys/girls, 1.8 and 1.7 for children five to fourteen). For all accidents the sex ratio is 1.6 (children one to four) and 2.2 (children five to fourteen) in Europe and 1.4 (children one to four) and 2.1 (children five to fourteen) in North America (see table 5.1).

Race. A number of studies report that children of ethnic minorities are more at risk than white children. However, Kurokawa (1967) found lower accident rates for minority group children. In a California sample he found that the rates for whites varied between 257 and 277 (per thousand children, and for the different SES-categories). For blacks, accident rates varied between 182 and 236, and for Orientals between 135 and 168.

Junger and Steehouwer (1990) found relatively large difference among three ethnic groups in the Netherlands. It appeared that Moroccan and Turkish children (age two to twelve) have a higher risk of becoming involved in traffic accidents than Dutch children. Among Dutch children, 14 per thousand were involved in a traffic accident (during four and a half years); among Turks and Moroccans these rates were 43 and 44 per thousand. These differences persisted after controlling for the neighborhood in which the accident happened. Van Rijn et al. (1987) also found that children of ethnic minorities were more at risk for burn injuries than a control group of Amsterdam (the Netherlands) children. Thirteen percent of the children treated for burn injuries belonged to an ethnic minority in comparison with 3 percent among the control group.

In the United Kingdom, however, Alwash and McCarthy (1988) did not find an association between country of birth (British Isles, Asian, Caribbean, other) and accidents requiring medical treatment in the hospital among five-year-old children. However, they mention that mortality rates (all causes), do show that the mortality is higher for persons born in Ireland and Africa. Asians do not have higher mortality rates then British citizens.

Similarly, in the United States, national statistics show that black children one to nine years of age die more often from accidental causes than white children. The race mortality ratio for children one to four years old from all accidental causes is 1.6 for males and 1.7 for females (Fingerhut et al. 1988). For homicide and fire the race ratio is much larger and varies between 3.1 and 4.3 (see table 5.2, and Wicklund, Moss, and Frost 1984).

Overall, it seems warranted to conclude that there is a relation between ethnic background and involvement in accidents and that some ethnic minority groups are more at risk than others.

How can the sex and race differences be explained? No study has tried systematically to "explain away" sex or racial differences. However, with

TABLE 5.1
Accident Mortality in Europe and North America from Motor Vehicle Accidents,
Accidents Caused by Fire, Accidental Drownings, and All Causes, by Age and Sex
(Rates per 100,000)

ACCIDENTS	AGE:	Europe		North America	
		1-4	5-14	1-4	5-14
Motor vehicle	Boys	11.22	11.66	12.82	12.79
accidents	Girls	7.11	6.63	10.37	7.44
	Ratio[1]	1.6	1.8	1.2	1.7
Accidental	Boys	7.29	4.21	6.93	5.49
drowning	Girls	3.17	0.97	3.05	1.47
	Ratio[1]	2.3	4.3	2.3	3.7
Accidents	Boys	1.85	0.37	6.08	1.66
caused by fire	Girls	1.38	0.24	5.26	1.52
	Ratio[1]	1.3	1.5	1.2	1.1
Total	Boys	31.21	22.55	35.75	27.44
	Girls	19.1	10.45	26.32	12.86
	Ratio[1]	1.6	2.2	1.4	2.1

Source: Marcusson and Oehmisch (1977).
1 Ratio boys/girls, computation by the author

respect to the differences between sexes several authors have noted behavior differences as well as exposure differences between boys and girls, especially when one looks at traffic accidents (see Firth 1982; Langley 1984). For example, girls are usually more careful in traffic. Finlayson (1972) observed boys and girls as they came from school. The children (five to seven years old) were filmed crossing the road (188 children were filmed 405 times alltogether). In this study it appears that girls behave more safely, while boys act more unpredictably and, therefore, put themselves more at risk. Similarly, Langley (1984) concludes, on the basis of the literature, that in twenty-two of the twenty-five studies he reviewed, behavior disorders were larger for boys than for girls and these differences might be connected to behavior in traffic.

Other studies have focused on the exposure factor, with several finding that girls are less exposed than boys (e.g., Sandels 1968; Firth 1982; Langley, Silva, and Williams 1987b). After reviewing the literature,

TABLE 5.2
Race Mortality Ratios of Children by Age and Sex
(U.S., 1982–1984)

	Children 1-4 Males	Children 1-4 Females	Children 5-9 Males	Children 5-9 Females
Homicide	3.9	4.3	3.6	3.1
Fire	3.5	4.2	3.4	4.1
Pedestrian/cyclist	1.6	1.6	1.8	1.9
All causes	1.6	1.7	1.5	1.5

Source: Fingerhut et al. (1988:401).

Sheehy (1982) concluded that control over girls by mothers is more stringent than for boys. There are no differences in relation to trips to and from school or during shopping. But streets are more often used as recreational sites by boys than by girls. He concludes that "while there may be only minor variations in exposure to traffic when boys and girls are engaged in purposive journeys, such as running errands, there may be substantially greater variations for less obviously goal-directed street activity" (1982:217).

Not all studies find relevant differences in exposure. For example, Routledge, Repetto-Wright, and Howarth (1974) asked a representative sample of schoolchildren about their journeys in the previous twenty-four hours. They found few differences in exposure between boys and girls. However, girls were more often accompanied by adults than boys. The authors conclude that differences in behavior among young children when crossing roads are probably responsible for the difference in accident liability. Overall, however, most authors seem to find that boys are more exposed to danger than girls.

Racial differences can be explained by pointing to differences on several of the factors mentioned above, especially social disadvantage. Wicklund, Moss, and Frost (1984) looked at the mortality statistics of North Carolina and Washington. They found that racial differences in accidental mortality of babies largely disappear when maternal age, educational level, and parity are controlled. However, variables such as

educational level and maternal age do not explain the underlying processes leading to the racial differences. As mentioned above, the evidence
concerning social disadvantage in relation to accidents is inconsistent.
Therefore, differences in socialization might explain (at least in part) the
racial difference just as they explain the sex difference.

Many criminological studies have looked at sex and race in relation
to crime. They have always found, just as in studies of accidents, that
boys are more at risk of delinquency (see Rutter and Giller 1983; Wilson
and Herrnstein 1985; Rutenfrans 1989; Braithwaite 1989; Gottfredson
and Hirschi 1990).

Similarly, research on crime also establishes that blacks are more at
risk of delinquent behavior. In many countries ethnic minorities are
overrepresented in the official criminal statistics. This has been established for the United States, the United Kingdom, France, the Netherlands, Sweden, Belgium and Germany.[13] In general, immigrants and
blacks are overrepresented in the judicial system, although Asians are
underrepresented in most countries. In the Netherlands it appears that
Turks and Moroccans, who are more at risk for accidents are also more
likely to be involved in delinquent behavior.

The Relationship between Accidents
and Other Types of Problematic Behavior

Many researchers who study young children have looked at various
forms of problem behavior, such as aggression, or being difficult with
adults, as forms of deviant behavior, and several have found an association between these types of deviant behavior and accident liability.

For example, Langley, Silva, and Williams (1983) assembled information on the activity level of the children (measured by emotional
reactivity, assertiveness, nature of activity, nature of communication,
bullying other children) and on antisocial behavior (measured by a
discipline questionnaire submitted to the parents that contained fifteen
items on shouting, times sent out of room, and talk about what he/she
had done wrong). They found that the best predictor of accidents at age
seven was the activity level of the child. The next best predictor was
antisocial behavior. Information in this study came from parents and
teachers. Both sources of data led to the same conclusions. Several
studies report that accident children are relatively daring and defiant
(Read et al. 1963), present discipline problems to their mothers and

teachers, are more aggressive (Manheimer and Mellinger 1967; Bijur and Stewart-Brown 1986), and overactive (Bijur and Stewart-Brown 1986), or present other forms of problematic and deviant behavior (Suchman 1970; Wadsworth et al. 1983).

Yeager and Otnow-Lewis (1990) studied 118 juvenile delinquents (97 males, 21 females) incarcerated in a correctional school in Connecticut. They located the delinquents seven years after they left the school when they were twenty-five years of age. They found that six males and one female had died. This is a rate of 5,932/100,000 (almost 6 percent), which is fifty-eight times the national mortality rate for those fifteen to twenty-five years of age. All met a violent death: two were involved in traffic accidents, two overdosed on drugs, one was stabbed in jail, one was shot by the police, and one committed suicide. Apparently, children involved in much criminal behavior lead lives that put them at risk of dying from other than natural causes. In this case, it seems that accidents follow from a life-style that also includes delinquent behavior.

Similarly, in criminology, the Gluecks (1950) found that their 500 delinquent boys had a much higher accident rate than their matched nondelinquent boys. The mean age of the boys at the time of the comparison was fourteen years (table 5.3).

TABLE 5.3
Serious Accidents among Delinquents and Nondelinquents, in Percentages

	Delinquents $\underline{N} = 500$	Nondelinquents $\underline{N} = 500$
Had serious accidents	33.2	15.4
Hit by moving vehicle or run over	14.0	5.0
All other	19.2	10.4
Did not have serious accidents	66.8	84.6

Source: Glueck and Glueck (1950:162).
x^2=43.06, p < .01

Finally, Rutter and Giller (1983) mention a study that showed that delinquents had more accidents and injuries and more hospital admissions than nondelinquents, especially before age four. The accident children were largely found in the group with a criminal father. Rutter and Giller explain this difference by relating the accidents to parental problems.

Summary and Discussion

First, it should be emphasized that the findings of this chapter have mainly a tentative character. Some studies mentioned above had to cope with methodological problems. Several studies were not designed to test the idea that accident liability and crime might be related. As a result, much more research is needed to study the relations between accident liability and delinquency among children. It might also be mentioned that the relation between accidents and crime should be interpreted in terms of increased likelihood: involvement in crime increases the probability of getting involved in accidents of all kinds.

This chapter presented empirical evidence on three questions:

1. What are the personal and social correlates of involvement in accidents among young children?
2. Are these correlates the same as the correlates of criminal behavior?
3. Is involvement in accidents related to involvement in other problem behavior among children?

The following conclusions can be drawn. With respect to the first two questions a number of social and individual correlates of accident liability have been examined: health problems and psychiatric problems in the family, education of mother, age of mother, mother's employment, marital tensions, mobility, family type, home environment, socialization practices, adverse life events, the influence of individual factors (psychosocial problems, hyperactivity), social disadvantage, sex, and ethnic group. Generally, most of these factors are related to accident liability and in the same way to crime (see table 5.4). In studies of accidents and studies of crime the authors mention the central role of socialization processes within the family frame as the key concept to explain the correlations with other independent variables.

With respect to the third question, it appears from the literature that there is a relation between accident liability and other problem behavior among children. First, children involved in accidents are more often difficult to handle than nonaccident children and more often display aggressive behavior. Second, delinquent children are involved in accidents more often than nondelinquents.

These results support the idea of a "syndrome of problem behavior" as argued by, among others, Jessor and Jessor (1977), Robins and Wish (1977), Osgood et al. (1988), and Gottfredson and Hirschi (1990). The relation between involvement in crime as well as in accidents supports the thesis of a latent factor that could be named problem behavior. It seems to follow that these various forms of problem behavior are related because they all are the result of the same causal factor(s). Several authors have tried to find an explanation for the interrelation of diverse forms of problem behavior, in criminology and in other disciplines. Sheehy (1982) focused on the influence family factors have on both accident liability and crime.

How should one interpret this association, especially the influence family factors have on both accident liability and crime? There are two paths by which an aspect of family functioning can lead to higher vulnerability to traffic accidents:

The first is through the intervening variable "chronic stress" (resulting from recurring conflict or anxiety, or rapid changes in the family). This may weaken a person's defense and generally lead to impaired or reduced performance, thus leading to increased vulnerability. However, there may be a number of intervening variables, such as constitutional predispositions, personality, coping abilities. This is the psycho-pathological path.

The second path results from the stabilization and repetition of a potentially dysfunctional form of behavior. For example, a child may be encouraged to play outside the home, increasing the exposure to traffic. This type of child-care practice may be passed on from one generation to another. This is essentially a nonpathological path and constitutes a more fundamental failure in adaptive behavior to accommodate continuing change in the environment. While behavior associated with the first pathway may be expected to disappear as soon as the family disturbances disappear, behavior arising from the second pathway is likely to prove more enduring and resistant to change (Sheehy 1982: 220, see also Beautrais, Fergusson, and Shannon 1982).

It seems likely that when one considers the information contained in this chapter, that the relations between family problems and accidents

TABLE 5.4
Factors Related to Accidents and to Delinquency among Juveniles

	Accident Liability among Children (high)	Juvenile Delinquency (much)
Health/ psychiatric problems	+	+
Education of mother (low)	+	+
Age of mother (young)	+	+
Mother employed (yes)	+/-	+/-
Marital tensions (yes)	+	+
Mobility rate (high)	+	+
Family type (incomplete)	+	+
Socialization (permissive)	+	+
Supervision (low)	+	+
Individual factors:		
Psychological problems (present)	+	+
Hyperactivity (yes)	+	+
Social disadvantage (present)	+/-	+/-
Socio-demographic factors:		
Sex (boys)	+	+
Ethnic background (some ethnic background)	+	+

+ Positive relation
+/- Inconsistent results

and other forms of problem behavior are not merely temporary. This would indicate that the second pathway is more plausible. But it is also possible that both causal directions do to some extent play a role.

For criminologists the question is to what extent the present findings have implications for theories on delinquency. According to Osgood et al. (1988) several criminological theories can explain the fact that there are relations among diverse forms of problem behavior. Although this might be true for the behavior of the adolescents who have been studied in most research up to now, the question is whether all criminological theories can explain why factors predicting involvement in accidents among sometimes very young children would be, to some extent, the same as the factors predicting crime.

Suchman (1970) formulated explicitly the relation between accidents and social deviance: Social controls serve the function of protecting the individual from harm. "Social controls may also serve to regulate hazardous consumer products such as poisons and lethal weapons. Obviously, a great many social controls—traffic laws and safety regulations, for example are aimed directly at reducing harmful anti-social behavior. To the extent that social controls are violated by the individual, we may hypothesize that he places himself in a situation of additional risk of injury or death" (1970:5). The same person will be more likely to commit crimes.

These results seem to fit very well within the formulation of Gottfredson and Hirschi's (1990) theory of low self-control. Low self-control will lead to more involvement in crime. Gottfredson and Hirschi (1990) emphasize the importance of socialization, especially socialization within the family frame, during the first years of life in order to learn self-control. The authors also argue that crime is but one of the many manifestations of low self-control. Other consequences of a low self-control are illnesses, deaths at higher rates, and becoming involved in traffic accidents. Consequently, the idea that accidents and crime have common causes follows from their theory of crime causation.

The author would like to thank David Farrington, Rolf Loeber, and Marc LeBlanc for their comments and advice.

Notes

1. In most countries there also exist crimes by omission and criminal negligence. These crimes are usually not committed by juveniles but by adults.
2. From National Health Statistics (cited by Rivara and Mueller 1987:14). Percentages computed by the author.
3. In two provinces children were selected for the study when they were registered for prenatal care. In some towns the most recent children registered at the municipality at birth were selected. Nurses followed the infants and other children below age six in twenty families. They visited the families twice a month, and noted everything related to accidents.
4. See also Beautrais, Fergusson, and Shannon (1982), and Langley, Silva, and Williams (1987a).
5. Nederlands Instituut voor Preventieve Geneeskunde (N.I.P.G.) and Stichting Wetenschapelijk Onderzoek Verkeersveiligheid (S.W.O.V.).

6. For example, Marcus et al. (1960) assembled information on very small samples (total: sixty-eight), and Christoffel et al. (1986) had information on six families.
7. However, it is well documented that the neighborhood is an important factor in accident rates. Neighborhoods having relatively dense traffic and few play yards do have higher accident rates than neighborhoods with less dense traffic and more space for children to play (see, e.g., Foot, Chapman, and Wade [1982], and the special issue of *Social Problems* [1987]).
8. The Gluecks (1950) matched the 500 delinquent boys with 500 control boys on age, intelligence, nationality, and residence in an underprivileged neighborhood.
9. (1) 200 children matched by hospital, age (+/- 2 years), sex, and socioeconomic area of residence; (2) a random sample of 200 children matched only by age and hospital. As the controls did not differ, they were analyzed as one group.
10. The teachers were unaware that injury records were being analyzed and some of the ratings precede and some follow the dates the injuries occur.
11. Often operationalized as SES of father, but also as crowding, and renting versus home ownership.
12. See among others Gould 1969, Chambliss and Nagasawa 1969, Nadjafi 1983, Stevens and Willis 1979, Hindelang, Hirschi, and Weis 1979, Rutter and Giller 1983, Wilson and Herrnstein 1985, Block 1985, Jager 1984, Craen 1984, Albrecht 1984, Van der Hoeven 1986, Killias 1989, Gottfredson and Hirschi 1990, and Junger 1990.

References

Albrecht, H.J. 1984. "Problems of Policing Ethnic Minorities in the Federal Republic of Germany." In *Policing and Social Policy: The Cranfield-Wolfson Colloquium on Multi-Ethnic Areas in Europe*, ed. J. Brown, 28–34. London: Police Review Publication.

Alwash, Rafi, and Mark McCarthy. 1988. "Accidents in the Home among Children under Five: Ethnic Differences or Social Disadvantage?" *British Medical Journal* 296:1450–53.

Backett, Maurice E., and A.M. Johnston. 1959, February 14. "Social Patterns of Road Accidents to Children." *British Medical Journal*, pp. 409–13.

Beautrais, A.L., D.M. Fergusson, and F.T. Shannon. 1982. "Childhood Accidents in a New Zealand Birth Cohort." *Australian Paediatric Journal* 18:238–42.

Bijur, Polly E., and Sarah Stewart-Brown. 1986. "Child Behaviour and Accidental Injury in 11,966 Preschool Children." *American Journal of Diseases of Children* 140:487–93.

Block, C. R. 1985. "Race/Ethnicity and Patterns of Chicago Homicide 1965–1981." *Crime and Delinquency* 31:104–16.

Braithwaite, John. 1989. *Crime, Shame and Reintegration*. Cambridge: Cambridge University Press.

Brown, George W., and Susan Davidson. 1978, February 18. "Social Class, Psychiatric Disorder of Mother and Accidents to Children." *The Lancet*, pp. 378–80.

Cernkovitch, S.A., and P.G. Giordano. 1987. "Family Relationships and Delinquency." *Criminology* 25:295–321.

Chambliss, W.J., and R.H. Nagasawa. 1969. "On the Validity of Official Statistics: A Comparative Study of White, Black and Japanese High-School Boys." *Journal of Research in Crime and Delinquency* 6:71–83.

Christoffel, Katherine K., Joseph L. Schofer, Paul P. Jovanis, Barbara Brandt, Barbara White, and Robert Tanz. 1986. "Childhood Pedestrian Injury: A Pilot Study Concerning Etiology." *Accident Analysis and Prevention* 18:125-35.

Craen, A. 1984. "Policing and Social Policy in the Multi-Ethnic Area of Genk." In *Policing and Social Policy: The Cranfield-Wolfson Colloquium on Multi-Ethnic Areas in Europe*, edited by J. Brown, 89-96. London: Police Review Publication.

Dershewitz, Robert A. 1978. "Are Poor Children at Greater Risk of Household Injuries?" *Public Health Reports* 93:395.

Donovan, John E., and Richard Jessor. 1985. "Structure of Problem Behavior in Adolescence and Young Adulthood." *Journal of Consulting and Clinical Psychology* 53:890-904.

Donovan, John E., Richard Jessor, and Frances M. Costa. 1988. "Syndrome of Problem Behavior in Adolescence: A Replication." *Journal of Consulting and Clinical Psychology* 56:762-765.

Emerick, Sara J., Laurence R. Foster, and Douglas T. Campbell. 1986. "Risk Factors for Traumatic Infant Death in Oregon, 1973-1982." *Pediatrics* 77:518-22.

Farrington, David P. 1989, July. "Implications of Criminal Career Research for the Prevention of Offending." Paper presented at the British Criminology Conference, Bristol.

Farrington, David P., Rolf Loeber, and Welmoet B. van Kammen. 1990a. "Long-term Criminal Outcomes of Hyperactivity-Impulsivity-Attention Deficit and Conduct Problems in Childhood." In *Straight and Devious Pathways from Childhood to Adulthood*, ed. Lee N. Robins and Michael Rutter, 62-81. Cambridge: Cambridge University Press.

Farrington, D. P., R. Loeber, D. S. Elliott, J. D. Hawkins, D. B. Kandel, M. W. Klein, J. McCord, D. Rowe, and R. Tremblay. 1990b. "Advancing Knowledge About the Onset of Delinquency and Crime." In *Advances in Clinical Child Psychology*, vol. 13, ed. Benjamin B. Lahey and Alan E. Kazdin, 283-342. New York: Plenum Press.

Fingerhut, Lois A., Joel C. Kleinman, Michael H. Malloy, and Jacob J. Feldman. 1988. "Injury Fatalities Among Young Children." *Public Health Reports* 103:399-405.

Finlayson, H.M. 1972. "Children's Road Behaviour and Personality." Crowthorne, Berkshire, Transport and Road Research Laboratory.

Firth, D.E. 1982. "Pedestrian Behaviour." In *Pedestrian Accidents*, ed. Anthony J. Chapman, Frances M. Wade, and Hugh C. Foot, 41-69. Chichester: John Wiley & Sons.

Foot, H.C., A.J. Chapman, and F.M. Wade, eds. 1982. *Pedestrian Accidents*. Chichester: John Wiley & Sons.

Fuller, E.M. 1947. "Injury-Prone Children." *American Journal of Orthopsychiatry* 17:708-23.

Glueck, Sheldon, and Eleanor Glueck. 1950. *Unraveling Juvenile Delinquency*. Cambridge, MA: Harvard University Press.

Gottfredson, Michael, and Travis Hirschi. 1990. *A General Theory of Crime*. Stanford, CA: Stanford University Press.

Gould, L.C. 1969. "Who Defines Delinquency: A Comparison of Self-Reported and Officially Reported Indices of Delinquency for Three Racial Groups." *Social Problems* 16:325-36.

Hindelang, Michael J., Travis Hirschi, and Joseph G. Weis. 1981. *Measuring Delinquency*. Beverly Hills, CA: Sage.

_____. 1979. "Correlates of Delinquency: The Illusion of Discrepancy between Self-Report and Official Measures." *American Sociological Review* 44:999-1014.

Jager, J. 1984. "Ethnic Minorities and the Police Problems in Germany." In *Policing and Social Policy: The Cranfield-Wolfson Colloquium on Multi-Ethnic Areas in Europe*, ed. J. Brown, 44–50. London: Police Review Publication.

Jessor, Richard, and Shirley L. Jessor. 1977. *Problem Behaviour and Psychosocial Development*. New York: Academic Press.

Junger, M. 1990. "Delinquency and Ethnicity: An Investigation on Social Factors Relating to Delinquency among Moroccan, Turkish, Surinamese and Dutch Boys." Deventer, NL: Kluwer Law and Taxation Publishers.

_____. 1988. "Social Control Theory Versus Differential Association: A Test on Panel Data." In *Juvenile Delinquency in the Netherlands*, ed. J. Junger-Tas and R. Block, 77–104. Netherlands: Kugler.

Junger, M., and L. Steehouwer. 1990. "Traffic Accidents Involving Children from Ethnic Minorities." Den Haag: WODC, Ministerie van Justitie.

Junger-Tas, J., and M. Junger. 1984. "Juvenile Delinquency; Backgrounds of Delinquent Behavior." The Hague: Ministry of Justice, Netherlands.

Killias, Martin. 1989. "Criminality Among Second-Generation Immigrants in Western Europe: A Review of the Evidence." *Criminal Justice Review* 14:13–42.

Kurokawa, Minako. 1967. "Childhood Accident as a Measure of Social Integration." *Canadian Review of Sociology and Anthropology* 3:99–107.

LaGrange, R.L., and H.R. White. 1985. "Age Differences in Delinquency." *Criminology* 23:19–46.

Langley, John D. 1984. "Injury Control - Psychosocial Considerations." *Journal of Child Psychology and Psychiatry* 25:349–56.

Langley, John D., Phil A. Silva, and Sheila M. Williams. 1983. "Child Behaviour and Accidents." *Journal of Pediatric Psychology* 8:181–189.

Langley, John D., Phil A. Silva, and Sheila M. Williams. 1987a. "Psychosocial Factors in Unintentional Childhood Injuries: Results from a Longitudinal Study." *Journal of Safety Research* 187:73–89.

_____. 1987b. "Cycling Experiences and Knowledge of the Road Code of Nine-Years-Old." *Accident Analysis and Prevention* 19:141–45.

Larson, Charles P., and I. Barry Pless. 1988. "Risk Factors for Injury in a 3-Year-Old Birth Cohort." *American Journal of Diseases of Children* 142:1052–57.

Larzelere, Robert E., and Gerald R. Patterson. 1990. "Parental Management: Mediator of the Effect of Socio-economic Status on Early Delinquency." *Criminology* 28:301–24.

Laub, John H., and Robert J. Sampson. 1988. "Unraveling Families and Delinquency: A Reanalysis of the Gluecks' Data." *Criminology* 26:355–80.

Laybourn, A. 1986. "Traditional Strict Working Class Parenting: An Undervalued System." *British Journal of Social Work* 16:625–44.

Loeber, Rolf, and Magda Stouthamer-Loeber. 1986. "Family Factors as Correlates and Predictors of Juvenile Conduct Problems and Delinquency." In *Crime and Justice: An Annual Review of Research*, vol. 7, ed. M. Tonry and N. Morris, 29–149. Chicago: University of Chicago Press.

Mak, Anita S. 1990. "Testing a Psychosocial Control Theory of Delinquency." *Criminal Justice and Behaviour* 17:215–30.

_____. 1991. "Psychosocial Control Characteristics of Delinquents and Non-delinquents." *Criminal Justice and Behaviour* 18:287–303.

Manheimer, Dean I., and Glen D. Mellinger. 1967. "Personality Characteristics of the Child Accident Repeater." *Child Development* 38:491–513.

Marcusson, H., and W. Oehmisch. 1977. "Accident Mortality in Childhood in Selected Countries of Different Continents, 1950-1971." *World Health Statistics*, 57-92.

Matheny, Adam P. 1986. "Injuries Among Toddlers: Contributions from Child, Mother, and Family." *Journal of Pediatric Psychology* 11:163-76.

Nadjafi, Abrandabadi A.H. 1983. "L'évolution de la criminalité des étrangers en France." *Revue Penitentiare et de Droit Penal* 2:147-55.

Nyman, Gote. 1987. "Infant Temperament, Childhood Accidents, and Hospitalization." *Clinical Pediatrics* 6:389-404.

Osgood, D. Wayne, Loyd Johnston, Patrick O'Malley, and Jerald Bachman. 1988. "The Generality of Deviance in Late Adolescence and Early Adulthood." *American Sociological Review* 53:81-93.

Osgood, Wayne D. 1990. "Covariation Among Adolescent Problem Behaviours." Paper presented at the meetings of the American Society of Criminology, Baltimore.

Patterson, Gerald R. 1980. "Children Who Steal." In *Understanding Crime*, ed. T. Hirschi and M. Gottfredson, 73-90. Beverly Hills, CA: Sage.

_____. 1986. "Performance Models for Antisocial Boys." *American Psychologist* 41:432-44.

Patterson, G.R., and T.J. Dishion. 1985. "Contributions of Families and Peers to Delinquency." *Criminology* 23:63-79.

Pless, Barry I., Rene Verreault, and Sonia Tennia. 1989. "A Case-Control Study of Pedestrians and Bicycle Injuries in Childhood." *American Journal of Public Health* 79:995-98.

Read, John H., Eleonor J. Bradley, Joan D. Morison, David Lewall, and David A. Clarke. 1963. "The Epidemiology and Prevention of Traffic Accidents Involving Child Pedestrians." *Canadian Medical Association Journal* 89:687-701.

Riley, D., and M. Shaw. 1985. *Parental Supervision and Juvenile Delinquency*. London: HMSO, Home Office Research Study, nr. 83.

Rivara, Frederick P., and Beth A. Mueller. 1987. "The Epidemiology and Causes of Childhood Injuries." *Journal of Social Issues* 43:13-31.

Robins, Lee N., and Eric Wish. 1977. "Childhood Deviance as a Developmental Process: A Study of 233 Urban Black Men from Birth to 18." *Social Forces* 34:448-73.

Rosen, L. 1985. "Family and Delinquency: Structure or Function." *Criminology* 23:553-71.

Routledge, D.A., R. Repetto-Wright, and C.L. Howarth. 1974. "The Exposure of Young Children to Accident Risk as Pedestrians." *Ergonomics* 17:457-80.

Rutenfrans, C.J.C. 1989. *Criminaliteit en Sexe* (Criminality and sex). Arnhem, The Netherlands: Gouda Quint.

Rutter, M., and H. Giller. 1983. *Juvenile Delinquency, Trends and Perspectives*. Harmondsworth, Penguin Books.

Sandels, Stina. 1968. *Children in Traffic*. London: Elek Books.

Sharples, P.M., A. Storey, A. Aynsley-Green, and J.A. Eyre. 1990. "Causes of Fatal Childhood Accidents Involving Head Injury in Northern Region." *British Medical Journal* 301:1193-97.

Sheehy, N. P. 1982. "Accidents and the Social Environment." In *Pedestrian Accidents*, ed. Anthony J. Chapman, Francis M. Wade, and Hugh C. Foot, 205-35. Chichester: John Wiley & Sons.

Snyder, J., and G. Patterson. 1987. "Family Interaction and Delinquent Behavior." In *Handbook of Juvenile Delinquency*, ed. H.C. Quay, 216-43. New York: John Wiley & Sons.

Social Problems. 1987. "Children's Injuries Prevention and Public Policy." 43:1-162.

Stevens, P., and C.F. Willis. 1979. "Race, Crime and Arrests." London, HMSO, Home Office Research Study No. 58.

Stewart-Brown, Sarah, Tim J. Peters, Jean Golding, and Polly Bijur. 1986. "Case Definition in Childhood Accident Studies: A Vital Factor in Determining Results." *International Journal of Epidemiology* 15:352-59.

Suchman, Edward A. 1970. "Accidents and Social Deviance." *Journal of Health and Social Behavior* 11:4-15.

Van der Hoeven, E. 1986. "De jeugdpolitie: een Observatie-Onderzoek" (The youth police: An observation study). Den Haag: CWOK.

Van Rijn, O.J.L., L.M. Bouter, R.M. Meertens, M.E.C. Grol, G.J. Kok, and S. Mulder. 1987. "Brandwonden bij 0-4 jarige kinderen" (Burn injuries among 0-4 Year old children). Amsterdam: Stichting Consument en Veiligheid.

Van Voorhis, P., F.T. Cullen, R.A. Mathers, and C. Chenoweth Garner. 1988. "The Impact of Family Structure and Quality on Delinquency: A Comparative Assessment of Structural and Functional Factors." *Criminology* 26:235-61.

Wadsworth, Jane, Iona Burnell, Brent Taylor, and Neville Butler. 1983. "Family Type and Accidents in Preschool Children," *Journal of Epidemiology and Community Health* 37:100-104.

Werner, E.E. 1987. "Vulnerability and Resiliency in Children at Risk for Delinquency: A Longitudinal Study from Birth to Young Adulthood." In *Prevention of Delinquent Behavior*, ed. J.D. Burchard and S.N. Burchard, 16-43. Newbury Park: Sage.

Wiatrowski, Michael D., and Kristine L. Anderson. 1987. "The Dimensionality of the Social Bond." *Journal of Quantitative Criminology* 3:65-81.

Wicklund, Kristine, Sheila Moss, and Floyd Frost. 1984. "Effect of Maternal Education, Age, and Parity on Fatal Infant Accidents." *American Journal of Public Health* 74:1150-52.

Willemijns, F, and J.V. Corbisier. 1961. "Een nieuw enkwest over ongevallen bij kinderen." *Het Kind*, Nrs. 5-6, 1-64.

Wilson, H. 1987. "Parental Supervision Re-Examined." *British Journal of Criminology* 27:275-301.

Wilson, James Q., and Richard J. Herrnstein. 1985. *Crime and Human Nature*. New York: Simon & Schuster.

Yeager, Catherine A., and Dorothy Otnow-Lewis. 1990. "Mortality in a Group of Formally Incarcerated Juvenile Delinquents." *American Journal of Psychiatry* 147:612-14.

6

Motor Vehicle Accidents

David W. M. Sorensen

Motor vehicle accidents are the result of driver, roadway, or vehicular factors, or some combination of these variables. The term *accident* conjures up images of chance happenings, unknown causes, and unavoidable outcomes. The roles of ignorance and negligence are diminished by both dictionary definition and standard usage. But under such a "fortuitous happening" paradigm, the frequency distribution of accidents would be expected to take the shape of a normal bell curve. It does not. Seventy years of empirical research have shown that certain individuals have more accidents than are explainable by chance alone. Furthermore, it has been demonstrated that the high accident rate for many of these specific individuals is stable over time, and that high-rate individuals are distinguishable from accident-free individuals on a number of dimensions. This insight indicates nothing about the *overall* causes of motor vehicle mishap, but it does imply that for some individuals the causes of accidents, or lack of them, lie in personal characteristics of the actor rather than uncontrollable circumstances in the environment.

This chapter will draw on some of the more important studies in the fields of accident analysis and criminology. Our purpose is twofold: first, to describe the concept of accident proneness, its development, and proposed explanations; and second, to explore the relation between accident proneness and crime by defining each as deviance, with the same correlates, age structures, and relatively stable manifestations.

Accident Proneness

Coined in the late 1930s, the term *accident prone* has become a household word. It is used by the layman to describe the clumsy, the repeatedly unfortunate, or any individual who appears to have had more than his or her share of accidental injury. In the worlds of social science and accident analysis the term *accident prone* is defined more specifically. Yet even within these scientific communities the seventy-year history of accident proneness research has been plagued by, and rightfully criticized for, a lack of definitional, and thus conceptual, congruency (e.g., Arbous and Kerrich 1951). Simply stated, accident proneness refers to "an enduring or stable personality characteristic that predisposes an individual toward having more accidents than explainable by chance alone" (Shaw and Sichel 1971). Such a concept implies that even controlling for physiological (vision, audition, reaction-time, etc.) and environmental factors, some individuals are intrinsically more likely to have accidents than others. Accident proneness refers solely to "affairs of personality," and is not to be confused with *initial accident liability*, a broader term encompassing all individual differences (psychological and physiological) that might affect one's overall chances of accidental injury (Greenwood and Wood 1919).

Greenwood and Wood first demonstrated the existence of unequal initial accident liability in 1919. They analyzed the accident records of a group of 750 similarly exposed and experienced female British munitions workers and noted that a small percentage of the women accounted for the vast majority of accident victims (Greenwood and Wood 1919). Greenwood and Wood suggested that some biographical, physiological, or psychological characteristic must account for the high rate of injury among this group. Observations of this skewed distribution continued most notably through the work of Newbold (1926). While these early statistical studies are applauded still for their precise methodological controls for exposure, reporting, and experience, controls for physiological factors were absent, allowing these experimenters to conclude no more than the finding of unequal initial accident liability.

Scientific enthusiasm for a psychological theory of accidents peaked in the late 1930s with the coining of the term *accident proneness* and the writing of many hundreds of papers on that subject. The more fashionable the concept, the more loosely its research was conducted, and the more unjustifiably grandiose its conclusionary statements became (e.g., Farmer and Chambers 1939). Though much insightful research did continue (e.g., Tillmann and Hobbs 1949; Hakkinen 1958; Shaw 1965), the previous lack of scientific objectivity on the part of some researchers had left the field open to question in the 1950s (Arbous and Kerrich 1951), and rejection in the 1960s (Haddon, Suchman, and Klein 1964) on methodological, statistical, and even conceptual bases. Nevertheless, the concept has enjoyed something of a scientific renaissance in the 1970s and 1980s due to a renewed concern with methodological precision, coupled with continually mounting evidence of the accident proneness phenomenon.

Methods

Myriad factors combine to define an individual's total accident liability. One aim of accident proneness research has been to separate the psychological contributors to accidents from confounding causal variables. To this end researchers have most generally followed one of two broad approaches: the clinical or the statistical.

The clinical approach examines identified high- and low-risk drivers for distinguishing psychological, sociological, or biographical features. Personality factors can be assessed by use of any means from a self-administered questionnaire to an in-depth psychological investigation. Discriminating variables are later correlated with accident record. From this analysis a composite of the accident prone, and the safe driver, emerges.

Clinical Findings on Accidents, Crime, and Social Deviance

McGuire (1976:433) describes the accident prone individual as being "emotionally less mature, less responsible, more a/antisocial, and not as well-adjusted." He adds that these individuals "tend to have a more disturbed history, such as an unhappy childhood, delinquency, family disruption and an uneven work record." More extensive descriptions, but similar in essence, are found throughout the accident proneness literature. Correlations between a proclivity for accidents and a variety of social deviance, including criminal activity have been repeatedly documented.

The belief that crime and a high propensity for accidents are in some way interrelated dates back at least forty years. The first systematic

clinical study of accidents and social pathology was undertaken by
Tillmann and Hobbs in 1949. Two experiments were conducted. The first
involved seventy taxi drivers in London, Ontario. Tillmann and Hobbs
rode with the seventy drivers over a two-and-one-half-month period,
giving them a chance to evaluate both the drivers and their driving habits.
Two groups of twenty each were then selected as a high- and low-accident sample. The groups were comparable in age and miles driven.

Extensive interviews were undertaken with these forty men to obtain
comprehensive biographical and psychological information. All self-
report information was cross-checked against official sources (i.e., police
records), management, and recollections of fellow cab drivers. Results
of comparisons between the twenty high-accident and twenty low-accident drivers have been reproduced in table 6.1. While the population of
the study was small, and the hazard of observer bias great, Tillmann and
Hobbs concluded that the high accident personality was "characterized
by aggressiveness and inability to tolerate authority either at the parental
or community level." They hypothesized further that this personality
"would appear to have its origin in the home background of the individual" (Tillmann and Hobbs 1949:327).

While small sample size and the possibility of observer bias were
obvious points of methodological concern, there was also a problem with
generalizing the findings of an experiment with a highly select group
(taxi drivers) to the general population. Realizing these problems,
Tillmann and Hobbs devised a second study. They obtained the names
and addresses of ninety-six male drivers in the area who had official
records of four or more serious (damage > $50) automobile accidents.
The names of 100 accident-free male drivers in the same district were
obtained as a control group. The names of both groups were submitted
to the juvenile court, the adult court (for non-traffic-related records), to
the "public health agencies" and venereal disease clinics, and to three
social service agencies. "These were the Family Service Bureau, which
handles difficulties of a family nature, and to the two Children's Aids
societies, Catholic and Protestant" (Tillmann and Hobbs 1949:328). In
addition, the names were checked by the local credit bureau, which
reported name recogition only when such names appeared two or more
times in their records. It was Tillmann and Hobbs's hope to turn up
evidence which would support and generalize their findings in the taxi
driver study. Table 6.2 summarizes the findings of the second study.

TABLE 6.1
Personality Survey on Group of Taxi Drivers

Personality	Characteristic	High Accident Group, 20 Men	Low Accident Group 20 Men	Statistical Significance X^2
Birth place.............	Urban.............................	15	15	....
History of parents.......	Parents divorced................	6	1	4.63
	Excessive strictness and disharmony................	13	5	6.28
Neurotic traits in childhood life...........	Excess childhood phobias*....	11	5	4.48
	Excess aggression in childhood**......................	11	0	23.60
School adjustment.......	Completing grade school......	15	15	....
	Truancy and disciplinary problems........................	12	2	10.98
Employment record.....	Five or more previous jobs....	13	7	3.60
	History of being fired.........	10	4	3.98
Armed service record...	Member of armed service.....	15	9	....
	Frequent A.W.L.'s.............	11	1	8.60
Marital status and sexual adjustment.......	Married..........................	8	11	....
	Admitting sexual promiscuity	8	2	4.00
Social adjustment.......	Having two or more hobbies..	9	17	8.50
	Admitting bootlegging on the job...........................	14	3	12.20
	Conscious of physique.........	11	3	5.40

*Source:*W.A. Tillmann and G.E. Hobbs,"The Accident-Prone Driver" *American Journal of Psychiatry* 106 (1949): 324. Copyright 1949, the American Psychiatric Association. Reprinted by permission.
*Enuresis, fear of fights, dark, deep water, excessive daydreaming, etc.
**Leader of gang, bully, temper tantrums, juvenile court record, etc.
When P=.05, X^2=3.84.

Tillmann and Hobbs report that 66 percent of the high-accident group were known to one or more agencies. Among the 100 accident-free drivers, only nine were known to any agency, and in no case was a person known to more than one. They conclude (1949:328) that "social maladjustment of various types is to be found quite as frequently among the general driving population with a high accident record as among the high accident taxi drivers, and that one is justified in feeling that the same pattern exists in both groups."

These findings, while vigorously criticized by Haddon, Suchman, and Klein (1964) as lacking in methodological precision (most notably controls on exposure), have been replicated many times since. Following the same line of inquiry with a population of professional truck drivers equitable on exposure, McFarland and Moseley (1954) reached identical

TABLE 6.2
Social Records of 96 Accident Repeaters and 100 Accident-Free Drivers,
in Percentages

	Repeaters	Accident Free
Credit Bureau Record	34.3%	6%
Social Service Agencies	17.7	1
Public Health and V.D. Clinic	14.4	0
Adult Court	34.3	1
Juvenile Court	16.6	1

Source: Tillmann and Hobbs (1949), fig. 2.

conclusions. Accident repeaters were more likely to have been involved with the criminal justice system and various social service agencies, and to have had childhood histories of "emotional disturbance" (McFarland and Moseley 1954). Correlations between childhood home life and future accidents have been found by Rommel (1959, cited by OECD 1975), Shaw and Sichel (1971), Harrington (1971, cited by Naatanen and Summala 1976), Sobel and Underhill (1974), Tillmann and Hobbs (1949), and McFarland and Moseley (1954).

The inverse relation between accident potential and academic achievement further illustrates the formation of attitudes and behaviors predictive of high-accident potential long before the age of driver eligibility. While Tillmann and Hobbs found no difference between high- and low-accident groups in terms of completion of grade school (perhaps a function of the Canadian school system), significant differences were found in regard to a history of "truancy and disciplinary problems."

Subsequent research has shown accident repeaters significantly more likely to have failed an elementary school grade (Kraus et al. 1970, cited by Robertson 1983), to have played "hooky" from high school (Harrington 1971), to have been enrolled in a "vocational track" curriculum (Kraus et al. 1970), and to have terminated their education at a younger age than their non-accident-repeating counterparts (Schuman et al. 1967, cited by Naatanen and Summala 1976, Harrington 1971). In fact, Harrington (1971) finds poor academic achievement and school adjustment to be among the best predictors of accident potential (see also Carlson and Klein 1970). Such findings are not new to criminology (Gottfredson and Hirschi 1990:105-7).

Most of the traditional correlates of criminality have also been found to be correlated with accident involvement. The accident repeater is more likely to have begun dating (Harrington 1971), working (Schuman et al. 1967, Kraus et al. 1970), and smoking (Kraus et al. 1970) at an early age. The fact that smoking has been consistently tied to accident involvement led DiFranza et al. to suggest that "the common denominator here may be the willingness to take risks" (1986:466).[1] The accident repeater is more likely than average to be single or divorced than married (Coppin & van Oldenbeek 1966, cited by Shaw and Sichel 1971; Michalowski 1977), and has more often fathered illegitimate children than his non-accident-repeating counterparts (McFarland and Moseley 1954). Those in low-skill occupations and the unemployed are overrepresented in accident statistics (Coppin and van Oldenbeek 1966; Michalowski 1977). Accident repeaters are disproportionately young and overwhelmingly male (National Safety Council 1989). As of 1988, approximately 51.8 percent of the estimated 164 million drivers were male. Yet males comprised 69 percent of those killed in, and 78 percent of those involved in, the motor vehicle fatilities of 1986 (National Safety Council 1989).

The potential for accidents would thus seem highest among the single, socioeconomically and educationally disadvantaged young male. Such a composite is all too familiar to the criminologist, who should not be surprised by the fact that a number of other studies, in addition to those of Tillmann and Hobbs (1949), and McFarland and Moseley (1954), have uncovered similar evidence of the connection between repeated motor vehicle accidents and crime. Larsen (1956) found that the greater the number of recorded traffic violations, the more likely a juvenile would have a (nontraffic) criminal arrest record (see also Carlson and Klein (1970), and Kraus et al. (1970). Willett (1964) found traffic offenders in Great Britain to have a rate of criminal arrests three times that of the general populace. Haviland and Wiseman (1974) found criminals who drive in Dade County, Florida, to have 3.25 as many traffic citations, and to have been involved in 19.5 as many motor vehicle fatalities as the noncriminal driving public.

A General Theory of Accidents

A general theory of accidents may begin with the assumption that human behavior is motivated by the pursuit of pleasure. Accidents are, of course, not widely regarded as pleasurable. But neither are criminal arrests nor social stigmatization. The factor common to accidents, crime, and social deviance is a pattern of involvement in risky activities without regard, or with little regard, for the long-term or low probability consequences of one's acts. Although the literature speaks of a "propensity for accidents," this is like speaking of a "propensity" for arrests. Accidents and arrests are unintended or unsought *consequences* of immediately pleasurable activity. The propensity, if any, must be toward those reckless behaviors that tend to increase the risk of accident occurrence. Such recklessness offers certain or immediate rewards that are often pursued without concern for distant or uncertain penalties.

While the odds of crash involvement are affected by a host of variables, human factors, and recklessness in particular, would seem paramount. It is estimated that "driver error" is a primary factor in 90 percent of motor vehicle accidents (Treat et al. 1977, as cited by Shinar 1978).[2] While reckless driving is merely one component of the many factors labeled "driver error," a number of statistics indicate its significance. For example, The National Safety Council (1989) has cited "improper driving" (consisting of reckless and predominantly illegal maneuvers) as a factor in 67 percent of motor vehicle accidents.[3] In such incidents, excessive speed and right-of-way violations were the most commonly specified factors.

Convictions for traffic violations are highly correlated with accident incidence (Campbell 1959; Sobel and Underhill 1974; Robertson 1983) and are, in fact, a better predictor of future accidents than accidents themselves (Miller and Schuster 1983). Explanation of the finding that violations predict future accidents better than accidents themselves may lie in the fact that while accidents are the result of both recklessness and chance, recklessness itself, which invites both citation and casualty, is a purely behavioral factor. Such correlations are further accentuated by analysis of only those drivers deemed responsible for their accidents (Banks 1977, cited in Robertson 1983). While traffic citation records are admittedly an imperfect measure of a propensity for recklessness, common sense would suggest a strong correlation between them.

Human action offers psychic as well as material rewards. On the whole, exciting, risky, or thrilling activities are perceived as more pleasurable than routine, harmless, or dull ones. Thus, driving fast and daringly is more pleasurable than driving slowly. But mere thrill-seeking is not the only motivation for traffic law violation. Widely held values regarding self-autonomy, competitiveness, and the efficient use of one's time are similarly thwarted by the rigid observance of traffic regulation. The driver must therefore balance the immediate, and often substantial benefits of a risky maneuver (such as passing a line of slow-moving vehicles in an extended "no-passing" zone) against the possibilities of collision or citation, both of which he justifiably views as unlikely. Collision, while severe, is a rare occurrence, and extremely unlikely to result from any given *single* violation. Citation, while still improbable, is more likely than collision, but also much less severe. While the probability of either event resulting from a single violation is extremely low, the odds increase with the frequency of the violating behavior. Those high on self-control are more likely to consider not only the immediate possible consequences of violating the law, but also the much increased long-term risks of forming a pattern of recklessness.

In a similar vein, the odds of arrest for a single unbungled burglary, while clearly dependent upon a variety of variables, are relatively low. U. S. Department of Justice statistics (1989) show clearance of only 13.8 percent of all *reported* burglaries in 1988. However, given the estimate that only 51 percent of total burglaries were reported in that year, the actual odds of apprehension for any single burglary (all else being equal) are more likely in the neighborhood of one in fourteen. Despite these seemingly favorable odds, repeated involvement in burglary almost always leads to arrest, or if not, clearly increases the odds of that outcome. A single standard traffic violation is, of course, infinitely less likely to result in physical or political sanction than the single standard burglary. Nevertheless, while both traffic law violation and burglary may "pay" in the short run, perpetual involvement invites disaster. The individual high on self-control, while equally tempted by the benefits inherent in reck-lessness, is more likely to consider the long-term risks, and is thus less likely to engage in reckless driving.

Age

The relationship between crime and motor vehicle accidents is further enhanced by an examination of the age curves of the two phenomena. Figure 6.1 displays the age curve of Part I Index property crime arrests and that of drivers involved (but not necessarily killed) in fatal motor vehicle accidents.[4] Like crime, involvement in fatal traffic accidents peaks in the late teens and steadily declines thereafter. Unlike crime, the motor vehicle fatality age curve is bimodal, displaying a second, though vastly less sizable rise beginning around age sixty. It is the contention here that while the high accident rate of youths ages sixteen to twenty-four is attributable to a greater disregard for consequences, increased casualty among elder adults is more likely a function of physiological factors. Such factors affect both the odds of crash involvement and the ability of the individual to survive physical trauma.

FIGURE 6.1: Age-Specific Accident and Arrest Rates

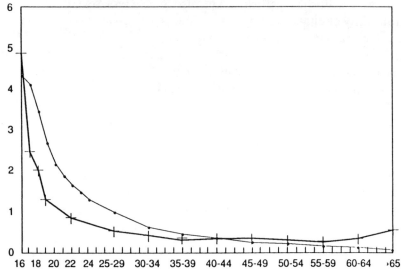

+++Male drivers involved in fatal crashes per 10,000,000 vehicle miles traveled, 1978 (Source: Robertson (1983:57))
***Male and female Part I property crime arrests per 100 persons, 1979 (Source: U.S. Department of Justice (1990))

Young Drivers

The belief that young people make up an especially dangerous class of drivers is not without foundation. In 1988, drivers age sixteen to twenty-four made up less than one-fifth (18.6 percent) of all licensed drivers, but accounted for nearly one-third (31.1 percent) of the 64,000 drivers involved in fatal accidents (National Safety Council 1989). Motor vehicle accidents are the leading cause of death in this age group, accounting for more fatalities than all other causes of death combined (National Safety Council 1989). The involvement of young adults in a considerably greater proportion of single-vehicle accidents leaves little doubt as to their culpability (Klein and Waller 1970). Costs for this age group in terms of permanent disablement and lesser injury are similarly disproportionate.

Because young adults have been shown to be at the prime of physical acuity, such variables as vision, audition, and reaction time cannot be used to explain their high rate of accidents. Efforts to account for the high incidence of accidents among the young have focused on exposure, alcohol consumption, and experience. But even these explanations are far from fully satisfying.

Quantitative exposure, as measured by miles traveled, is a significant predictor of accident involvement. But ironically, young adults actually drive fewer miles than their older counterparts (Carlson 1973, as cited by Lewis 1985). Thus, exposure cannot explain their overrepresentation in fatality statistics. Furthermore, the age curve depicting drivers involved in fatal accidents (fig. 6.1) is based on a *rate* of fatalities per vehicle miles driven by each age group. Exposure has therefore already been taken into account.

Of course, the quality of exposure also affects total accident liability. While young adults drive fewer total miles, a greater proportion of their total mileage is accumulated during recreational (Klein and Waller 1970) and nighttime driving (Carlson 1973). Lewis (1985) cites a study by Mayhew, Warren, and Simpson (1981) demonstrating young drivers to be between 1.2 and 2.3 times more likely (depending on specific age) to be fatally injured during nighttime driving than the general population of nighttime drivers. Such results have led Lewis (1985) to ponder whether this is "because of the inherent risks of night-time driving or because adolescents choose night-time as suitable for particularly dangerous types of driving which they favor?" Cameron (1982, as cited by Lewis 1985) has reviewed a number of studies examining the combined effects of quantitative and qualitative exposure for the sixteen- to twenty-four-year-old driving population. It was concluded that exposure alone could not account for the overrepresentation of young adults in fatal motor vehicle accidents.

Alcohol was implicated as a factor in 50 to 55 percent of fatal motor vehicle accidents in 1988 (National Safety Council 1989).[5] The percentage of motor vehicle fatalities involving alcohol was, however, highest among young adults (National Highway Traffic Safety Administration

1988). This age group's percentage of alcohol-related accidents was also far higher than would be expected on the basis of vehicle miles of travel, all else being equal (Lewis 1985). Have we now found our explanation of the increased motor vehicle fatality liability of young adult drivers? According to studies reviewed by Lewis (1985), we have not. Lewis cites the Grand Rapids Study by Zylman (1973) that shows young adult male drivers to have a higher risk of motor vehicle accidents than older drivers even at blood-alcohol levels of zero. In fact, it is reported that the effects of age are most pronounced in non-alcohol-related accidents (Zylman 1973). After the examination of one such group of non-alcohol-related accidents, Zylman found sixteen to seventeen year olds, and eighteen to nineteen year olds to be overrepresented by 53 percent and 25 percent, respectively. While no doubt exists as to the significance of intoxication as a principal cause of motor vehicle fatalities, the evidence suggests that alcohol alone cannot account for the overrepresentation of young adults in traffic accidents.

The effects of age and those of experience are intricately interwoven. Attempts to isolate their individual effects have proven difficult. Experience with driving would be expected to improve proficiency. Given such conventional wisdom, it has been argued that the high accident rate of young adults could be largely attributable to a lack of comparable driving experience. Yet despite the palatability of such an argument, evidence to the contrary can be found. For example, Robertson (1983:56) describes a study by Pierce (1977) in which

> 14.2% of drivers licensed at sixteen had crashes reported to the police in their first year, compared to 13.4% in their second year and 11.5% in their third year at age eighteen. Among those who waited until eighteen to be licensed, 11.9% reported crashes in their first year, about the same percent as eighteen year olds with two years of experience. Nineteen-year-old drivers licensed since they were sixteen had 10.2 crashes per hundred drivers compared to 10.5 per 100 newly licensed nineteen year olds. (Robertson 1983:56)

Swedish researchers Kritz and Nilsson (1967, cited by OECD 1975) arrived at similar findings.

Evidence thus far has demonstrated that the high accident rate of young adults cannot be attributed exclusively to the effects of exposure, intoxication, or a lack of experience. Some other variable is in simultaneous operation.

Stability

After controlling for exposure, age, experience, reporting, and vision, Hakkinen (1958) found the accident rates of fifty-two bus, and forty-four tram drivers to be relatively stable over a period of eight years. Split-half correlations between the first and second four-year periods, and between odd/even year periods were r = +0.577 and +0.678 for bus drivers, and r = +0.674 and +0.726 for tram drivers, respectively, all coefficients being significant at the .001 level (Hakkinen 1958, cited by Shaw and Sichel 1971). Shaw and Sichel (1971), after controlling for exposure, experience, and a number of physiological factors, found split-half correlations of r = .64 over a six-year period for eighty-two South African bus drivers, again significant at the .001 level. While neither study directly controlled for alcohol consumption, long-term employment and strict company policies regarding intoxication all but precluded that variable.

Studies of industrial populations have yielded similar results. In a recent, and very exacting study by Boyle (1980), exposure, experience, and reporting were controlled for in a group of eighty-four press operators. The split-half (Spearman's Rank) correlation coefficient obtained for accident involvement over a period of eight years and nine months was p = .67 (significant at the .01 level). The correlation coefficients produced are good evidence of the stability of long-term accident involvement.

Predicting Accident Potential

Attempts at devising tests predictive of accident involvement on the basis of social and individual variables have met with much success. Such tests predict or identify inherent, psychologically based accident risk under controlled circumstances. As far back as 1954, McFarland and Moseley (1954) were able accurately to identify 85 percent of the accident repeaters in a professional driver sample on the basis of motor vehicle files, court records, and "derogatory inspection report(s)." Shaw (1965) reports 78.5 percent accuracy in the prediction of future accidents for a group of South African bus drivers on the basis of two psychological tests. Shaw employed a South African version of the Thematic Apperception Test (TAT) and the Social Relations Test (SRT), both of which were constructed by her research team. Mayer and Treat (1977) have reported accurate accident record classification for a (very small, N = 14) sample of private automobile drivers. Classification was based on a number of tests, the most discriminating of which examined levels of "citizenship" (voting frequency, church and club attendance, etc.), antisocial tendencies, and psychopathology.

It has been argued that paper and pencil tests should be incorporated into the Department of Motor Vehicle's general licensing criteria. Under such a scenario, applicants deemed "psychologically unfit to drive," like those deemed visually, or otherwise physically below par, would be denied driver's licenses. While such a program might in fact save a great many lives, public reaction would be passionately negative, and justifiably so. Using a test demonstrated to be 80 percent accurate, one out of every five low-risk drivers would be misclassified as high risk, and on this basis denied driver's license eligibility. Given the integral role of the automobile in the American life-style, the accuracy rate of any such test would need drastic improvement before meeting acceptable standards.

In lieu of license ineligibility, it has been argued that psychological testing could be used, reasonably and justifiably, for the purpose of recommending "high risk" individuals for driver education seminars. Yet the long-term stability of violating behavior would suggest the hardy resilience of unsafe driving practices to such deterrent/educational measures (Miller and Schuster 1983).

Conclusion

One's concept of the "accidental" changes with knowledge. The more thoroughly one understands the causes and consequences of a phenomenon, the less likely one is to attribute that phenomenon to chance, destiny, or supernatural forces. There was a time when contagious disease was ascribed to the work of fate; a time when criminality was attributed to the power of demons; a time when accidents were considered no more than a matter of chance.

The research on motor vehicle accidents fits reasonably well with the general theory of self-control, including the concepts of versatility and stability, and decline with increasing age. Those lacking self-control show tendency to violate not one, but a host of social mores both simultaneously and consistently. So why shouldn't this individual's consistence extend also to his driving habits? It was a similar thought that led Tillmann and Hobbs (1949) to conclude, "a man drives as he lives."

Notes

1. DiFranza's study found smokers to have 50 percent more accidents and 46 percent more traffic violations than nonsmokers. Such differences remained when age, alcohol consumption, education, and driving experience were controlled. See also Harrington (1971).
2. After the on-site investigation of 2258 motor vehicle accidents of varying severity, Treat et al. (1977) concluded that "driver error" was the exclusive cause of 57.1 percent of these accidents. An additional 33.2 percent of the accidents examined were caused by some combination of driver *and* vehicular *or* environmental factors, thus bringing the total percentage of accidents involving apparent driver error to 90.3 percent. "Driver error" was defined as the commission of, or failure to take, an action "that an otherwise alert, reasonably skilled, and defensive driver would have taken—and which would have prevented the accident" (Shinar 1978:112).
3. "Improper driving" was cited as a factor in 61.4 percent and 69.5 percent of all fatal and severe injury accidents, respectively. In such incidents, excessive speed and right-of-way violations (failure to yield, passed stop sign, disregarded signal) were the most commonly specified factors, being implicated in 30.3 percent and 11.3 percent of fatal accidents, and 25.1 percent and 23.8 percent of severe injury accidents, respectively (National Safety Council, 1989).
4. An age curve based on drivers *involved* in fatalities rather than (a) driver fatalities or (b) total fatalities is superior because (a) takes no account of culpability (many times those killed are not those who caused the accident), and (b) is diluted by the ages of passenger fatalities who (while very often similar in age to their driver) are incidental to the accident.
5. "Implicated" refers to "alcohol-related" as determined by the presence of blood alcohol content ≥ .01 percent in any involved party. Legal intoxication, on the other hand, requires a BAC of ≥ .10 in most states.

References

Arbous, A.G., and J.E. Kerrick. 1951. "Accident Statistics and the Concept of Accident Proneness." *Biometrics* 7:340-432.

Banks, W.W. 1977. "The Relationship Between Previous Driving Record and Driver Culpability in Fatal, Multiple-Vehicle Collisions." *Accident Analysis and Prevention* 9:9.

Boyle, A.J. 1980. "'Found Experiments' in Accident Research: Report of a Study of Accident Rates and Implications for Future Research." *Journal of Occupational Psychology* 53:53-64.

Cameron, T.L. 1982. "Drinking and Driving Among American Youth: Beliefs and Behaviors." *Drug and Alcohol Dependence* 10:1-33.

Campbell, B.J. 1959. "The Effects of Driver Improvement Actions on Driving Behavior." *Traffic Safety Research Review* 3:19-31.

Carlson, W.L. 1973. "Age, Exposure, and Alcohol Involvement in Night Crashes." *Journal of Safety Research* 5:247-59.

Carlson, W.L., and D. Klein. 1970. "Familial vs. Institutional Socialization of the Young Traffic Offender." *Journal of Safety Research* 2:13-25.

Chipman, M.L., and P.P. Morgan. 1974. "The Predictive Value of Driver Demerit Points in Ontario." Proceedings of the 18th Annual Conference of the American Association for Automotive Medicine, Toronto, Canada.

Coppin, R.S., and G. van Oldenbeek. 1966. "The Fatal Accident Reexamination Program in California." Sacramento, CA: Department Motor Vehicles.

DiFranza, J.R., T.H. Winters, R.J. Goldberg, L. Cirillo, and T. Biliouris. 1986. "The Relationship of Smoking to Motor Vehicle Accidents and Traffic Violations." *New York State Journal of Medicine* 86:464-67.

Farmer, E. and E.G. Chambers. 1939. *A Study of Accident Proneness Amongst Motor Drivers*. London: Industrial Health Research Board. (Report No. 84)

Goldstein, L.G. 1972. "Youthful Drivers as a Special Safety Problem." *Accident Analysis and Prevention* 4:153-89.

Gottfredson, M., and T. Hirschi. 1990. *A General Theory of Crime*. Stanford: Stanford University Press.

Greenwood, M., and H.W. Wood. 1919. *A Report on the Incidence of Industrial Accidents upon Individuals with Special Reference to Multiple Accidents*. London: British Industrial Fatigue Research Board. (No. 4)

Haddon, Jr., W., E.A. Suchman, and D. Klein, eds. 1964. *Accident Research: Methods and Approaches*. New York: Harper & Row.

Hakkinen, S. 1958. "Traffic Accidents and Driver Characteristics: A Statistical and Psychological Study." *Scientific Researches*, No. 13. Helsinki: Finland's Institute of Technology.

Harrington, D.M. 1971. *The Young Driver Follow-up Study: An Evaluation of the Role of Human Factors in the First Four Years of Driving*. California Department of Motor Vehicles. (Report No. 38)

Haviland, C.V., and H.A.B. Wiseman. 1974. "Criminals Who Drive." Proceedings of the 18th Annual Conference of the American Association for Automotive Medicine, Toronto, Canada.

Klein, D., and J.A. Waller. 1970. *Causation, Culpability, and Deterrence in Highway Crashes*. Washington, DC: U.S. Department of Transportation.

Kraus, A.S., R. Steele, W.R. Ghent, and M.G. Thompson. 1970. "Pre-driving Identification of Young Drivers with a High Risk of Accidents." *Journal of Safety Research* 2:55-66.

Kritz, L.B. and G. Nillson. 1967. *Young Drivers and Road Accidents*. (Report from TRAG, No. 100). Official Swedish Council on Road Safety Research.

Larsen, J.C. 1956. "Rehabilitating Chronic Traffic Offenders." *Journal of Criminal Law, Criminology, and Police Science* 47:46-50.

Lewis, C. 1985. "Adolescents' Traffic Casualties: Causes and Interventions." In *Human Safety and Traffic Behaviors*, ed. L. Evans and R.C. Schwing, General Motors Research Laboratories. New York: Plenum Press.

Mayer, R.E., and J.R. Treat. 1977. "Psychological, Social, and Cognitive Characteristics of High-Risk Drivers: A Pilot Study." *Accident Analysis and Prevention* 9:1-8.

Mayhew, D.R., R.A. Warren, and H.M. Simpson. 1981. *Young Driver Accidents*. Ottawa, Canada: T.I.R.F.

McFarland, R.A., and A. Moseley. 1954. "Human Factors in Highway Traffic Safety." Boston, MA: Harvard School of Public Health.

McGuire, F.L. 1976. "Personality Factors in Highway Accidents." *Human Factors* 18:433-42.

Michalowski, R.J. 1977. "The Social and Criminal Patterns of Urban Traffic Fatalities." *British Journal of Criminology* 17:126-40.

Miller, T.M., and D.H. Schuster. 1983. "Long Term Predictability of Driver Behavior." *Accident Analysis and Prevention* 15:11-22.

Naatanen, R., and H. Summala. 1976. *Road-User Behavior and Traffic Accidents*. The Netherlands: North-Holland Publishing Co.

National Highway Traffic Safety Administration. 1988. *Fatal Accident Reporting System, 1987*. Washington, DC: U.S. Department of Transportation.

National Safety Council. 1989. *Accident Facts*. Chicago, IL: National Safety Council.

Newbold, E.M. 1926. *A Contribution to the Study of the Human Factor in the Causation of Accidents*. London: Report of the Industrial Health Research Board, No. 34.

Organization for Economic Cooperation and Development (OECD). 1975. "Young Driver Accidents." Paris: OECD.

Pierce, J.A. 1977. "Drivers First Licensed in Ontario, October 1969 to October 1975." Toronto: Ontario Ministry of Transportation and Communications.

Robertson, L.S. 1983. *Injuries: Causes, Control Strategies and Public Policy*. Lexington, MA: D. C. Heath & Company.

Rommel, R.C.S. 1959. "Personality Characteristics and Attitudes of Youthful Accident-Repeating Drivers." *Traffic Safety Research Review* 3:13-14.

Schuman, S.H., D.C. Pelz, N.J. Ehrlich, and M.L. Selzer. 1967. "Young Male Drivers: Impulse Expression, Accidents, and Violations." *Journal of The American Medical Association* 200:1026-30.

Shaw, L. 1965. "The Practical Use of Projective Personality Tests as Accident Predictors." *Traffic Safety Research Review* 9:34-72.

Shaw, L., and H.S. Sichel. 1971. *Accident Proneness*. Oxford: Pergamon Press.

Shinar, D. 1978. *Psychology on the Road*. New York: John Wiley & Sons.

Sobel, R., and R. Underhill. 1974. "Psychosocial Antecedents of Automobile Accidents in Rural Adolescents." Proceedings of the 19th Annual Conference of the American Association for Automotive Medicine, Toronto, Canada.

Tillmann, W.A., and G.E. Hobbs. 1949. "The Accident-Prone Automobile Driver." *American Journal of Psychiatry* 106:321-31.

Treat, J.R., N.S. Tumbas, S.T. McDonald, R.D. Hume, R.E. Mayer, R.L. Stansifer, and N.J. Castellan. 1977. *Tri-Level Study of the Causes of Traffic Accidents*. (Report No. DOT-HS-034-3-535-77 [TAC]). Indiana University.

U. S. Department of Justice. 1990. *Uniform Crime Reports*. Washington, DC: U. S. Goverment Printing Office.

U.S. Department of Justice, Bureau of Justice Statistics. 1989. *Sourcebook of Criminal Justice Statistics-1988*, ed. K.M. Jamieson and T.J. Flanagan. Washington, DC: United States Government Printing Office.

Willett, T.C. 1964. *Criminal on the Road*. London: Tavistock Publications.

Zylman, R. 1973. "Youth, Alcohol, and Collision Involvement." *Journal of Safety Research* 5:58-72.

7

Driving Under the Influence

George C. Strand, Jr. and Michael S. Garr

Today, the general public views driving under the influence (DUI) as a serious crime—serious in terms of its prevalance and its consequences (Gusfield 1988; Jacobs 1989). In 1986 there was approximately one arrest for DUI for every eighty-eight licensed drivers. The National Highway Traffic Safety Administration estimates that perhaps as many as a quarter million persons were killed in alcohol-related motor vehicle crashes over the last ten years. "For many years, people interested in highway safety in the United States have been aware of two virtually unchanging statistics. First, approximately 50,000 lives are lost each year as a result of highway crashes and, second, about half the fatal crashes involve the presence of significant amounts of alcohol in the driver's blood" (Ross 1984:24). More than 650,000 persons are injured in drug related crashes every year. The annual cost in property damage, medical costs, and other costs of drunk driving may total more than $24 billion (Greenfeld 1988).

This chapter seeks to show that the extant scholarship on drinking and driving lacks theoretical direction. After reviewing the literature, a theory, based on the rational choice paradigm and classical assumptions of human nature, is offered as a plausible guiding theory to explain DUI and related behaviors. Developed by Gottfredson and Hirschi (1990), the theory posits that low self-control (acts that satisfy immediate gratification, without concern for long-term consequences) is the general cause of criminal and deviant behavior. To test this theory we employed a sample of high school seniors. Self-report questionnaires provided data on DUI and related behaviors. The theory was then reassessed in terms of the findings, and its implications for DUI research elaborated.

Review of the Literature

During the 1960s researchers and policymakers interested in DUI concentrated on three kinds of studies (Gusfield 1981). The majority of studies examined the correlation between blood alcohol concentration (BAC) and fatalities resulting from auto accidents (e.g., McCarroll and Haddon 1961). This series of studies was the major source of statements about the significance and magnitude of the "drinking-driving problem" (Gusfield 1981).

Other studies focused on the characteristics that distinguished drinking drivers from drivers in the general population. These studies were concerned with the role of the problem drinker or alcoholic in DUI events (e.g., Waller and Turkel 1966). The third type of study utilized the measurement of blood-alcohol levels in an attempt to gauge the increased risk of accident due to alcohol (e.g., Borkenstein et al. 1964).

DUI research in the 1970s followed the pattern developed in the previous decade. In general, these studies (e.g., Perrine, Waller, and Harris 1971) were more methodolgically sound, employing control groups, and being concerned with BAC rather than with the nature of the drinking driver as a causal agent. Subsequent studies concentrated on variables such as age (Pelz and Schuman 1974; Zylman 1973) rather than the personality characteristics of the drinking driver involved in auto accidents.

The research of the 1980s has given greater attention to other factors associated with alcohol than was true of past research and has developed multivariate perspectives (Holder 1989; Pernanen 1989; Moskalewicz and Wald 1989). During this period, researchers and policymakers became interested in documenting levels of impairment due to drug consumption. Several experiments have been conducted in order to ascertain the effect of alcohol or marijuana on various aspects of driving performance. These studies indicate that, generally, essential skills such as judgment, reaction time, and muscle coordination are impaired while one is under the influence of these drugs (Attwood et al. 1981; Peck et al. 1986; Sutton 1983).

Other researchers were interested in locating psychological variables associated with the DUI offender. Personality traits claimed to be correlated with DUI (among those involved in violations and accidents) include externally focused locus of control, heightened levels of impulsivity, hostility, aggression, depression, paranoid ideation, anxiety, exhibitionism, and decreased levels of self-esteem (Bradstock et al. 1987; Cameron 1982; Donovan et al. 1985; McCord 1984; Wilson and Jonah 1985). Johnson and White (1989) reported that risk-taking orientation was a strong predictor of DUI, both directly and indirectly. They suggest that impaired driving may be part of a global syndrome of risk-taking behavior and is an activity engaged in most often by those who frequently use alcohol and other drugs to cope with problems.

While a vast amount of scholarship has been devoted to the study of DUI, it tends to be data rich and theory poor. A further conceptual weakness in this literature is found in the definition and measurement of its dependent variable. The majority of recent studies aimed at a multivariate approach opt for the location of variables that are associated with DUI without proffering an a priori theoretical position. After observing what "comes out in the wash," post hoc theorizing commences. The ensuing explanations of DUI range from biological models to systems models of complex social relationships.

Researchers continue to seek the causes of DUI as distinct from the the causes of other deviant, criminal, or reckless behavior (for important exceptions to this general trend, see Argeriou, McCarty, and Blacker 1985; Gould and MacKenzie, 1990). As Gottfredson and Hirschi have noted, a major tenet of positivism is the view that acts have causes. This idea is frequently translated, via the research literature, into the idea that specific acts have specific causes (Gottfredson and Hirschi 1990). In this regard, the DUI literature is similar to the bulk of criminological literature.

A General Theory of Crime and DUI

Any theory of crime presupposes a conception of human nature. In the classical tradition, represented by Thomas Hobbes, Jeremy Bentham, and Cesare Beccaria, human nature was easily described: "Nature has placed mankind under the governance of two sovereign masters, pain and pleasure" (Bentham 1970 [1789]:11). In this view, all human conduct can be understood as the self-interested pursuit of pleasure or the avoidance of pain.

> By definition, therefore, crimes too are merely acts designed to satisfy some combination of these basic tendencies. The idea that criminal acts are an expression of fundamental human tendencies has straightforward and profound implications. It tells us that crime is not unique with respect to the motives or desires it is intended to satisfy. . . . It tells us that people behave rationally when they commit crimes and when they do not. . . . And it tells us that people think of and act first for themselves, that they are not naturally inclined to subordinate their interests to the interests of others. (Gottfredson and Hirschi 1990: 5)

While Gottfredson and Hirschi believe their theory is not "just another rehash of rational choice theory" (1990:274), it is important to understand that all rational choice theories share underlying principles and basic assumptions. In an excellent paper addressing these topics, Friedman and Hechter trace the model shared by rational choice theorists, excluding "the flesh of any specific rational choice model" (1988:201–2).

> Rational choice models rely on conceptions of actors as purposive and intentional. These actors are conceived to have given preferences, values or utilities. They act with the express purpose of attaining ends that are consistent with their hierarchy of preferences. . . . In any specific rational choice theory, however, actor's ends (and the preferences implied by those ends) must be specified in advance. Without such prespecification of actors' ends, rational choice explanations are liable to be tautological. Yet individual action is not solely the product of intention. . . . It is also subject to constraints that derive from opportunity costs and social institutions. . . . Further, rational choice models contain an aggregation mechanism by which the separate individual actions are combined to produce the social outcome." (Friedman and Hechter 1988: 202–3)

Crime, in general, and DUI more specifically can be considered the social outcome. People make individual choices regarding drinking and driving. Society views these choices in the aggregate, thereby constructing the "problem" of DUI.

Given the seriousness of the consequences of DUI, it can be argued that it is far from a rational action ("If I get drunk and drive, I may lose my driver's license, I may incur heavy fines, my automobile insurance may increase, or I may kill myself or others"). Coleman provides a general response to this argument:

> [S]ince social scientists take as their purpose the understanding of social organization that is derivative from actions of individuals and since understanding an individual's action ordinarily means seeing the reasons behind the action, then the theoretical aim of social science must be to conceive of that action in a way that makes it rational from the point of view of the actor. Or put another way, much of what is ordinarily described as nonrational or irrational is merely so because the observers have not

discovered the point of view of the actor, from which the action *is* rational. (Coleman 1990: 17–18)

With this in mind, it is quite plausible to conceive of DUI as a rational act ("If I take a cab home, I have to come all the way back for my car tomorrow. Besides, I'm not that drunk").

While the choice to drink and drive may provide benefits to the driver, such decisions also incur possible costs. Classical theory is also a theory of social or external control, a theory based on the idea that the costs of crime depend on the individual's current location in or bond to society. "What classical theory lacks is an explicit idea of self-control, the idea that people also differ in the extent to which they are vulnerable to the temptations of the moment. Combining the two ideas thus merely recognizes the simultaneous existence of social and individual restraints on behavior" (Gottfredson and Hirschi 1990: 87–88). Thus, social restraints, such as legal sanctions and implorements by others, serve to reduce drinking and driving. Despite these restraints, many individuals continue to engage in DUI. These individuals possess low self-control.

Gottfredson and Hirschi claim that crimes result from the pursuit of immediate, certain, easy benefits. The nature of crime, including DUI, indicates that nearly all crimes are mundane, simple, trivial, easy acts aimed at satisfying desires of the moment, as are many other acts of little concern to the criminal law.

The essence of criminality (the propensities of individuals committing criminal acts) is low self-control. Crime and analogous behaviors will be engaged in at a relatively high rate by people with low self-control. People with low self-control are more likely to smoke, drink, use drugs, skip school, be involved in most types of accidents, engage in risk-taking behavior (i.e., speeding), get in fights, and engage in several other noncriminal acts psychologically or theoretically equivalent to crime.

Gottfredson and Hirschi's theory is directly testable. If they are correct in their conceptions of the nature of crime and criminality, people who report DUI should also report higher rates of smoking, drinking, drug use, traffic ciatations for speeding, and accident involvement, and will attain lower grades than those who do not report DUI. In addition, since they assert that self-control is a continuum, it follows that persons who exhibit low self-control will engage in more serious deviant and criminal acts than persons who exhibit higher levels of self-control. One can therefore expect that persons who commit law-breaking acts, will also engage in DUI more than persons who commit less serious acts.

Offenses differ in their validity as measures of self-control: Those offenses with large risk of public awareness are better measures than those with little risk. "Drinking alcohol stolen from parents and consumed in the family garage is less likely to receive official notice than drinking in the parking lot outside a concert hall" (Gottfredson and Hirschi 1990: 90). Consuming alcohol or marijuana, which impair essential driving skills, and driving on public roads can certainly be considered an activity that carries a high risk of public awareness.

This study seeks to provide empirical support for Gottfredson and Hirschi's theory. Many teenagers of driving age use alcohol and marijuana (Johnston, O'Malley, and Bachman 1986) and 10–50 percent of these teens have reported driving after consuming these drugs (Beck and Summons 1987; Hingston et al. 1982; Williams, Lund, and Preusser 1986). In the present study, 37 percent of the seventeen to eighteen year olds reported DUI at least once in the last six months. It should be noted that use of alcohol and marijuana are both crimes for this population. From Gottfredson and Hirschi, we predict that (1) deviant and criminal behaviors of all types will be correlated with one another, and (2) more serious behaviors will be better predictors of DUI than less serious behaviors.

Method

Sample and Data Collection

The sample consisted of 691 high school seniors from a county in Northeastern Pennsylvania. The sample is predominately white (97 percent), a proportion equal to that found for the population of this county and a somewhat higher proportion than the 89 percent of whites in Pennsylvania (State Health Data Center 1988). Slightly more than half of the respondents are male (53 percent) a proportion somewhat higher than the 49.8 percent of males (age seventeen to eighteen) in Pennsylvania (State Health Data Center 1988). Family income broke down as follows: less than $15,000 (10 percent), $15,00–30,000 (27 percent), $30,00–45,000 (33 percent), $45,00–60,000 (20 percent), over $60,000 (10 percent); a distribution also comparable to that for the entire state. In addition, the prevalence of alcohol and drug use in our sample is comparable to national surveys (e.g., Johnston, O'Malley, and Bachman 1986) and other studies employing alternative methods of data collection (e.g., Johnson and White 1989).

Self-report questionnaires provide the data used in this study. Self-reports are generally accepted as a valid and reliable indicator of alcohol and drug use (Rouse, Kozel, and Richards 1985; Sobell and Sobell 1982, 1986) and related problems (Polich 1982). Research assistants administered the surveys in five area high schools during school hours. Respondents were instructed not to put their name on any questionnaire or response sheet and were repeatedly assured of the complete confidentiality of all data, especially with regard to parents, teachers, and public authorities. They were told that only aggregated data would be analyzed and reported. Further, respondents were informed that participation was voluntary, they did not have to complete the survey nor answer any question they did not want to. The students responded on general purpose NCS answer sheets which were scanned directly by mark sensing equipment. This procedure cuts the cost of data-entry personnel and lowers the risk of data entry error.

Independent Variables

Two conformity variables were used, grade point average (GPA) and the importance of education. Attaining good grades displays a concern for the future and indicates a willingness to cooperate within the confines of the educational institution. Students with low GPAs and who felt that school was relatively unimportant would exhibit less self-control. GPA was measured by the question, "What is your grade point average in school this year?" The range of grades was from failing to 4.0 on a 5-point scale. Importance of education was measured by the question, "How important is school in your life?" Responses ranged from "not very important" to "very important" on a four-point scale.

Drug use was assessed by asking students about their use of alcohol, cigarettes, and marijuana. Alcohol was measured by the question, "How often do you drink alcoholic beverages (beer, wine, hard liquor)?" Responses ranged from "I do not drink" to "at least once a day" on a five-point scale. Cigarette use was measured by the question, "How often do you smoke cigarettes? Response categories ranged from "I do not smoke" to "3 or more packs a day" on a four-point scale. Marijuana use was measured by the question, "How often do you smoke marijuana?"

Responses ranged from "I do not smoke" to "at least once a day" on a five-point scale.

Risk-taking driving behaviors were measured by asking students about their use of seat belts and the number of tickets they received and accidents in which they were involved. Seat-belt use was measured by the question, "Do you wear seat belts when you are in a car?" Response categories ranged from "never" to "always" on a four-point scale. Tickets were measured by the question, "In the past six months, how many traffic tickets have you received?" Response categories ranged from "none" to "four or more" on a five-point scale. Accidents were measured by the question, "In the past six months, how many automobile accidents were you involved in while you were driving?" The same response categories as with tickets were used.

Dependent Variable

DUI was measured by the question, "In the past six months, how many times have you driven a car or some other vehicle after or while drinking/doing drugs?" Response categories ranged from "never" to "7 times or more" on a five-point scale.

In order to enhance the validity of the self-reports, we employed a technique recommended by Converse and Presser. "The effort in recent years to narrow the reference period for survey reporting is a welcome corrective, in general. . . . It is common now to reduce the reference period to six months or less" (1986: 21). We asked about behaviors "in the past six months" in order to balance overreporting due to telescoping and underreporting due to the inability of many respondents to recall the past.

The data indicated that 256 (37 percent) respondents reported DUI in the past six months. Crosstab analyses on alcohol and marijuana consumption and DUI were performed as a check for internal validity. These analyses revealed that five individuals reported DUI and "I do not drink," while 251 individuals reported DUI and some level of alcohol consumption. Further, 97 individuals reported DUI and "I do not smoke (marijuana)," while 159 individuals reported DUI and some level of marijuana consumption. It is plausible that the 5 individuals who do not drink, smoke and drive, while the 97 individuals who do not smoke, drink and drive. In any event, it is evident that the majority of those who report DUI drink alcohol and smoke marijuana.

Results

Bivariate Results

Following Gottfredson and Hirschi (1990), it was hypothesized that deviant and criminal acts are intercorrelated. That is, people do not specialize in particular deviant or criminal acts. Because some people lack self-control, they engage in all types of deviant and criminal acts more than people with higher self-control. Therefore, people who engage in one kind of deviant act should also engage in other kinds of deviant acts. Table 7.1 presents a correlation matrix of GPA, importance of education, use of alcohol, cigarettes, marijuana, and seat belts, number of tickets and accidents in the past six months, and DUI.

TABLE 7.1. Correlation Matrix of Conforming, Drug Use, Risky Driving, and DUI Variables

VARIABLES	1	2	3	4	5	6	7	8	9
1. GPA	-								
2. Edimp	.38	-							
3. Alcohol	-.24	-.29	-						
4. Cigarette	-.38	.25	.42	-					
5. Marijuana	-.35	-.30	.53	.52	-				
6. Seatbelts	.20	.17	-.29	-.22	-.26	-			
7. Tickets	-.21	-.22	.22	.20	.23	-.06*	-		
8. Accidents	-.14	-.25	.16	.22	.19	-.08**	.32	-	
9. DUI	-.23	-.28	.52	.29	.53	-.23	.28	.25	-

** p. < .01
All other correlations significant at p. < .001
n = 681–691

The first thing to note in table 7.1 is that each of the variables is significantly correlated with all other variables. With the exception of two correlations involving the use of seat belts, all of the correlations are highly significant (p. .001). Second, with the exception of the conformity indicators—GPA and importance of education—the signs of all of the correlations are positive. Consequently, the bivariate results support Gottfredson and Hirschi's theory of crime. High school seniors who drink and drive are more likely than those who do not drink and drive to have low GPAs (r = .23, p. .001), smoke cigarettes (r = -.29, p. .001), smoke marijuana (r = .28, p. .001), and get into accidents (r = .25, p. .001).

Alcohol and marijuana use, which for this population are definitely delinquent or criminal behaviors, have the highest correlations with DUI, another act that is definitely criminal. The slopes are doubled for the criminal behaviors compared to the noncriminal behaviors. While marijuana and alcohol have standardized coefficients between .52 and .53, the other noncriminal variables have standardized coefficients ranging from .23 to .29. This finding is consistent with Gottfredson and Hirschi's argument that the lower the self-control possessed by people, the more likely they are to commit serious deviant and criminal acts.

Multivariate Analysis

A hierarchical regression model[1] was used to assess the independent effects of the conforming behaviors, drug use, and unsafe driving practices. In the first stage, conforming behaviors are regressed against drinking and driving. In the second stage, the drug use measures are added to the measures of conformity. Finally in the third stage, unsafe driving practices are added to the conforming behaviors and the drug use measures. The results of this analysis are shown in table 7.2.

The conformity variables, GPA and the importance of education, account for almost 10 percent of the variance in DUI (R^2 = .098). GPA and importance of education are each significantly related to DUI (b = -.14, p. < .001 and b = -.22, p < .001, respectively). Hence, the more students conform to school, the less likely they are to drink and drive.

Adding the drug use variables to the model increases the R^2 from .098 to .375, thereby explaining an additional 28 percent of the variance of DUI. As with the bivariate case, drinking and marijuana use are highly related to DUI (b = .34, p. < .001 and b = .35, p. < .001, respectively). Meanwhile cigarette smoking is less important in predicting DUI (b = .08, p. < .05). These results make sense because using alcohol or marijuana are prerequisite to DUI. However, they are necessary, not sufficient, conditions for DUI. That is, not everyone who uses alcohol or marijuana gets in a car and drives.

When the drug use variables are added to the model, the conformity variables lose some of their strength. Importance of education remains significant (b = -.10, p. < .01) while the effect of GPA drops almost to zero (b = -.01, ns). The change in GPA indicates that it has no direct effect on DUI. The relation between GPA and DUI is mediated by drug use. (An alternative interpretation, inconsistent with the general theory of crime, is that the relation between GPA and DUI is spurious. Drug use leads to both lower GPA and higher rates of DUI [Johnson and Kaplan 1990].)

TABLE 7.2.

Hierarchical Multiple Regression Model of DUI with Conforming, Drug Use, and Risky Driving Variables (Standardized Coefficients)

MODELS VARIABLES	I	II	III
Grade point average	-.14***	-.01	-.01
Importance of education	-.22***	-.10**	-.07*
Alcohol		.34***	.32***
Cigarettes		.08*	.10**
Marijuana		.35***	.33***
Seatbelt			-.05
Tickets			.12***
Accidents			.08*
R^2	.097	.375	.402
R^2 Change	.097	.278	.028

* p.< .05
** p. < .01
*** p.< .001

In the last stage, risk-taking driving practices are added to the model. The R^2 increases from .375 to .402. Consequently, risk-taking driving practices add just under 3 percent to the explained variance of DUI. Seat belt use is unrelated to DUI (b = -.05, ns) when controlling for the effects of conformity behavior and drug use. Perhaps, the habitual use of seat belts is increasing among all segments of the population. On the other hand, the number of accidents and traffic tickets were found to be significantly related to DUI. With other factors being equal, the more accidents people have, the more likely they are to drink and drive (b =

likely they are to drink and drive, other factors being equal (b = .12, p < .001). In general, risk-taking driving practices increase the probability of drinking and driving.

When risk-taking driving practices are added to the model, the conformity and drug use variables change very little. Drug use variables remain most strongly related to DUI, explaining most of the variance, followed by the unsafe driving habits. The conformity variables are the least important in explaining the variation in DUI.

It is tempting to posit that DUI causes accidents and risk-taking driving behaviors. If this were true, the relationship between accidents and risk-taking driving behaviors, as indicated by the number of traffic violations, should be spurious. In fact it is not. Accidents and traffic violations have a standardized coefficient of .32 (r_{yx1} = .32). Using a partial regression model controlling for the effects of DUI, the relationship between accidents and traffic violations remains generally unchanged ($r_{yx1.x2}$ = .28). If the relationship were spurious, we would expect a partial correlation closer to zero.

The hierarchical regression model provides support for Gottfredson and Hirschi's theory. When controlling for the effects of other types of deviant and criminal behaviors, most of the variables examined had an independent effect on drinking and driving. Similar to the bivariate results, drug use seems to have a greater impact in explaining DUI than conforming and risk-taking driving behaviors.

Conclusion

We find strong support for Gottfredson and Hirschi's general theory of crime. Using data from self-report DUI questionnaires completed by 691 high school seniors, we expected that deviant and criminal behaviors would be intercorrelated and that DUI would be more strongly predicted by more serious offenses than minor offenses. The bivariate results shows that all the variables were significantly correlated with one another. Further, the multivariate analysis showed that DUI was most strongly predicted by the use of alcohol and marijuana, clearly crimes for this population, and cigarettes. In addition, risk-taking driving practices moderately predicted DUI. Use of seat belts and the conformity variables predicted DUI weakly, if at all.

A limitation with this study is that self-control remains an unmeasured, latent construct. A valid and reliable measure of self-control (as defined by Gottfredson and Hirschi) needs to be developed. While a number of psychological tests purport to measure personality traits that distinguish offending and nonoffending populations, these measures of personality are either direct indicators of crime or conceptually indistinguishable from low self-control.

While DUI is significantly correlated with other low self-control behaviors, the opportunity costs and institutional constraints operating on DUI need to be evaluated. Hirschi and Gottfredson (1983) cite the fact that young people engage in crime more often than their elders. Friedman and Hechter argue that this is true because "in general, young people have less to lose if they are apprehended (that is, they have lower opportunity costs)" (1988:203). Hirschi and Gottfredson (1983) do not accept this explanation, arguing instead that age has a direct effect on crime—that is, an effect that cannot be explained by social or self-control. Be that as it may, future research can concentrate on ascertaining the effects of opportunity costs and institutional constraints that impinge on the decision to drive after drinking.

The literature on DUI remains problematic in several respects when viewed from the theoretical perspective presented in this paper. Joye (1986) echoes the dominant view found in the DUI literature in the statement "DWI is the crime most commonly committed by the non-criminal." Depending on how the nature of crime and criminality are conceived, researchers will continue to seek the specific cause(s) of DUI and the specific attributes of DUI offenders. In our view, this approach has yielded little in the way of substantive findings because it focuses on what makes the DUI offender unique. Howevere, Gould and Mackenzie (1990) empirically demonstrate that statements such as Joye's are false. They find a strong connection between DUI arrests and prior criminal history. This finding supports Gottfredson and Hirschi's assertion that criminals, and therefore DUI offenders, are "versatile."

The vast majority of the scholarship on DUI measures the dependent variable by ascertaining blood-alcohol content (BAC). All legislation in the United States defines being under the influence in terms of BAC. However, Gusfield argues that "the object of concern is not alcohol in the blood but the effect of alcohol on driving ability. In other words, a physiological-chemical condition is transformed into a behavioral one. BAC is considered isometric, similar in measure, to the psychic state of being influenced" (Gusfield 1981:64). Gottfredson and Hirschi's theory does not require this transformation. It is evident that people with low self-control are more likely to drink and drive. DUI is a behavior that certainly fits the model of satisfying immediate gratification without concern for long-term consequences.

Wilson and Herrnstein (1985) critically reviewed the literature on alcohol use and crime. They noted that many scholars who study the association between alcohol and crime are by no means convinced that the former causes the latter. The statistics show an association between drinking and crime, not a causal connection. Gottfredson and Hirschi's general theory of crime posits the common cause as low self control. "In our view, the relation between drug use and delinquency is not a causal question. The correlates are the same because drug use and delinquency are both manifestations of an underlying tendency to pursue short-term, immediate pleasure" (1990:93). This view is also supported by the connection between crime and drugs that do not affect mood or behavior sufficiently to cause crime (such as nicotine).

A further problem with much of the DUI literature is the varying definitions of the problem drinker and the alcoholic. There is little or no consensus on who is an alcoholic. This makes comparing different studies inherently problematic. Gottfredson and Hirschi's theory does not rely on definitions of alcoholics and problem drinkers. Individuals who drink, no matter how you define them, are seen as possessing low self-control. In our view, as well, these definitions can be irrelevant and misleading when studying DUI.

While the carnage continues on American highways, research and policy efforts that focus on ascertaining the specific cause(s) of DUI are unlikely to be effective in reducing the number of automobile fatalities. As long as drunk driving is viewed as a unique event, and the drunk driver a unique kind of person, researchers and policymakers will fail to see the general cause of deviant behavior, including drinking and driving. We have met the drunk driver and he may be any one of us, particularly if we ignore the long-term consequences of our behavior and focus on satisfying the passion of the moment—getting home.

We thank Richard Alba, Richard Felson, Travis Hirschi, Allen Liska, Steven Messner, and Mary Ann Zager for their helpful comments on previous drafts of this paper. Funding for this research was provided through a grant from the Pennsylvania Department of Transportation.

Note

1. We also employed logistic regression analyses. The dependent variable was dichotomized into the categories of "never DUI" and "ever DUI" (within the last six months). In logistic regression, the probability of an event occurring is directly estimated. These analyses yielded substantive conclusions similar to the hierarchical regression analysis.

References

Argeriou, M., D. McCarty, and E. Blacker. 1985. "Criminality Among Individuals Arraigned for Drinking and Driving in Massachusetts." *Journal of Studies on Alcohol* 46:483-85.

Attwood, D.A., R. D. Williams, L.J. McBurney, and R.C. Frecker. 1981. "Cannabis, Alcohol and Driving: Effects on Selected Closed-Course Tasks." In *Alcohol, Drugs and Traffic Safety*, vol. 3, ed. L. Goldberg, 938-53. Proceedings of the Eighth International Conference on Alcohol, Drugs and Traffic Safety, Stockholm, Sweden, 15-19 June, 1980, Stockholm: Almqvist & Wiksell International.

Beck, K.H., and T.G. Summons. 1987. "The Social Context of Drinking among High School Drinking Drivers." *American Journal of Drug and Alcohol Abuse* 13:181-98.

Bentham, J. [1789] 1970 . *An Introduction to the Principles of Morals and Legislation*. London: The Athlone Press.

Borkenstein, M.K., R.F. Crowther, R.P. Shumate, W.B. Ziel, and R. Zylman. 1964. *The Role of the Drinking Driver in Traffic Accidents*. Bloomington, IN: Dept. Police Admin., Indiana University.

Bradstock, M.K., J.S. Marks, M.R. Forman, E.M. Gentry, G.C. Hogelin, N.J. Binkin, and F.L. Trowbridge. 1987. "Drinking-Driving and Health Lifestyle in the United States: Behavioral Risk Factors Surveys." *Journal of Studies on Alcohol* 48:147-52.

Cameron, T.L. 1982. "Drinking and Driving Among American Youth: Beliefs and Behaviors." *Drug and Alcohol Dependence* 10:1-33.

Coleman, James S. 1990. *Foundations of Social Theory*. Cambridge: The Belknap Press/Harvard University Press.

Converse, J.M., and S. Presser. 1986. *Survey Questions: Handcrafting the Standardized Questionnaire*. Newbury Park, CA: Sage Publications.

Donovan, D.M., H.R. Queisser, P.M. Salzberg, and R.L. Umlauf. 1985. "Intoxicated and Bad Drivers: Subgroups Within the Same Population of High-Risk Men Drivers." *Journal of Studies on Alcohol* 46:375-82.

Friedman, Debra, and Michael Hechter. 1988. "The Contribution of Rational Choice Theory to Macrosociological Research." *Sociological Theory* 6:201-18.

Gottfredson, Michael R., and Travis Hirschi. 1990. *A General Theory of Crime*. Stanford, CA: Stanford University Press.

Gould, Larry A., and Doris Layton MacKenzie. 1990. "DWI: An Isolated Incident or a Continuous Pattern of Criminal Activity?" In *Drugs and the Criminal Justice System*, ed. Ralph Weisheit, 257-72. Cincinnati, OH: Anderson.

Greenfeld, L.A. 1988. *Drunk Driving*. Washington, DC: U.S. Department of Justice, Bureau of Justice Statistics Special Report. U.S. Government Printing Office.

Gusfield, Joseph R. 1981. *The Culture of Public Problems: Drinking-Driving and the Symbolic Order*. Chicago: University of Chicago Press.

_____. 1988. "The Control of Drinking-Driving in the United States: A Period in Transition?" In *Social Control of the Drinking Driver*, ed. M. Laurence, J.R. Snortum, and F.E. Zimring. Chicago: University of Chicago Press.

Hingston, R., T. Heeren, T. Mongione, S. Morelock, and M. Mucatel. 1982. "Teenage Driving After Using Marijuana or Drinking and Traffic Accident Involvement." *Journal of Safety Research.* 13:33-37.

Hirschi, T., and M. Gottfredson. 1983. "Age and the Explanation of Crime." *American Journal of Sociology* 89:552-84.

Holder, H.D. 1989. "Drinking, Alcohol Availability and Injuries: A Systems Model of Complex Relationships." In *Drinking and Casualties: Accidents, Poisonings and Violence in an International Perspective*, ed. N. Giesbrecht, R. Gonzalez, M. Grant, E. Osterberg, R. Room, I. Rootman, and L. Towle, 133-48. London: Tavistock/Routledge.

Jacobs, James B. 1989. *Drunk Driving: An American Dilemma.* Chicago, IL: University of Chicago Press.

Johnson, R.J., and H.B. Kaplan. 1990. "Stability of Psychological Symptoms: Drug Use Consequences and Intervening Processes." *Journal of Health and Social Behavior* 31:277-91.

Johnson, V., and H.R. White. 1989. "An Investigation of Factors Related to Intoxicated Driving Behaviors Among Youth." *Journal of Studies of Alcohol* 50:320-30.

Johnston, L.D., P.M. O'Malley, and J.G. Bachman. 1986. *Drug Use among American High School Students, College Students, and Other Young Adults: National Trends through 1985.* Washington, DC: Government Printing Office.

Joye, R.I. 1986. "Drunk Driving: Recommendations for Safer Highways." In *Stop DWI: Successful Community Responses to Drunk Driving*, ed. D. Foley. Lexington, MA: Lexington Books.

McCarroll, J.R., and W. Haddon. 1961. "A Controlled Study of Fatal Automobile Accidents in New York City." *Journal of Chronic Diseases* 15:811-26.

McCord, J. 1984. "Drunken Drivers in Longitudinal Perspective." *Journal of Studies on Alcohol* 45:316-20.

Moskalewicz, J., and I. Wald. 1989. "Alcohol and Casualties: Divergences and Convergences in the Researcher's and Policy Maker's Agenda." In *Drinking and Casualties: Accidents, Poisonings, and Violence in an International Perspective*, ed. R. Giesbrecht, M. Gonzalez, M. E. Grant, R. Osterberg, R. Room, I. Rootman, and L. Towle, 131-48. London: Tavistock/Routledge.

Peck, R.C., A. Biasotti, P.N. Boland, C. Mallory, and V. Reeve. 1986. "The Effects of Marijuana and Alcohol on Actual Driving Performance." *Alcohol Drugs and Driving* 2:135-54.

Pelz, D.C., and S.H. Schuman. 1974. "Drinking, hostility and Alienation in Driving Young Men." In *Proceedings of the Third Annual Alcoholism Conference of the National Institute on Alcohol Abuse and Alcoholism*, ed. by M.E. Chafetz, 50-74. Washington, DC: Government Printing Office.

Pernanen, K. 1989. "Causal Inferences About the Role of Alcohol in Accidents, Poisonings and Violence." *In Drinking and Casualties: Accidents, Poisonings and Violence in an International Perspective*, ed. N. Giesbrecht, R. Gonzales, M. Grant, E. Osterberg, R. Room, I. Rootman, and L. Towle, 133-148. London: Tavistock/Routledge.

Perrine, M.W., J.A. Waller, and L.S. Harris. 1971. *Alcohol and Highway Safety: Behavioral and Medical Aspects.* Washington, DC: U.S. Department of Transportation. Washington, DC: Government Printing Office.

Polich, J.M. 1982. "The Validity of Self-Reports in Alcoholism Research." *Addictive Behaviors* 7:123-32.

Ross, H. Laurence. 1984. "Social Control Through Deterrence: Drinking-and-Driving Laws." *Annual Review of Sociology* 10:21-35.

Rouse, B.A., N.J. Kozel, and L.G. Richards, eds. 1985. *Self-Report Methods of Estimating Drug Use: Meeting Current Challenges to Validity* (NIDA Research Monograph No. 57.) Washington, DC: Government Printing Office.

Sobell, L.C. and M.B. Sobell. 1982. "Alcoholism Treatment Outcome Evaluation Methodology." In *Alcohol and Health Research Monograph* (No. 3, 293-321). National Institute on Alcohol Abuse and Alcoholism. Washington. DC: Government Printing Office.

_____. 1986. "Can We Do Without Alcohol Abusers' Self-Reports?" *Behavioral Therapist* 7:141-46.

State Health Data Center. 1988. *Pennsylvania Vital Statistics, 1988*. Harrisburg, PA (May).

Sutton, L.R. 1983. "The Effects of Alcohol, Marijuana and Their Combination on Driving Ability." *Journal of Studies on Alcohol* 44:438-45.

Waller, J., and H.W. Turkel. 1966. "Alcoholism and Traffic Deaths." *New England Journal of Medicine* 275:532-36.

Williams, A.F., A.K. Lund, and D.F. Preusser. 1986. "Drinking and Driving Among High School Students." *International Journal of the Addictions* 21:643-55.

Wilson, J.Q., and R.J. Herrnstein. 1985. *Crime and Human Nature*. New York: Simon and Schuster.

Wilson, R.J., and B.A. Jonah. 1985. "Identifying Impaired Drivers Among the General Driving Population." *Journal of Studies on Alcohol* 46:531-37.

Zylman, R. 1973. "Youth, Alcohol and Collision Involvement." *Journal of Safety Research* 5:58-72.

8

Drugs and Alcohol

Carolyn Uihlein

This chapter attempts to show the relevance of the general theory of crime to drug use and to the well-established association between drug use and crime. The strong relationship between crime and drugs has been shown to hold regardless of age, race, gender, or country (Chaiken and Chaiken 1990). There is, however, little agreement about why drug use and criminal or delinquent behavior are associated (cf. Akers 1992 with Gottfredson and Hirschi 1990; and Elliott, Huizinga, and Ageton 1985). According to the general theory of crime, drug use, criminal acts, and reckless behavior are all manifestations of low self-control. According to alternative perspectives, they are consequences of common causal factors or actually cause one another.

The choice between these views requires that we spell out and test their implications with appropriate data. If the general theory is correct, several empirical consequences follow: Diverse delinquent acts and forms of drug use should be highly correlated; they should have the same correlates (causes and consequences); they should behave similarly over time (their age curves should be approximately the same); there should be no specialization in one rather than another type of behavior; and differences among individuals should be stable over age.

The data are from the National Youth Survey (Elliott, Huizinga, and Ageton 1985). This longitudinal study of drug use and delinquency is based on a national probability sample of youths aged eleven to seventeen at Wave 1. The sample was selected and interviewed for the first time in 1975 and has been followed up each year. The current analysis is based on data from Waves 1 through 4. The sample consisted of 1,725 youths.

(Previous exploration of the crime-drug relation in these data may be found in several sources—e.g., Elliott, Huizinga, and Ageton 1985; Elliott, Huizinga, and Menard 1989; Chaiken and Chaiken 1990).

Scales were constructed to measure delinquency, drug use, and sufficient outside variables to address the questions raised earlier, including attachment to the family, attachment to peers, long-term plans and goals, and school achievement (details of scale construction are provided in an appendix.)

Gottfredson and Hirschi (1990) tell us that those with low self-control will be short-sighted and less attached in general. It would seem that those who are less attached at this age would not have a firm attachment to their primary groups, that is, parents and peers, and those who are short-sighted would not have long-term plans, nor see the benefits in school work.

Age and Drug Use

The age-crime relation has been thoroughly investigated (see chap. 1). The relation between age and drug use is depicted in table 8.1, with data from the National Survey on Drug Abuse (U.S. Department of Health and Human Services 1982). It shows that marijuana use conforms to the same general pattern over age as other forms of crime and deviance. Of course this conclusion is not new. In his thorough review of the drug literature, Akers (1992:51–52) has noted that "there is a relationship between age and drug use with the peak years of drug involvement coming in young adulthood."

TABLE 8.1
Recency of Marijuana Use, 1982, by Age (N = 5,624)

AGE	Percent using marijuana: Ever	Past month	Past year not past month	Not past year
12-13	8	2	4	3
14-15	24	8	10	6
16-17	46	23	13	9
18-21	64	28	15	20
22-25	64	27	10	27
26-29	60	19	11	29
30-34	53	15	8	29
35-49	24	8	4	12
50+	5	*	1	4

Source: U.S. Department of Health and Human Services 1982.
*p < .05

Drug Use and Delinquency

Table 8.2 shows for the National Youth Survey data the correlations between drug and delinquency measures both within and across waves of data collection. These data show that crime and delinquency are indeed highly correlated, with correlations of .47 to .58 for the cross-sectional correlations The cross-lagged correlations range from .25 to .37, showing that current drug use predicts subsequent delinquency, and current delinquency predicts subsequent drug use.

TABLE 8.2
Correlations of Delinquency and Drug Use between and across Waves,
National Youth Survey (N=1725)

| Delinquency | Drug Use | | | |
	Wave 1	Wave 2	Wave 3	Wave 4
Wave 1	.49	.29	.36	.37
	(1719)	(1719)	(1620)	(1538)
Wave 2	.37	.49	.43	.45
	(1655)	(1655)	(1605)	(1520)
Wave 3	.33	.35	.47	.49
	(1626)	(1626)	(1626)	(1529)
Wave 4	.25	.27	.41	.58
	(1543)	(1543)	(1529)	(1543)

All correlations significant at p < .05
Correlations computed by author.

The robust positive correlations in table 8.2 between drug use and delinquency are consistent with the view of the general theory that these behaviors reflect an underlying tendency or common cause. They are inconsistent with the view that juveniles specialize in delinquency *or* drug use, and they are inconsistent with the view that the relationship between drug use and crime depends on the stage of the life course.

Stability

Another test of generality suggested by Gottfredson and Hirschi is stability. They state that differences in self-control remain stable over time, that those who have high self-control during adolescence will have high self-control later in life, relative to others. Because the data I use are longitudinal, I am able to test this idea by examining correlations for delinquency and drug use over time. Tables 8.3 and 8.4 reveal the findings. The stability coefficients here range from .45 to .68 for delinquency and from .48 to .72 for drug use. All of these coefficients are large and significant, suggesting stability in individual differences in drug use over time, a stability on the whole equivalent to that found for delinquency.

TABLE 8.3
Correlations of Delinquency across Waves 1–4 of National Youth Survey

	Wave 1	Wave 2	Wave 3
Wave 2	.58 (1649)		
Wave 3	.50 (1620)	.63 (1605)	
Wave 4	.45 (1538)	.56 (1520)	.68 (1529)

All correlations significant at the .000 level

TABLE 8.4
Correlations of Drug Use across Waves 1–4 of National Youth Survey

	Wave 1	Wave 2	Wave 3
Wave 2	.53 (1725)		
Wave 3	.55 (1626)	.71 (1626)	
Wave 4	.48 (1548)	.50 (1543)	.67 (1529)

All correlations significant at the .000 level

Versatility

Gottfredson and Hirschi tell us that those who have low self-control will commit diverse deviant acts. In other words, there is no specialization except that which is created by opportunity. The use of one drug should thus be correlated with the use of other drugs. Easily obtainable drugs, such as alcohol and cigarettes, should be for that reason relatively highly correlated with general drug use (this same pattern of versatility will hold for criminal acts as well; see Britt, chap. 10 below). Table 8.5 shows correlations among the individual drug items. Although the coefficients for heroin tend to be small, due no doubt to the substantial skew on this item, overall the pattern of correlations is consistent with the versatility hypothesis. The frequency of use of one type of drug predicts the frequency of use of other types of drugs, including alcohol.

Common Correlates

A final test of the generality hypothesis is the question of the similarity of correlates of drug use and delinquency. Table 8.6 shows the results of a correlational analysis for both drug use and delinquency, repeated for each wave of the National Youth Survey. Those who score high on all independent variables tend to be less delinquent and, in addition, less likely to use drugs. Clearly, there are few differences between the correlation coefficients when the dependent variable is drug use and when it is delinquency. Parental attachment, school achievement, plans and goals, and peer attachment are all similarly related to delinquency and drug use. The average difference in the coefficients is .03, a difference well within the range of error for the data. The "drug" and "crime" variables do, in fact, appear indistinguishable from one another.

Discussion and Conclusions

In addition to showing that attachment and achievement are important predictors of criminal behavior and drug use, the data presented here also support the suggestion that drug use shares the three general properties of crime and delinquency identified by Gottfredson and Hirschi. The age curve for both follows, at the very least, the same general road, peaking in young adulthood and then declining sharply with age. Both drug use and delinquency are comparatively stable over time, as our four waves of data show. Finally, drug use is versatile. Although this test is not exhaustive, the data presented support an underlying variable hypothesis. Further testing is needed to better identify this variable. However, this exploratory study presents a good case for describing drug use and delinquency as manifestations of low self-control.

TABLE 8.5
Correlations among Individual Drug Variables, National Youth Survey, by Wave

	Alcohol	Marijuana	Barbiturates	Heroin
Wave 1 (N = 1725)				
Marijuana	.45*			
Barbiturates	.16*	.25*		
Heroin	.08**	.18*	.39*	
Cocaine	.14*	.28*	.36*	.42*
Wave 2 (N = 1725)				
Marijuana	.49*			
Barbiturates	.11*	.38*		
Heroin	.04	.33*	.79*	
Cocaine	.14*	.41*	.79*	.81*
Wave 3 (N = 1625)				
Marijuana	.48*			
Barbiturates	.14*	.22*		
Heroin	.05**	.08*	.11*	
Cocaine	.17*	.30*	.39*	.17*
Wave 4 (N = 1542)				
Marijuana	.51*			
Barbiturates	.21*	.23*		
Heroin	.11*	.11*	.28*	
Cocaine	.30*	.34*	.35*	.25*

* - Significant at the .000 level
** - Significant at the .001 level

TABLE 8.6
Correlations between Delinquency, Drug Use, and Independent Variables, by
Wave

	Parental Attachment	School Achievement	Plans & Goals	Peer Attachment
Wave 1				
Delinquency	-.22*	-.24*	-.13*	.18*
	(1719)	(1703)	(1719)	(1717)
Drug use	-.23*	-.30*	-.15*	.18*
	(1719)	(1703)	(1719)	(1717)
Wave 2				
Delinquency	-.21*	-.28*	-.13*	.15*
	(1655)	(1617)	(1655)	(1655)
Drug use	-.25*	-.31*	-.16*	.18*
	(1655)	(1617)	(1655)	(1655)
Wave 3				
Delinquency	-.26*	-.32*	-.19*	.18*
	(1626)	(1526)	(1626)	(1625)
Drug use	-.26*	-.30*	-.13*	.18*
	(1626)	(1526)	(1626)	(1625)
Wave 4				
Delinquency	-.25*	-.25*	-.12*	.22*
	(1543)	(1326)	(1543)	(1543)
Drug use	-.28*	-.34*	-.14*	.22*
	(1543)	(1326)	(1543)	(1543)

* = Significant at the .001 level

Appendix: Scale Construction

Delinquency Scale

The scale for general delinquency used for the analysis in this chapter
was based on the one used by Elliott, Huizinga, and Ageton (1985) with
minor alterations. Twenty-three delinquency items were dichotomized
and then summed.

Drug Use Scale

This scale was created by summing the dichotomized frequencies for the five drug items mentioned in the text.

Parental Attachment Scale

This scale was created by summing the responses to the following items. Responses were scored 1 = Not Important through 5 = Very Important.

1. How important is getting along with your parents?
2. How important is it that your parents think you do well?
3. How important is doing things with your family?
4. How important is it to have parents who comfort you?
5. How important is it for you to have parents you can talk to?

School Achievement Scale

This scale was created by summing the responses to the following items. Responses were scored 1 = Not Important through 5 = Very Important.

1. How important is having a high GPA?
2. How important is having others think you are a good student?
3. How important is doing your own work?
4. How important is it to do well in hard subjects?
5. How important is having teachers think you are a good student?

Long-Term Plans and Goals

This scale was created by summing the responses to the following items. Responses were scored 1 = Not Important through 5 = Very Important.

1. How important to you is getting a good job?
2. How important to you is going to college?
3. How important to you is getting married?
4. How important to you is having children?

Peer Attachment Scale

This scale was created by summing responses to the following items. (All items had five ordered response categories.)

1. How important is it to have a particular group of friends?
2. How many afternoons a week do you spend with your friends?
3. How many evenings a week do you spend with your friends?
4. How much time to you spend with your friends on the weekend?
5. How much influence do you think your friends have on you?

References

Akers, Ronald L. 1992. *Drugs, Alcohol, and Society: Social Structure, Process and Policy.* Belmont, CA: Wadsworth Publishing Company.

Chaiken, Jan M., and Marcia R. Chaiken. 1990. "Drugs and Predatory Crime." In *Drugs and Crime*, ed. Michael Tonry and James Q. Wilson, 203–39. Chicago: University of Chicago Press.

Elliott, Delbert S., David Huizinga, and Suzanne S. Ageton. 1985. *Explaining Delinquency and Drug Use.* Beverly Hills, CA: Sage Publications.

Elliott, Delbert S., David Huizinga, and Scott Menard. 1989. *Multiple Problem Youth.* New York: Springer Verlag.

Gottfredson, Michael, and Travis Hirschi. 1990. *A General Theory of Crime.* Stanford: Stanford University Press.

U.S. Department of Health and Human Services. 1982. *National Survey on Drug Abuse: Main Findings, 1982.* Washington, DC: Government Printing Office.

9

Rape

Victor Larragoite

There is no escaping the question of rape and the adequacy of most current theories to explain it (Martin and Hummer 1989; Messerschmidt 1986; Griffin 1977). To say this is to risk, almost guarantee, giving offense: it is impossible to talk honestly about the causes of rape without offending men and women alike. The truth is too terrible, on all sides; and we are all too familiar with the soothing euphemisms and inflammatory rhetoric with which the subject is cloaked. It is, therefore, regrettable that the impetus for most current rape explanations is limited to theories that describe patriarchal social structures and processes (see MacKinnon 1987; Brownmiller 1975).

Despite the increased research and public concern, it is perplexing that most feminist theories of rape are not rooted in any fundamental criminological perspective, although principles of social learning, subcultures of deviance, and/or conflict theory are implicit in some of them (Baron and Straus 1987; Schur 1984; Sanday 1990; Smart 1976). By their lack of attention to established crime theories, current theories of rape serve to confuse rather than clarify. For that matter, there is little value in a theory that explains only one specific crime. A better understanding of particular crimes would be provided by a theory that explains all crimes at the individual level. An alternative to current theorizing is thus the theory of self-control, which accounts for rape in the same way it accounts for all other offenses.

In this chapter I (1) review feminist explanations of rape, (2) offer Gottfredson and Hirschi's (1990) self-control theory as an alternative explanation, and (3) analyze characteristics of rapists and rape victims to support Gottfredson and Hirschi's self-control hypothesis.

Feminism and Rape

Though bringing into existence new interest in the causes of rape, recent theories have been criticized by some criminologists as suffering from radical overstatement, sweeping generalizations, and limited research (Gilbert 1991; Smith and Bennet 1985; Deming and Eppy 1981). Various strains of feminist criminology may be identified (e.g., Marxist, radical, and socialist), and each makes different assumptions about the nature of patriarchy. Nonetheless, they all adhere to a common set of assumptions about the nature of sexual assault.

Most notably the feminist literature has shifted the conception of rape as a phenomenon of "sick" males to one in which the offender is seen as reacting to prescribed social norms (Schur 1984; Griffin 1977; Smart 1976; Brownmiller 1975). The image of the rapist as abnormal, with a definite psychotic profile, has been supplanted by one in which "the rapist is the man next door" (Medea and Thompson 1974:36). In fact, Brownmiller asserts that "[t]he typical American rapist is no weirdo, psycho schizophrenic beset by timidity, sexual deprivation, and a domineering wife or mother" (1975:191). In this respect, Brownmiller and other feminist theorists are probably correct. But, as we will see, if the rapist is not a weirdo, neither is he typically a Sunday school teacher, nor is he likely to be the man next door.

The shared primary assumption of feminist perspectives, then, is that rape results from institutionalized sexism and/or violent subcultures (Sanday 1990; Martin and Hummer 1989; Amir 1971), rather than psychopathology (Schur 1984) or victim precipitation (Spohn and Horney 1991; Galvin 1985). Feminists view rape, as well as gender stratification, as by-products of specific cultural, economic, and political arrangements (Scully and Marolla 1985; Brownmiller 1975). Specifically, they argue that a patriarchal society leads to a "set of social relations of power, in which men control the labor power and sexuality of women" (Messerschmidt 1986:32). Rape emerges from this perspective as an instrument of males to enforce their dominance in society. Messerschmidt (1986:32) writes:

Certain aspects of patriarchal capitalism contribute to the prevalence of rape in U.S. society. . . . By establishing and maintaining women in a subordinate position, rape contributes to maintaining capitalism by reproducing a cheap reserve army of labor and to continuing patriarchy by insuring masculine dominance.

Central to all variants of feminism is the idea that "rape is a crime of domination" (Kleck and Sayles 1990:149). Feminists consistently argue that patriarchy develops conceptions of masculinity and femininity that have particular implications for rape (see Alder 1985; Rose 1977; Brownmiller 1975). Traditional gender socialization promotes the notion of masculinity as dominant and powerful and femininity as passive and submissive, thus perpetuating violence toward women. Sexual assault is thus an invocation of male power. Messerschmidt writes, "In short, patriarchal capitalism maintains a culture supportive of rape. Thus, the existence of rape is structural at root. Very simply, males are in positions of power, while women are powerless" (1986:136). Male sexuality and power are inextricably intertwined in this literature. Rape has nothing to do with sexual desires, or, for that matter, with the individual rapist. Rape is merely a natural product of a patriarchal society.

Objections can be made to some of the feminist conceptions of these relationships. First, while rape may be used to support male supremacy in some societies, it is in fact censured in most of them (Schwendinger and Schwendinger 1983). There are laws in every one of the United States that condemn violence against women. In particular, most states possess legislative statutes that mandate severe punishment for rape offenders (Harlow 1991). Indeed, among felony offenders, only murderers receive harsher sentences than rapists, and actual time served for the two groups are nearly equivalent (Langan and Dawson 1990). Further, there is little evidence that male and female police officers, prosecutors, judges, and juries respond differently to rape cases (LaFree 1989). Clearly, convicted rapists are being punished by the criminal justice system.

Although some researchers might argue about the efficacy and original intent of these laws (Spohn and Horney 1991, LaFree 1989), it is well documented that "the attitudes expressed by officials toward rape cases and rape victims appear to have shifted considerably from the attitudes cited in the early calls for reforms" (Spohn and Horney 1991:158). The feminist movement has had an impact on (1) the reforming of rape statutes; (2) the increase in reported incidents of rape due to increased reporting, arrests, prosecutions, and convictions; and (3) the response of society in dealing with rape victims (Galvin 1985). Whatever the situation in the past, a recent study shows that male police officers are by no means insensitive to the plight of rape victims (LeDoux and Hazelwood 1985). Even if these attitudes may be to some extent ascribed to the success of the feminist movement, they would nevertheless undercut the conclusion that "patriarchal capitalism maintains a culture supportive of rape" (Messerschmidt 1986:136).

Given that rapists are severely sanctioned, it seems odd that feminist theorists do not attempt to explain why most male justice officials find rapists repugnant. Do these officials suffer from false consciousness because they willingly prosecute their nefarious brethren? It seems unlikely. Even males convicted of crimes are unsympathetic toward violence against women. Studying prisoners, Irwin writes, "The prisoners divided themselves into a variety of special types. These types were arranged in a hierarchy of prestige, power, and privilege. At the bottom of the pile were the 'rapos,' persons serving sentences for sexual acts which were repulsive to most prisoners" (1980:12–14). In a prison setting, where one could argue society's most violent reside, rape of women is not honored but condemned.

Brownmiller's supposition that "rape is nothing more or less than a conscious process of intimidation by which all men keep all women in a state of fear" (1975:15) promotes the idea of a male conspiracy to subjugate women. This theory is weakened by evidence indicating large regional variation in rape rates across communities in the United States (Baron and Strauss 1987, Smith and Bennet 1985). Also, arrest records indicate that rape is relatively rare compared to other violent crimes. Likewise, victimization reports show that one in 2000 women report being raped (Bureau of Justice Statistics 1991). Can we accept the assertion that all men consciously intend to intimidate women through rape? If patriarchal norms are in place, the question remains why most men refrain from committing rape.

Rape as Learned Behavior

Central to feminist explanations of rape is that a conditioned attitude exists that dehumanizes, objectifies, and debases the victim (Schur 1984). Young men are socialized into sex roles in which "they learn to be rapists" (Alder 1985:308). It follows then that men would not commit rape if they were not taught and reinforced to act this way. A canon prevalent in the feminist literature on rape is that male subcultures exist that teach and emphasize an aggressive masculinity conducive to rape. Fraternity houses are depicted as bastions that provide a social context where sexual coercion of women is tolerated if not encouraged (Copenhaver and Grauerholz 1991). For example Martin and Hummer write:

> Analyses that lay blame for rapes by fraternity men on "peer pressure" are, we feel, overly simplistic. We suggest, rather, that fraternities create a sociocultural context in which the mechanisms to keep this pattern of behavior in check are minimal at best and absent at worst. We conclude that unless fraternities change in fundamental ways, little improvement can be expected. (1989:459)

Martin and Hummer advance feminist assertions that stress that men are concerned "more than anything else with masculinity" (1989: 460). They argue that fraternities offer a prime example of male bonding taking place through inculcated norms. This particular subculture values narrow conceptions of masculinity such as "competition, athleticism, dominance, winning, conflict, wealth, material possessions, willingness to drink alcohol, and sexual prowess visavis women" (1989:460). Women are objectified as sexual conquests by members so they may gain acceptance and status within the fraternity.

For feminists who espouse a subcultural deviance model, rape is not an intrinsic proclivity within mankind, but rather an act that must be learned through subculture socialization. Subculture theories suggest that fraternity brothers never violate norms, for they are well-socialized members of well-knit subsocieties to whose cultural codes they invariably conform (see Kornhauser 1978:181). There is no deviant individual, only a deviant subculture. The fraternity brother is only a norm violator in the viewpoint of those whose norms differ and who can impose sanctions on him for his behavior. In the eyes of his fraternity brothers, he is simply conforming to group norms. Further, feminists argue that fraternities work within a cloak of secrecy that contributes to the sexual coercion of women (for a detailed case study of this phenomenon see Sanday 1990). Through the practices of brotherhood (i.e., loyalty, group protection, and secrecy) the members act according to strong norms that supercede their own conceptions of what is right and wrong (Sanday 1990; Martin and Hummer 1989). "Rape then becomes an overconforming act rather than a deviant one" (Messerschmidt 1986:132). That is, even though some members do not agree with the practice of "gang rape," most will not divulge details about the incident because of strong ties to the fraternity.

Somewhat confusingly, then, rape is explained by a strong subculture in which the act of rape must be kept secret from a weaker patriarchal society that purportedly condones the behavior? Thus we see that feminist theorists cannot decide whether rape is the result of a strong patriarchal system, or the result of a thriving subculture, or both.

Feminist theorists assert that pornography compels men to rape women (MacKinnon 1987, Brownmiller 1975). They maintain that pornography objectifies women by glamorizing violence and legitimizing the sexual oppression of women (Schur 1984). Sexism and male dominance are depicted and celebrated in pornography. Intuitively, then, "it is through the process of sexual objectification that women become identified as the appropriate victims of sexual violence" (Baron and Straus 1987: 468). Yet in spite of presumptions that there is a direct link between pornography and rape, other researchers find evidence that denies such a causal relationship. For examples, Gentry (1991) reports finding no correlation between circulation of pornographic magazines and rape rates in 244 cities, and Scott and Schwalm (1988) find a lower rate of rapes in those states with the most adult theaters per capita. By the same token, Kutchinsky (1991) reports that in countries where pornography has become increasingly available, rape rates have not increased as much as rates for nonsexual assault. One scholar in fact concludes that "the most important finding [of such research] is that sex criminals, not only as adolescents but also as adults, see less pornography than do [nonoffenders]" (Holmes 1991:87).

It is not clear whether the long-range consequences of pornography provide a stepping-stone to more violent deviant behaviors like sexual assault. If we accept that some men would commit rape if the conditions were right, can we accept that they all must be properly socialized by a patriarchal society in order to complete the act? If we accept that to be true, can we accept the notion that rape cannot otherwise be invented spontaneously by those men? Clearly, we must accept that rape need not be learned.

Rape as Frustration

There is a long tradition in criminology that attributes deviance to a lack of legitimate opportunities (see especially Merton 1957). Within this paradigm, humans are viewed as inherently good by nature. Deviant impulses are socially induced. Strain theorists describe these inducements as a condition of strain, of psychological dissonance that is a necessary bridge between blocked opportunity and high aspirations (Agnew 1992). For example, a great emphasis on monetary success and prestige leads wanting lower-class individuals to seek illegitimate means to obtain such fruits. "A cardinal American virtue, 'ambition,' promotes a cardinal American vice, 'deviant behavior'" (Merton 1957:146).

For feminists, patriarchal pressures corrupt innocent boys. Norms condition young men to believe that they must have great sexual prowess to be accepted or to realize their dominant gender position. Intuitively, then, we can deduce that the central premise for rape (within strain theory) is that deviance is an adaptation to the frustration of an unfulfilled sex drive. Simply put, sexual frustration results in sexual assault. Kanin, however, finds in his study that "the rapist appears considerably more sexually successful and active [than nonoffenders]" (1985: 222). He further contends that "[i]t is sexually less frustrating to encounter rejection when one's socialization has provided for a lower level of aspiration than when one's socialization has instilled a high expectancy of sexual success" (1985:229). Thus, we see that relative deprivation does not lead to sexual frustration and rape. On the contrary, rape appears less likely among those in a condition of strain.

In truth, most strain rape explanations avoid depicting the offender as sexually frustrated. They deny that sex is the motivation for the act but rather conclude (in the feminist tradition described earlier) that power frustration leads men to rape (recall that sex and power are defined as interchangeable). Feminist rape theorists essentially substitute one form of impotence (thus frustration) for another. Still, the assertion that rapists are seeking power, control, violence, and/or domination instead of sex is disputed (Palmer 1988). Finding that sex is an important goal, Palmer concludes that feminist assertions are "logically unsound, based upon inaccurate definitions, untestable, or inconsistent with actual behavior of rapists" (1988:529–30).

In sum, we see that patriarchal models are flawed (Why don't all men commit rape?), subculture models are confused (Why must rape be learned?), and strain theories are misguided (Why do sexually active men commit rape?). So, how do we approach the rape question? Structural models do not seem to get to the root of the problem, namely the rape offender. Thus what is needed is an individual-level explanation for rape. Where should we look for such an explanation? According to Ruth Kornhauser, control models offer the best hope of success: "Cultural deviance models are without foundation in fact. To the more definitive formulation of control models, to the more adequate linking of macrosocial and microsocial control theories, and to their more rigorous testing, the study of delinquency might profitably turn" (1978: 252). Following Kornhauser's advice, I turn to Gottfredson and Hirschi's (1990) theory of self-control. This theory is meant to explain all deviant behavior, a category that certainly encompasses the act of rape.

A Self-Control Explanation of Rape

Understanding the nature of rape requires examining the role of individual deviance as compared to social pressure in the genesis of the offense. Within the feminist perspective, motivation and pressure do not fully account for deviant behavior any more than they account for conforming behavior. The potential rapist, like the potential priest, is merely conforming to norms governed by a patriarchal structure. Therefore, perhaps the most likely avenue for understanding rape is to reexamine the perpetrator.

Before going to the perpetrator we might note, however, that a central tenent of the general theory of crime is that crime can be understood by examining the logical structure of criminal events. That is, besides emphasizing the characteristics of offenders, the theory also emphasizes the conditions in which crime takes place. Each completed offense requires an *offender* who has low self-control. There must also be present a victim or object that provides a *suitable* (i.e., attractive) *target*, and there must be an *absence of guardians* capable of preventing the behavior. The lack of any one of these conditions precludes the crime. Gottfredson and Hirschi accept the ecological notions put forth by opportunity theory, but go a step further by explaining why people differ in their propensity to seize the moment. The theory proposes that self-control varies between individuals but remains reasonably constant for individuals because they are socialized differently.

Consistent with the feminist formulation that rapists are not abnormal, Gottfredson and Hirschi are "suspicious of images of an antisocial, psychopathic, or career offender whose motives to crime are somehow larger than those given in the crimes themselves" (1990: 86). Rapists do not suffer from a psychological defect, nor are they merely products of a sexist tutelage as imputed by feminists. In contrast to strain and social learning models that see society as creating rapists, control theory sees society as attempting to create model citizens. Rapists are not sophisticated plotting souls who rape because they have learned it is one way to reinforce their dominant position in society. The rape offender, in the self control model, has simply not internalized norms that call for restraint of immediate gratification. The rapist is simply someone who has little control over his desires. The "man next door" (Medea and Thompson 1974:36) most likely commands the requisite self-control, at least with regard to rape.

The elements of self-control are clearly outlined by Gottfredson and Hirschi:

> Criminal acts provide *immediate* gratification of desires. Criminal acts provide *easy or simple* gratification of desires. Criminal acts are *exciting, risky, or thrilling*. Crimes provide *few or meager long-term benefits*. Crimes require *little skill or planning*. Crimes often result in *pain or discomfort* for the victim. (1990:89–90)

Sexual assault clearly involves immediate, simple gratification of desires. The desire may be sex or it may be power. Regardless, the individual with low self-control finds this relatively uncomplicated (if heinous) activity fulfilling. Certainly the act itself does not provide any long-term benefits. The pain inflicted upon the woman is not a by-product of patriarchal socialization, but rather the terrible consequence of a selfish act. The rapist is not an individual entrenched in a subculture, nor is he perfectly socialized within a greater patriarchal system. Instead, the rapist is someone who is "insufficiently restrained" by controls (Gottfredson and Hirschi 1990:37). Low self-control is not a product of socialization, but rather a consequence or its absence or failure.

Feminists argue that "the basic fallacy of the male sex-drive myth lies in the belief that rape is a spontaneous act (an immediate response to desire) and that it is a purely sexual act engaged in for the purpose of sexual satisfaction" (Smart 1976:95). Unfortunately in the case of rape, sexual desire is a classic example of the low-self-control principle. An analysis of 155 standard metropolitan statistical areas (SMSAs) taken from the 1980 Uniform Crime Reports shows that a substantial portion of rapes occur inside homes following an unlawful entry of the residence (Warr 1988). Rape and burglary show similar opportunity structures: characteristics that place particular types of homes at greater risk of burglary also place female residents at greater risk of rape (Warr 1988). Thus, rape may be seen as a spontaneous act within the framework of the ecological conditions set forth in the general theory of crime.

A typical reported rapist is likely to be young and poor. He may or may not be married. He is also likely to have had previous arrests for offenses other than rape (Amir 1971). One of the most revealing statistics is the high occurrence of criminal records among rape offenders (Amir 1971). This finding fits in well with the profile of the spontaneous, versatile, low- self-control offender. Henn, Herjanic, and Vanderpearl write: "The profile of the rapist is similar to that of the felon involved in crimes against persons or property. He is a young, poor male; probably belongs to an ethnic minority; and is likely to have used alcohol or drugs prior to his crime. He has a history of previous criminal activity, but he is unlikely to suffer from a psychotic disorder" (1976: 695).

As we have seen, the feminist literature says that men are socialized into sex roles in which "they learn to be rapists" (Alder 1985:308). Implicit in self-control theory, in contrast, is the idea that men are socialized *not* to commit rape. They are taught to defer immediate gratification on all levels; to be goal-oriented. We see in table 9.1 that indeed rape is a rare phenomenom vis-a-vis other crimes. Even taking into consideration limitations of the National Crime Survey (e.g., only heads of household are interviewed), we see that rape victims tend to mirror their offenders (see table 9.2).

Notwithstanding the prior statistics, many studies assert that rape is much more prevalent in society than exhibited by official records (Alder 1985). The argument would be something like this: "Low self-control might only work with reported or convicted rapists. What about all the rapes that go unreported?" In contrast, some speculate that the problem of sexual assault has not reached epidemic proportions as indicated by feminists (Gilbert 1991). The problem lies in the definition of rape and the measures utilized to secure rape information. For example, some surveys broadly codify victimization, as can be seen in the Sexual Experiences Survey (Koss and Oros 1982, see also Copenhaver and Graulholz 1991), while others require acts of rape clearly actionable by legal authorities.

Feminists who promote an "epidemic" assertion may not be attempting to solve the question of rape but rather gallantly, and laudably, aiming to raise social consciousness. Even a single rape is deplorable, but as

TABLE 9.1
Average Annual Rate of Completed and Attempted Rape,
by Selected Characteristics of Female Victims, 1973–87

Victim Characteristics		Average annual rate of rape per 1,000 women age 12 or older		
		Total	Completed	Attempted
Total		1.6	.6	1.1
Race				
	White	1.5	.5	1.0
	Black	2.7	1.2	1.5
	Other	1.8	.9	.9
Ethnicity				
	Hispanic	1.5	.5	1.0
	non-Hispanic	1.6	.6	1.1
Age				
	12-15	2.3	.7	1.6
	16-19	4.8	1.7	3.1
	20-24	4.1	1.3	2.7
	25-34	2.3	.8	1.4
	35-49	.6	.2	.4
	50 or older	.2	.1	.1
Marital Status				
	Married	.5	.1	.4
	Widowed	.4	.1	.3
	Separated/divorced	4.3	1.7	2.6
	Never married	3.5	1.2	2.3

Source: Harlow, *Female Victims of Violent Crime.* (Washington, DC: Bureau of Justice Statistics, 1991), p. 8, table 16.
Note: Detail may not add to total because of rounding.

Gilbert argues, "the burgeoning rates of sexual assault advanced by radical feminists have been almost immune to critical examination" (1991:65). This is not to deny that a great many rapes go unreported, but rather that flawed sociological instruments used to gather data on acquaintance rape may ensnare the innocent with the guilty. When survey respondents are required to select from general conceptions that define sexual experiences as rape, the incident rate emerges with lofty figures such that 26 percent of female college students will have been raped or experienced an attempted rape before they finish school (Koss, Gidcyz, and Wisniewski 1987).

In table 9.2 the age distribution of rapists parallels the age distribution of victims. Men aged twenty or younger victimized women twenty or younger more than 50 percent of the time. Men twenty-one to twenty-nine years of age victimized women within five years of their age 85 percent of the time. And finally, men thirty years and older sexually assaulted those within five years of their age 41 percent of the time. Hence, we see that offenders are "attracted" to women roughly in their own age group if not younger. If a feminist conception of crime were accurate, there presumably would be a greater variation in the age and race of the offenders and their victims. Especially if a young minority male wanted to demonstrate his prowess and sexual domination over women, it seems he would choose older, nonminority women who are thought to be more powerful in their own right.

In conclusion, despite the growing research on rape, our knowledge of the rapist, and/or the etiology of rape, remains quite limited. Unfortunately, the capricious nature of the subject has greatly reduced its scrutiny on criminological grounds. Although there has been much conjecture and theorizing in the feminist literature on the causes of rape, this perspective still lacks adequate empirical support. The objective of this chapter was to examine the propositions put forth by feminist theorists and weigh them against the contentions found in Gottfredson and Hirschi's theory of self-control. Based on conceptual flaws in the feminist perspective, and the paucity of empirical validation, I find the low-self-control profile of the rapist a more convincing explanation of rape.

References

Agnew, Robert. 1992. "Foundation for a General Strain Theory of Crime." *Criminology* 30:47–87.

Alder, C. 1985. "An Exploration of Self-Reported Sexually Aggressive Behavior." *Crime and Delinquency* 31:306–31.

Amir, M. 1971. *Patterns in Forcible Rape*. Chicago: University of Chicago Press.

Baron, L., and M. Straus. 1987. "Four Theories of Rape: A Macrosociological Analysis." *Social Problems* 34:467–88.

Blumstein, Alfred, Jacqueline Cohen, Jeffrey Roth, and Christy Visher. 1986. *Criminal Careers and "Career Criminals,"* vol. 1 Washington, DC: National Academy Press.

Brownmiller, S. 1975. *Against Our Will: Men, Women, and Rape*. New York: Simon and Schuster.

Chappell, D., R. Geis, and G. Geis. 1977. *Forcible Rape: The Crime, the Victim, and the Offender*. New York: Columbia University Press.

Clark, L., and D. Lewis. 1977. *Rape: The Price of Coercive Sexuality*. Toronto: The Woman's Press.

Copenhaver, C., and E. Grauerholz. 1991. "Sexual Victimization among Sorority Women: Exploring the Link between Sexual Violence and Institutional Practices." *Sex Roles* 24:31–41.

TABLE 9.2
Age of Female Victims of Rape with One Victim and One Offender, by Age of Offender, 1979–87

Age of Victim	Age of offender 20 or younger	21-29	30 or older
Total	100%	100%	100%
12-15	27%	7%	6%
16-19	36%	22%	17%
20-24	21%	37%	19%
25-34	12%	25%	41%
35-49	3*	7%	3%
50-64	1*	1*	3*
65 or older	0	1*	1*
Number of rapes	207,100	504,300	428,600

Source: Harlow, *Female Victims of Violent Crime (Washington, DC: Bureau of Justice Statistics, 1991), p. 11, table 24.*
. *Too few cases to obtain a statistically reliable estimate.*

Deming, M.B., and A. Eppy. 1981. "The Sociology of Rape." *Sociology and Social Research* 65:357–80.

Galvin, J. 1985. "Rape: A Decade of Reform." *Crime & Delinquency* 31:163–68.

Gardner, C.B. 1990. "Safe Conduct: Women, Crime, and Self in Public Places." *Social Problems* 37:311–27.

Gentry, C.S. 1991. "Pornography and Rape: An Empirical Analysis." *Deviant Behavior* 12:277–88.

Gilbert, N. 1991. "The Phantom Epidemic of Sexual Assault." *The Public Interest* 103:54–65.

Gottfredson, Michael, and Travis Hirschi. 1990. *A General Theory of Crime.* Stanford, CA: Stanford University Press.

Griffin, S. 1977. "Rape: The All-American Crime." In *Forcible Rape: The Crime, the Victim, and the Offender,* ed. D. Chappel, R. Geis, and G. Geis, 47–67. New York: Columbia University Press.

Harlow, C. W. 1991. *Female Victims of Violence Crime.* Washington, DC: U.S. Department of Justice. Bureau of Justice Statistics.

Haas, L., and J. Haas. 1990. *Understanding Sexuality.* Boston: Mosby.

Henn, F.A., M. Herjanic, and R.H. Vanderpearl. 1976. "Forensic Psychiatry: Profiles of Two Types of Sex Offenders." *American Journal of Psychiatry* 133:694–96.

Holmes, R.H. 1991. *Sex Crimes.* Newbury Park, CA: Sage.

Irwin, John. 1980. *Prisons in Turmoil.* Boston: Little, Brown and Company.

Kanin, E. 1985. "Date Rapists: Differential Sexual Socialization and Relative Deprivation." *Archives of Sexual Behavior* 14:219–31.

Kleck, G., and S. Sayles. 1990. "Rape and Resistance." *Social Problems* 37:149–62.

Kornhauser, Ruth. 1978. *Social Sources of Delinquency.* Chicago: University of Chicago Press.

Koss, M., C. Gidycz, and N. Wisniewiski. 1987. "The Scope of Rape: Incidence and Prevalence of Sexual Aggression and Victimization in a National Sample of Higher Education Students." *Journal of Consulting and Clinical Psychology* 55:162–70.

Koss, M., and C. Oros. 1982. "Sexual Experiences Survey: Reliability and Validity." *Journal of Consulting and Clinical Psychology* 50:455–57.

Kutchinsky, B. 1991. "Pornography and Rape: Theory and Practice? Evidence from Crime Data in Four Countries Where Pornography Is Easily Available." *International Journal of Law and Psychiatry* 14:47–64.

LaFree, Gary. 1989. *Rape and Criminal Justice*. Belmont, CA: Wadsworth.

Langan, P., and J. Dawson. 1990. *Felony Sentences in State Courts, 1988*. Washington, DC: U.S. Department of Justice, Bureau of Justice Statistics.

LeDoux, J.C., and R.R. Hazelwood. 1985. "Police Attitudes and Beliefs toward Rape." *Journal of Police Science and Administration* 13:214–20.

MacKinnon, C. 1987. *Feminism Unmodified: Discourses on Law and Life*. Cambridge, MA: Harvard University Press.

Martin, P.Y., and R. Hummer. 1989. "Fraternities and Rape on Campus." *Gender & Society* 3:457–73.

Medea, A., and K. Thompson. 1974. *Against Rape*. New York: Farrar, Straus, and Giroux.

Merton, Robert K. 1957. *Social Theory and Social Structure*. New York: Free Press.

Messerschmidt, J.W. 1986. *Capitalism, Patriarchy, and Crime*. New Jersey: Rowan and Littlefield.

Palmer, Craig T. 1988. "Twelve Reasons Why Rape is not Sexually Motivated: A Skeptical Examination." *Journal of Sex Research* 25:512–30.

Rose, V.M. 1977. "Rape as a Social Problem: A By-Product of the Feminist Movement." *Social Problems* 25:75–89.

Sanday, P.R. 1990. *Fraternity Gang Rape*. New York: New York University Press.

Schur, E. 1984. *Labeling Women Deviant: Gender, Stigma, and Social Control*. New York: Random House.

Schwendinger, J.H., and H. Schwendinger. 1983. *Rape and Inequality*. Beverly Hills, CA: Sage.

Scott, J., and L. Schwalm. 1988. "Pornography and Rape: An Examination of Adult Theater Rates and Rape Rates by State." In *Controversial Issues in Crime and Justice*, ed. J. Scott and T. Hirschi, 40–53. Newbury Park, CA: Sage.

Scully, P., and J. Marolla. 1984. "Convicted Rapists' Vocabulary of Motives: Excuses and Justification." *Social Problems* 31:530–44.

Smart, C. 1976. *Women, Crime and Criminology: A Feminist Critique*. Boston: Routledge & Kegan Paul.

Smart, Carol. 1979. "The New Female Criminal: Reality or Myth?" *British Journal of Criminology* 19:50–59.

Smith, M.D., and N. Bennett. 1985. "Poverty, Inequality, and Theories of Forcible Rape." *Crime & Delinquency* 31:395–405.

Spohn, C., and J. Horney. 1991. "The Law's the Law, but Fair Is Fair: Rape Shield Laws and Officials' Assessment of Sexual History Evidence." *Criminology* 29:137–61.

Warr, Mark. 1988. "Rape, Burglary, and Opportunity." *Journal of Quantitative Criminology* 4:275–88.

10

Versatility

Chester L. Britt

A key element of the criminal career paradigm is the notion of specialization in offending, which Blumstein, Cohen, Roth, and Visher define as the "tendency to repeat the same offense type on successive arrests" (1986:81). Thus, over the course of an individual's criminal career, any single arrest should be predictable on the basis on the most recent prior arrest. However, in partial recognition of the narrowness of this definition, Blumstein, Cohen, and Moitra (1988) revised the definition of specialization to say that offenders will tend to cluster the type of their offenses, and that the nature of these offense clusters will change over time.[1] For example, rather than require that offenders arrested for burglary be subsequently charged with burglary to demonstrate specialization, the offense cluster could be called "theft," meaning that any subsequent property crime would be indicative of specialization in theft offenses. In the longitudinal sequence of offenses defining a criminal career, according to Blumstein et al. (1986), individuals should commit a variety of offenses at the start of their criminal careers (i.e., as adolescents), but as they age and become more successful and proficient at some crimes, they should tend to repeat those types of crimes in which they have been more successful. In other words, the criminal career view claims that specialization in criminal activity is more likely over time, the reason being that specialization is cost-effective. Individuals who have had some experience committing particular crimes in the past will recognize that they are more skillful at those crimes. In addition, increased levels of criminal expertise may lower the chances of being caught when the crime is committed again, and the person should know how to retrieve a greater reward from the criminal act (see Pyle 1983: chap. 2).[2] At a minimum, then, this view of offending assumes that successful execution of profitable crimes requires relatively high skill levels (see Cohen 1986; Blumstein, Cohen, and Moitra 1988). Thus, as individuals gain experience committing crimes, they should tend to concentrate (or cluster) their activities into more profitable crimes.

In contrast, control theories see crime as a general phenomenon that provides some pleasure to the individual committing the offense. The specific form of this pleasure could be as diverse as mood enhancement or monetary gain. The key is that crimes are seen as providing short-term gains that are more attractive to individuals with lower levels of self-control, because it is those individuals who will be least likely to consider the long-term consequences of their acts, and more likely to act impulsively. In short, control theory sees criminal offending as versatile, in stark contrast to the criminal career view that claims offenders specialize in offending due to more long-term concerns with a successful criminal career. Thus, where the criminal career view sees rational, long-term oriented offenders, control theories see rational, pleasure-seeking, short-term oriented individuals. On the basis of time orientation alone, then, the criminal career view expects offenders to specialize, while the control view expects offenders to commit a variety of crimes to satisfy immediate desires.

This chapter focuses on empirically testing the specialization hypothesis, using several data sources.[3] Prior to presenting the results from these analyses, however, the recent research purporting to test the specialization hypothesis is reviewed and critiqued. Cohen (1986) has reviewed and critiqued the research on specialization appearing prior to 1986, and readers are referred to that paper for a more detailed discussion of the early specialization research. Briefly, in her review of five studies on specialization, she notes that Wolfgang, Figlio, and Sellin (1972) and Rojek and Erickson (1982) found very little evidence of specialization in offending among juveniles, Bursik (1980) found weak evidence in support of specialization among juveniles, while Blumstein, Cohen, and Das (1985) and Moitra (1981) found more substantial support for offense specialization among adult offenders. Cohen then reanalyzes the data published in the Wolfgang and colleagues, Rojek and Erickson, and Bursik studies to statistically compare their results with those of Blumstein and colleagues (1985) and Moitra (1981). She concludes, based on these new findings, that all five studies show some minimal support for a general notion of offense specialization. More specifically, Cohen summarizes the specialization research by saying

> there are differences in the level of specialization by juvenile and adult offenders. Specialization is evident and strong in all offense types among adult offenders, but it is more sporadic and somewhat weaker among juvenile offenders. Among adults, specialization is strongest for drugs, fraud, and auto theft—all offenses that play a role in organized illicit markets. It is weakest, although still significant, for the more impulsive, violent crimes of murder, rape, and weapons offenses. (1986:395)

Since Cohen's review, there have been five additional attempts to test for specialization in offending. These studies all claim to demonstrate support for offense specialization. For example, Kempf (1987) analyzes a sample of males born in Philadelphia in 1958 who had five or more records of police contact (n=982). She split this group of offenders by race (white, nonwhite) and by police contacts before or after the individual's eighteenth birthday (adult offender, adult nonoffender). This partitioning created four subsamples: white adult offenders (n=125), nonwhite adult offenders (n =458), white adult nonoffenders (n=84), and nonwhite adult nonoffenders (n=315). Kempf uses transition matrices, similar to the studies reviewed by Cohen, to test for specialization. She finds few offenders tending to repeat immediate past crimes. This finding held regardless of the subsample used and the crime type considered. Kempf also looked at the proportion of offenses an individual committed that were in the same general crime type. Many of the values were between 10 and 20 percent, with the highest value being 32 percent for property crime among white adult offenders. In other words, among white adult offenders with five or more police contacts, 32 percent had been charged with property crimes more than once. Although Kempf concludes that her analysis clearly demonstrates support for the specialization hypothesis—since there was not perfect versatility among offenders—she appears to be mistaken. Her results show offending not to be entirely independent from one offense to the next offense, but there was much unpredictability in offending, especially since a person's next offense could not be predicted very well by knowing only the immediate past offense.

Wolfgang, Thornberry, and Figlio (1987) use the same data set as Kempf and conclude that adult offenders were as versatile in their offending as were juveniles. Specifically, Wolfgang and colleagues

(1987) find that offenders were most likely to commit a nonindex offense and/or stop committing crimes as they aged, similar to the pattern observed when the sample was younger (Wolfgang, Figlio, and Sellin 1972). Thus, not only were offenders found to be versatile in their criminal activity, but these same individuals committed less serious crimes or quit offending as they aged. These findings are at odds with the claim that specialization becomes more likely as individuals age and gain more experience committing crime.

Farrington, Snyder, and Finnegan's (1988) analysis is similar to both Kempf's and Wolfgang et al.'s, but uses information on 69,271 juveniles in Utah (n=34,134) and Maricopa County, Arizona (n=35,137). To test for specialization in offending, they focus on individuals with two or more referrals (n=28,201) and ten or more referrals (n=1,979), and compare these individuals across twenty-one different offenses. For the individuals with two or more referrals, the highest "Forward Specialization Coefficient" (FSC)[4] is 0.292 for runaway, and the lowest is 0.026 for trespassing, with the overall average across the twenty-one offenses being 0.107. The same pattern holds for the individuals with ten or more referrals. Runaway again has the highest FSC value at 0.301, trespassing the lowest at 0.012, and the overall average is 0.098. Interestingly, the overall average FSC shows the level of specialization to decrease as the number of referrals increased. In short, again contrary to the specialization hypothesis, individuals with more offenses (referrals in this case), demonstrate less offense specialization. Farrington, Snyder, and Finnegan thus err when they conclude, "Specialization tended to increase with successive referrals, however, especially for the persistent offenders with 10 or more referrals, and especially for liquor, drug, and robbery offenses" (1988:483).

It is unclear what results Farrington and associates' conclusion refer to, because liquor, drug, and robbery offenses also showed decreases in the level of specialization. Liquor's FSC declined from .218 to .175, drug's FSC from .129 to .120, and robbery's FSC from .116 to .052 (1988:476, table 4). Further, every table in their paper contradicts their conclusion about offense specialization. Nearly every offense shows a decrease in the value of the FSC when the sample is restricted to those individuals with ten or more referrals. This finding is contrary to the prediction of increased offense specialization among individuals who commit more crimes. In the end, although not apparently their intention,

Farrington, Snyder, and Finnegan (1988) show juvenile offenders to become more versatile, and not specialized, in their criminal behavior as they commit more crimes.

A fourth transition matrix analysis to test for specialization was published by Blumstein, Cohen, and Moitra (1988). They use a sample of 32,197 adults (aged seventeen or older) arrested in the period 1974 to 1977 for any of the six more serious index offenses[5] in the Detroit SMSA (n=18,635) or in the remaining Southern Michigan region (n=13,562). Blumstein and associates then focus on two groups of offenders—those with one or more prior arrests and those with four or more prior arrests. Again, the idea is to test for an effect of increasing specialization given increased levels of prior offending. Based on FSC values, Blumstein, Cohen, and Moitra (1988) reach two apparently contradictory conclusions. First, they claim that there is no trend in specialization (1988:326). Yet, they also note that "some specialization was found in all crime types for adult offenders" (1988:341). How can this be possible? Unfortunately, Blumstein, Cohen, and Moitra (1988) use the same faulty logic that Kempf (1987) and Farrington, Snyder, and Finnegan (1988) exhibited by concluding specialization in offending when no FSC value is found to be zero. In short, a double standard is used; specialization is imputed when offenders are not shown to be completely versatile in their offending, yet the reverse is not held to be true, namely, that lack of complete specialization is indicative of versatility. For example, an FSC value of 0.10 would be taken as evidence of specialization, since offenders are said to be 10 percent specialized. At the same time, however, offenders are not seen as being 90 percent versatile. In general, this approach makes little sense. The implication of this work is that researchers looking for specialization will always find it, since FSC values will likely always be greater than zero, which does not seem to be the most appropriate way of testing any kind of an explanation.

Brennan, Mednick, and John (1989) take a slightly different approach to assessing specialization, by not using transition matrices, in analyzing a sample of 28,884 Danish men to see if violent offenders are more likely to specialize than other offenders. Of the 28,884 men in the initial sample, a subsample of 735 had arrest records for at least one violent offense, and 147 had arrest records indicating two or more violent offenses. The analysis by Brennen, Mednick, and John is restricted to the 147 individuals with two or more prior violent offense arrests. Brennan and associates claim to find specialization in violence among this subsample by using a Bernoulli probability model, and comparing the predicted number of offenders under this model (assuming independence) to the observed number of offenders. It is unclear, however, just how many individuals are indeed specialists in violence. Brennan, Mednick, and John fail to give further sample size information once they focus on the 147 two-time offenders. However, computations based on several bar graphs in the paper suggest that Brennan et al. have found approximately 20 specialists in violence. And while these individuals may in fact be specialists in violence, a substantive question raised by this finding concerns whether 20 specialists in violence in a sample of 28,884 Danish men provide a meaningful group on which to validate theories of crime or base public policies?

In sum, the research on specialization in offending has emphasized the use of transition matrices, and generally reached similar conclusions, although many times at odds with the results presented in the corresponding tables (e.g., Kempf 1987; Farrington et al. 1988). Specialization is found to the extent that a small number of offenders commit the same general type of crime on two consecutive occasions. Otherwise, offenders show a great deal of versatility by committing different crimes for subsequent offenses. There are four serious problems with this research on specialization, however, that lead to questions about the validity of the conclusions in these five papers.

First, the use of transition matrices has focused only on the most serious charge that an individual received when they came into contact with the criminal justice system. Additional information about the other offenses the individual has either concurrently been charged with or been charged with in the past are lost, which may bias the potential results. For example, consider an offender who at Time 1 was charged with rape and burglary, and at Time 2 was charged with aggravated assault, arson, and auto theft. The two most serious offenses at each time are rape and aggravated assault (by the criteria in Wolfgang et al. 1985). Thus, if the offense categories in a specialization analysis are theft, personal, drug, and nonindex offenses, this individual would give the appearance of being a "violent" offender. This categorization would be quite misleading, since the same individual also committed three property crimes (burglary, arson, and auto theft). On the basis of some other criteria than the most serious offense (e.g., number of property as opposed to personal offenses), this same person could be a property offender. This example, while contrived, shows how the research claiming to find specialists in violent or property crime may be based on faulty measurement of criminal activity. If specialization research uses only part of an offender's criminal activity to reach conclusions, the corresponding measurement errors call into question the validity of the findings.

Second, the specialization hypothesis as recently stated—that as offenders age and commit more crimes they are more likely to commit the same types of crime—implies an interaction effect between age and criminal offending. Nowhere in the specialization research currently in print is this interaction effect explicitly tested. Kempf (1987) and Wolfgang, Thornberry, and Figlio (1987) indirectly test for this interaction when the transition matrices they construct are split by age (under eighteen years old and eighteen years old and above). However, without statistical tests to show whether these two tables are different, these authors may err when they conclude that there is an increased likelihood of specialization as individuals age.

Third, the criminal career paradigm emphasizes the offender's career in crime—that it is inappropriate to look at only a cross-section of an individual's illegal activity, and that a more extended period of time needs to be examined. However, with the exception of the Brennan, Mednick, and John (1989) paper, every other specialization paper considers crimes at only two points in time (i.e., a simple Markov model), rather than evaluate all this information simultaneously. Thus, even if it was granted that using only the most serious offense in transition matrices was somehow appropriate, latent class Markov models could be used to simultaneously test every transition matrix in a study to evaluate whether individuals really were clustering their offending in certain areas over time. The findings from such an analysis would provide a much more convincing test of increased specialization in offending as offenders aged and committed more crimes.

Fourth, Kempf (1987), Farrington et al. (1988), and Blumstein, Cohen, and Moitra (1988) all use the FSC to measure the degree of offense specialization in a sample. This is problematic for specialization research, however, in that the FSC is computed assuming a model of independence in a transition matrix. There are no alternative models suggested by the researchers claiming to have found specialization. Thus, while they can claim that an offense at Time 1 is not entirely independent of the offense committed at Time 2, this research has really missed an opportunity to specify the nature of the relationship between prior offense and current offense. More importantly, this research has failed to establish offense specialization as the statistical alternative to independence in offending. Without that specification, this research has failed to produce clear evidence that specialization in offending exists.

The following analyses do not use transition matrices to test for specialization among offenders. Rather, they use a variety of approaches—graphical, logistic regression, and latent class models—that may enlighten discussion on whatever offenders specialize in their illegal activity.

Uniform Crime Reports

Our first data set is based on FBI arrest statistics from the Uniform Crime Reports (UCR). Since the UCR does not contain individual level data, it is difficult to assess whether criminal offenders tend to commit the same types of offenses as they age and continue to offend. However, an indirect test, which still provides substantial information, looks at the age distribution of arrest for each offense. The idea here is that if offenders tend to commit some crimes more than others as they age, which has been argued in recent specialization research (i.e., Cohen 1986; Blumstein, Cohen, and Moitra 1988), the distribution of arrests for these crimes should be substantially different from the age distribution of total crime. In other words, the specialization hypothesis suggests that older offenders will tend to commit some types of crime more often than others. If the specialization hypothesis holds, this trend should manifest itself in different age distributions for specific forms of crime.

FIGURE 10.1
Offense-Specific Age Plots, Total, Murder, and Gambling Offenses

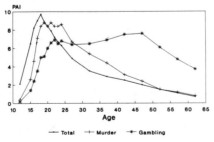

FIGURE 10.2
Offense-Specific Age Plots, Total, Rape, and Suspicion Offenses

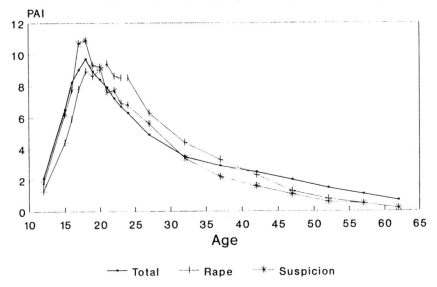

FIGURE 10.3
Offense-Specific Age Plots, Total, Robbery, and Vagrancy Offenses

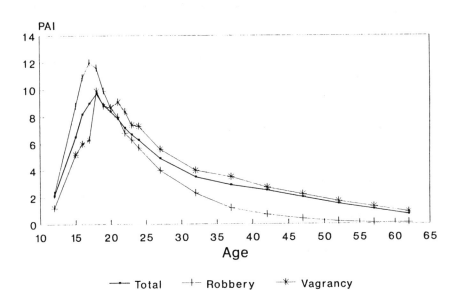

FIGURE 10.4
Offense-Specific Age Plots, Total, Assault, and Conduct Offenses

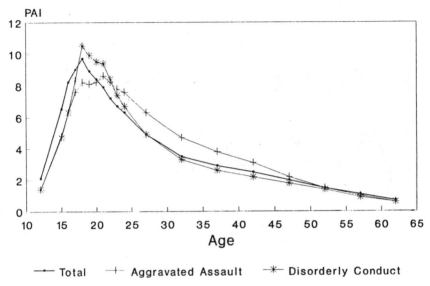

In the analyses that follow, percent age involvement (PAI) values are calculated for 1980 UCR data. To help interpret the offense specific PAI values, plots of the age distributions of offending were created for the various offenses recorded in the UCR. Figures 10.1 to 10.4 are illustrative of these plots. In each figure, the two offense-specific distributions were chosen by alternating top and bottom of the list of crimes contained in the UCR data. Thus, some figures contain very serious crimes, such as rape, along with less serious crimes, such as suspicion, in the same graph.

The rationale for choosing the 1980 UCR is to correct for a mistake in Steffensmeier et al.'s (1989) analysis of the same data. Specifically, their error was in using the age distribution of burglary arrests as the baseline distribution against which to compare all other offense-specific distributions. Their use of burglary arrests was arbitrary, and the use of any one of the other possible twenty-six offense distributions (including total arrests) would likely have provided substantially different results. The choice of total arrests as the baseline distribution provides a more meaningful comparison in that it can demonstrate how a single offense distribution is indeed different from all other types of crime.[6]

Findings

Only one offense—gambling—has an age distribution substantially different from that for the total age distribution of crime in 1980. Gambling offenses peak in the early twenties, not unlike many other offenses, and also begin a rather sharp decline. But, instead of continuing to decline, the PAI values for gambling offenses again increase, peaking a second time in the late forties. With the exception of this single offense, however, all other crimes follow a pattern very similar to that for total crimes.[7]

Clearly, the offense-specific distributions are not identical. The values of the means, modes, and medians vary from one distribution to the next. However, variation in these values should not detract from the underlying similarity among the curves. Thus, the figures show that with the exception of gambling, most crimes do not become more attractive as individuals age.

Bail Decision-making Study

The BDS data (see chap. 11) provide information on 3104 offenders with one or more prior arrests (of the initial 4800 offenders in the sample). The BDS data are particularly useful for testing specialization among offenders because they contain substantial information on the arrest histories of the offenders in the sample and permit a direct test of the interaction effect of age and prior criminal activity.

The dependent variable in the following analyses is current charge,[8] which has four categories—drug, property, personal, and other offense. To test for specialization, a model was constructed to use an offender's age and prior criminal activity to predict current charge. If specialization in offending exists, the type of offense involved in the current charge should be predictable from prior offenses and age.

The independent variables specified in the following analyses were age, proportion of prior arrests that were serious property offenses, proportion of prior arrests that were serious personal offenses, and proportion of prior arrests that were drug offenses. Interactions between age and each of the prior record variables were also included to specifically test the claim that increased age, along with increased offending, results in a greater tendency to specialization among offenders.

Due to the categorical nature of the dependent variable, logistic regression was used to test the model. The subsample of offenders with one or more prior arrests was further restricted in subsequent analyses to offenders with five or more prior arrests, and ten or more prior arrests. The additional partitioning of the sample by prior record focuses the analyses on more "active" criminals.

Again, the justification for the approach discussed here lies in the notion that people who have committed more of a particular type of offense in the past, and who are older, should be more likely to commit that same type of offense in the future. Support for offense specialization will be found if the odds that offenders tend to commit the type of crime they have currently been charged with increase as the proportion of prior offending in that type of crime increases and the age of the offender simultaneously increases. Otherwise, the data will support the claim that offenders are versatile in the types of crimes they commit.

Findings

Tables 10.1 and 10.2 present the results for the test of offense specialization in the subsample of offenders with one or more prior arrests. Table 10.1 displays the parameter estimates, while Table 10.2 displays the parameter estimates for the interaction effects. Clearly shown in Table 10.1 is that most of the individual parameter estimates are not statistically significant. Table 10.2 then adds to the interpretability of the initial estimates by summing the appropriate parameter values and computing the standard errors for the interaction effects.

In the total subsample, only two of the interaction effects are statistically significant. First, for a given age, an increase in the proportion of prior arrests for personal offenses increases the chances that the offender was currently charged with a personal offense as opposed to any other offense (drug, property, or other). Second, for a given age, an increase in the proportion of prior offenses that were drug related decreases the chances that the offender has currently been charged with a property offense as opposed to any other offense (drug, person, or other).

When this subsample is split by gender, the pattern is basically the same. For males of a given age, as the proportion of prior offending in drug related offenses increases, the chances that they have currently been charged with a property offense decrease compared to all other offenses. For females with a given level of prior property offense activity, as age

TABLE 10.1
Logistic Regression Results by Race and Gender for Offenders with One or More Prior Arrests

Parameter	Total Subsample Estimate (s.e.)	White Males Estimate (s.e.)	White Females Estimate (s.e.)	Nonwhite Males Estimate (s.e.)	Nonwhite Females Estimate (s.e.)
Age +	-0.036 (0.026)	-0.052 (0.028)	0.527 (0.277)	-0.107 (0.060)	-0.049 (0.033)
Age *	-0.024 (0.038)	-0.026 (0.041)	0.137 (0.283)	-0.114 (0.089)	-0.011 (0.053)
Proportion Property	0.016 (0.083)	0.009 (0.030)	0.358 (0.231)	-0.012 (0.060)	0.019 (0.035)
Age +	0.003 (0.019)	0.005 (0.020)	-0.002 (0.058)	0.084 (0.047)	0.007 (0.024)
Age *	0.025 (0.034)	0.019 (0.035)	0.102 (0.109)	0.078 (0.075)	0.019 (0.039)
Proportion Personal	0.058 (0.025)	0.052 (0.028)	0.094 (0.081)	0.031 (0.055)	0.048 (0.030)
Age +	-0.016 (0.031)	-0.016 (0.032)	0.002 (0.137)	0.082 (0.056)	0.001 (0.037)
Age *	-0.130 (0.034)	-0.069 (0.035)	-0.089 (0.149)	-0.015 (0.061)	-0.085 (0.040)
Proportion Drug	-0.026 (0.033)	-0.018 (0.035)	-0.113 (0.141)	-0.006 (0.057)	-0.019 (0.040)
Proportion	0.846 (0.766)	1.284 (0.815)	-20.222 (10.185)	3.149 (1.892)	0.578 (0.956)
Property +	1.120 (1.034)	1.124 (1.091)	-5.473 (12.487)	3.864 (2.726)	0.529 (1.420)
Age*	0.110 (0.678)	0.230 (0.713)	-13.800 (9.422)	-0.513 (1.725)	-0.024 (0.850)
Proportion Property					
Proportion	0.291 (0.554)	0.121 (0.589)	0.874 (1.841)	-1.439 (1.440)	-0.446 (0.643)
Personal +	0.377 (1.034)	0.602 (0.924)	-2.036 (2.715)	-1.312 (2.140)	0.027 (1.001)
Age *	0.737 (0.678)	0.845 (0.664)	-0.092 (2.141)	2.246 (1.598)	1.107 (0.736)
Proportion Personal					
Proportion	-0.803 (0.785)	-0.821 (0.815)	-2.036 (3.594)	-3.554 (1.701)	-1.697 (0.958)
Drug +	-0.005 (0.835)	-0.080 (0.861)	-0.214 (3.897)	-2.537 (1.873)	-0.110 (1.023)
Age *	1.412 (0.822)	1.197 (0.852)	3.169 (3.798)	1.036 (1.735)	1.377 (1.011)
Proportion Drug					

TABLE 10.2
Interaction Effects by Race and Gender for Offenders with One or More Prior Arrests

Parameter	Total Subsample Estimate (s.e.)	White Males Estimate (s.e.)	White Females Estimate (s.e.)	Nonwhite Males Estimate (s.e.)	Nonwhite Females Estimate (s.e.)
Intercept	1.016 (0.205)	1.104 (0.221)	0.459 (0.577)	0.263 (0.416)	1.595 (0.270)
	0.951 (0.342)	0.983 (0.367)	0.763 (0.988)	0.254 (0.642)	1.452 (0.455)
	-1.001 (0.221)	-0.975 (0.241)	-1.102 (0.580)	-0.764 (0.453)	-1.073 (0.291)
Age	-0.044 (0.006)	-0.047 (0.006)	-0.028 (0.017)	-0.035 (0.013)	-0.056 (0.007)
	0.013 (0.011)	0.013 (0.011)	0.018 (0.032)	0.020 (0.022)	0.005 (0.014)
	0.028 (0.007)	0.030 (0.008)	0.030 (0.008)	0.014 (0.015)	0.037 (0.009)
Proportion property	0.838 (0.766)	1.289 (0.814)	-20.777 (10.182)	2.799 (1.631)	0.571 (0.955)
	1.157 (1.033)	1.163 (1.084)	-5.592 (12.483)	2.385 (1.725)	0.545 (1.419)
	0.122 (0.677)	0.251 (0.712)	-14.139 (9.420)	0.898 (1.388)	-0.006 (0.850)
Proportion personal	0.244 (0.554)	0.069 (0.588)	0.848 (1.832)	1.691 (1.859)	-0.509 (0.642)
	0.365 (0.865)	0.596 (0.923)	-2.120 (2.713)	1.919 (2.854)	0.013 (1.001)
	0.707 (0.627)	0.823 (0.663)	-0.167 (2.139)	0.731 (1.805)	1.096 (0.736)
Proportion drug	-0.831 (0.784)	-0.852 (0.815)	-2.066 (3.591)	1.748 (1.734)	-1.754 (0.957)
	0.081 (0.834)	-0.002 (0.861)	-0.107 (3.894)	-0.481 (1.821)	-0.020 (1.022)
	1.467 (0.822)	1.245 (0.851)	3.301 (3.796)	1.221 (1.750)	1.433 (1.011)
Age* Proportion property	0.008 (0.026)	-0.005 (0.028)	0.555 (0.277)	-0.032 (0.059)	0.007 (0.032)
	-0.037 (0.037)	-0.039 (0.040)	0.119 (0.282)	-0.081 (0.065)	-0.016 (0.052)
	-0.012 (0.026)	-0.021 (0.028)	0.339 (0.231)	-0.028 (0.056)	-0.018 (0.033)
Age* Proportion personal	0.047 (0.019)	0.052 (0.020)	0.026 (0.056)	0.010 (0.069)	0.063 (0.021)
	0.012 (0.032)	0.006 (0.034)	0.084 (0.104)	-0.014 (0.111)	0.014 (0.036)
	0.030 (0.024)	0.022 (0.026)	0.075 (0.079)	0.021 (0.072)	0.011 (0.028)
Age* Proportion drug	0.028 (0.030)	0.031 (0.031)	0.030 (0.136)	-0.053 (0.071)	0.057 (0.036)
	-0.086 (0.031)	-0.082 (0.033)	0.107 (0.146)	-0.038 (0.076)	-0.090 (0.038)
	-0.055 (0.032)	-0.048 (0.034)	0.132 (0.140)	-0.043 (0.073)	-0.056 (0.039)

increases, they become much less likely to be charged with a drug-related offense compared to all other offenses.

When males are then split by race, no interaction effect is statistically significant for white males, indicating that age and prior offending activity have very little predictive value on future criminal activity. For nonwhite males, the same pattern holds, namely, that for a given age, as the proportion of prior offending in drug-related offenses increases, individuals become less likely to be charged with a property offense. Although the tables are not shown here, significant effects found for those with five or more or ten or more arrests is virtually the same as that found for those with only one prior.

The test for specialization in the BDS data thus suggests that very few offenders commit crimes in a predictable manner, based on their prior offending, and not their most serious prior offenses. Recall that the operationalization of the specialization hypothesis suggested that an offender's current charge type (drug, personal, property, or other) should have been predictable based on the proportion of all prior arrests that fell within given offense types. Further, all this was evaluated through an interaction effect of age and offending, that as offenders aged and committed increasingly more crime in a particular offense category, their current charge should have been more predictable.

Seattle Youth Survey

The SYS data provide a considerably different source of information on which to evaluate individuals and their specialization in offending. The approach taken in analyzing the SYS is to test whether individuals fall into different latent classes of offenders—personal, property, or nondelinquents.

Four delinquency items are used in the following analyses—theft of an item worth $2 or less, theft of an item worth between $2 and $50, hit a teacher, and fought with someone other than a sibling.[9] Each item was coded as 0-1, where a 1 indicated that the individual had ever committed the act, while the 0 indicated that the individual had never committed the act. Due to sample size limitations, only males were used in the following analyses.[10] The test for specialization involved searching for distinct classes of offenders. If the specialization hypothesis is to hold in these self-report data, there should be individuals who are nondelinquents, along with individuals who have concentrated their offending efforts in either personal or property offenses. Thus, the specific statistical test below examines whether there are three distinct classes of individuals in the SYS data and compares this to a model where there are only two classes of individuals—delinquents and nondelinquents. If the two-class model fits well, it implies that crime commission is general—that individuals do not concentrate their activity in one area, but commit a variety of offenses to satisfy some pleasure-seeking desire.

Findings

Tables 10.3 through 10.5 present the results for the independence, unrestricted two-class and three-class, and restricted three-class11 models for all males, white males, and black males, respectively.

In all three tables, the only model not fitting the data is the independence model, which implies that there is only one latent class of individuals. The other three models provide good fits to the data. Given that these three models fit well, some other criterion is needed to decide which of these models would be the best overall description. Using parsimony as that criterion results in the two-class model being more attractive for all three groups. Males in the SYS, then, show offending to be a fairly general phenomenon, where individuals committing the simple theft activities are also committing some personal crimes. And while the three-class models have a lower Index of Dissimilarity and Likelihood-Ratio, it is not convincing to argue that the slight improvement in overall model fit justifies the increased complication in the model structure by having three latent classes as opposed to two.

Summary

Similar to much of the previous research that has tested for specialization among juveniles (Bursik 1980; Kempf 1987; Wolfgang, Figlio, and Sellin 1972; Wolfgang, Thornberry, and Figlio 1988; Farrington, Snyder, and Finnegan 1988; Rojek and Erickson 1982), the SYS results show little evidence of specialization. Tests of four latent class models demonstrated the two-class model to be the most parsimonious model that best fits the data, where the two classes were delinquents and nondelinquents. The primary implication of these findings is that offense specialization is unnecessary to describe the pattern of offending among the male juveniles in the SYS data.

TABLE 10.3
Latent-Class Model Fits for All Males in the Seattle Youth Study

Model	LR-χ^2	χ^2	DF	D
Independence	256.026	266.544	10	0.166
Two-class (unrestricted)	25.772	26.861	6	0.040
Three-class (unrestricted)	7.171	6.837	3	0.021
Three-class (restricted)	6.884	7.527	3	0.014

TABLE 10.4
Latent-Class Model Fits for White Males in the Seattle Youth Study

Model	LR-χ^2	χ^2	DF	D
Independence	182.474	190.044	10	0.157
Two-class (unrestricted)	14.084	14.453	6	0.037
Three-class (unrestricted)	2.231	2.207	2	0.011
Three-class (restricted)	2.242	2.226	2	0.010

The SYS data also support the conclusion of no difference in offense specialization by race. Prior research on incarcerated offenders (e.g., Blumstein, Cohen, and Moitra 1988) using only transition matrices claimed there were significant differences between whites and blacks in their tendency to specialize. The SYS data do not replicate this claim.

Conclusions

The specialization hypothesis claims that as individual offenders age and continue to commit crimes, they become more likely to commit the same type of crime on successive offenses. The analyses in this chapter have examined this hypothesis in three different ways with three different

TABLE 10.5
Latent-Class Model Fits for Nonwhite Males in the Seattle Youth Study

Model	LR-χ^2	χ^2	DF	D
Independence	87.864	87.184	10	0.183
Two-class (unrestricted)	19.230	18.141	6	0.066
Three-class (unrestricted)	6.660	6.528	3	0.034
Three-class (restricted)	6.659	6.526	4	0.034

data sources. Overall, the findings were not supportive of the notion that older, more experienced offenders tend to commit the same type of crime.

Offense-specific data from the Uniform Crime Reports showed the age distribution of gambling offenses to be the only curve not comparable to the age distribution for total crimes. The logic of this test was that some crimes should be more attractive to older offenders because they are potentially more profitable and may require more skill to be successful (Cohen 1986; Blumstein, Cohen, and Moitra 1988). The data show this not to be the case, that most crimes exhibit virtually the same age-specific pattern of offending.

The Bail Decision-making Study data also failed to show offenders specializing in their illegal activity. Using logistic regression, a model that included age, prior record information (crime type), and interaction effects between age and prior offending to predict current charge was tested on multiple subsamples distinguished by the number of prior arrests (one or more, five or more, and ten or more), race (white, nonwhite), and gender. Overwhelmingly, the results showed the independent variables to not have an effect on predicting current charge. Thus, the specialization hypothesis was again not supported in a test of its predictive validity.

The Seattle Youth Survey also failed to support the specialization hypothesis. Latent class models testing whether adolescent males fell into two distinct classes of offenders (i.e., nondelinquent, personal, and property classes) showed the distinction between personal and property crimes not to be particularly helpful in explaining the distribution of individuals across the four-way cross-tabulation. The model that had the best overall fit was a two-class model of delinquents and nondelinquents, meaning that the individuals involved in the property crimes were also likely to be involved in the personal offenses. In addition, the conclusion that there are no differences in specialization between black and white males was also confirmed.

The findings in this chapter thus pose serious problems for the specialization hypothesis. There were virtually no findings here that support the specialization in offending notion, regardless of how specialization was operationalized or tested.

In part, the differences in findings from those previously published in studies of specialization are due to different methods used to test for specialization. However, the analyses conducted in this chapter—especially the logistic regression and latent class analyses—are far more comprehensive than any of the transition matrix approaches. The logistic regression analysis of the BDS data explicitly tested for an age and prior offense interaction effect implied in prior research, but never tested. The latent class analysis, while not incorporating age, tried to assess whether individuals committing illegal acts tended to commit those acts to the exclusion of other acts.

The results in this chapter suggest that the methods used to test for specialization may need modification. Interestingly, in the analyses here, where no transition matrix is used, no specialization is found. Yet, in virtually every study using these matrices, specialization is found. Prior to general refutation of the specialization hypothesis, a variety of additional analyses on previously published data needs to be undertaken to determine the extent to which the method of analysis produced findings of specialization. The validity of the specialization hypothesis must be held in doubt until these additional analyses are completed.

In addition to this methodological implication, the findings in this chapter also cast doubt on the accuracy of the criminal career view. While this view makes specialization in offending a key characteristic of offenders, the results here fail to find a minimal level of specialization. Conversely, control theory claims that criminal offending is a general phenomena, that all crimes, regardless of specific type, will appeal to individuals committing crimes. The results reported here clearly support the control theory view of criminal offending.

There will no doubt continue to be substantial research assessing the level of specialization or versatility in offending. The question that will need to be addressed in all these studies is: Does the analysis demonstrate actual offense specialization or that offenses are not entirely independent? The argument and analyses in this chapter claim that research needs to demonstrate that specialization occurs, not merely that subsequent offenses are not independent.

Notes

1. While this is a definition of specialization, it is also called the "specialization hypothesis."
2. Recall that the criminal career view does not explicitly claim offenders are rational actors. However, the criminal career paradigm is derived from microeconomic perspectives that rely heavily on the assumption of rational criminals (see Blumstein and Nagin 1978).
3. See chap. 11 for a discussion of these data sources.
4. An FSC value of 0 represents complete versatility, while an FSC value of 1 represents perfect specialization, and is based on Haberman's Adjusted Standardized Residuals (ASR). In the Farrington, Snyder, and Finnegan paper, as well as the other studies using the FSC, the independence model is used as the baseline against which to compute the ASR and the FSC.
5. These are criminal homicide, forcible rape, robbery, aggravated assault, burglary, and motor vehicle theft.
6. A way to think about this comparison is analogous to testing whether a single observation (an offense-specific age distribution of crime) is different from the mean (the total age distribution of crime).
7. While gambling offenses appear to imply specialization for gamblers, it is worthwhile to keep in mind that gambling offenses accounted for 0.38 percent of all crimes in 1980. Thus, while granting apparent specialization for this one offense implies support for the criminal career paradigm, among the other 99.62 percent of all crimes, there is no obvious difference in the age distribution of arrests for each offense and total crimes.
8. Only the first charge—the most serious—is used in these analyses, in order to make the results compatible with the research discussed above.
9. The National Youth Survey data do not produce any four-way cross-tabulations (coded as 0–1) where there are fewer than three zero cells. When there are only sixteen cells in a table, the estimation of a statistical model becomes difficult when there are so many empty cells. Thus, rather than produce results that have dubious accuracy, the National Youth Survey was not used to test for specialization.
10. This does not imply that female offense specialization may not be interesting to examine. It does mean there were too few females to provide a table with no empty cells.
11. The restriction introduced into this model is that individuals who have hit a teacher are assigned, with a probability of 1.0, to the personal offender latent class.

References

Blumstein, Alfred, Jacqueline Cohen, Jeffrey Roth, and Christy Visher, eds. 1986. *Criminal Careers and "Career Criminals,"* Volume 1 (Report of the Panel on Research on Criminal Careers). Washington, DC: National Research Council, National Academy Press.

Blumstein, Alfred, Jacqueline Cohen, and Soumyo Moitra. 1988. "Specialization and Seriousness During Adult Criminal Careers." *Journal of Quantitative Criminology* 4:303–45.

Blumstein, Alfred, Jacqueline Cohen, and Somnath Das. 1985. *Crime-Type Switching in Criminal Careers.* Unpublished paper, Urban Systems Institute, School of Urban and Public Affairs, Carnegie-Mellon University, Pittsburgh, PA.

Blumstein, Alfred, and Daniel Nagin. 1978. "On the Optimum Use of Incarceration for Crime Control." *Operations Research* 26:381–405.

Brennan, Patricia, Sarnoff Mednick, and Richard John. 1989. "Specialization in Violence: Evidence of a Criminal Subgroup." *Criminology* 27:437–53.

Bursik, Robert. 1980. "Dynamics of Specialization in Juvenile Offenders." *Social Forces* 58:850–64.

Cohen, Jacqueline. 1986. "Research on Criminal Careers." In *Criminal Careers and "Career Criminals, Volume 1,"* ed. A. Blumstein, J. Cohen, J. Roth, and C. Visher, 292–418. Washington, DC: National Academy Press.

Farrington, David P., Howard N. Snyder, and Terrance Finnegan. 1988. "Specialization in Juvenile Court Careers." *Criminology* 26:461–87.

Kempf, Kimberly. 1987. "Specialization and the Criminal Career." *Criminology* 25:399–420.

Moitra, Soumyo D. 1981. *The Analysis of Sentencing Policies Considering Crime Switching Patterns and Imprisonment Constraints.* Unpublished Ph.D. dissertation, School of Urban and Public Affairs, Carnegie-Mellon University, Pittsburgh, PA.

Pyle, Donald J. 1983. *The Economics of Crime and Law Enforcement.* London: The Macmillan Press.

Rojek, Dean G., and Maynard L. Erickson. 1982. "Delinquent Careers: A Test of the Career Escalation Model." *Criminology* 20:5–28.

Steffensmeier, Darrell J., Emilie Andersen Allan, Miles D. Harer, and Cathy Streifel. 1989. "Age and the Distribution of Crime." *American Journal of Sociology* 94:803–31.

Wolfgang, Marvin E., Robert M. Figlio, and Thorsten Sellin. 1972. *Delinquency in a Birth Cohort.* Chicago: University of Chicago Press.

Wolfgang, Marvin E., Robert M. Figlio, Paul E. Tracy, and Simon I. Singer. 1985. *The National Survey of Crime Severity.* Washington, DC: U.S.G.P.O.

Wolfgang, Marvin E., Terrence F. Thornberry, and Robert M. Figlio. 1987. *From Boy to Man: From Delinquency to Crime.* Chicago: University of Chicago Press.

11

Participation and Frequency

Chester L. Britt

Criminologists have long been concerned with the theoretical importance of the distinction between participation in crime and the frequency with which criminal acts are committed (see Reiss 1975). At issue has been concern that the causes of initial participation in crime may differ from the causes of continued involvement in criminal activity. Reiss (1975) among others, accurately notes that tests of criminological theory tend to operationalize crime or delinquency as participation (a yes-no dichotomy). While these measures can provide information, the argument goes, they cannot provide the full picture, because individuals committing only one crime may differ from individuals committing ten or twenty crimes. For example, Wolfgang, Figlio, and Sellin (1972) show that the frequency of offending varies substantially by race and socioeconomic status (SES) of the individual. Other studies operationalizing crime as a frequency show patterns of results different from those of studies using a simple dichotomy (Ball, Ross, and Simpson 1964; Douglas et al. 1966; Gordon 1976; Little 1965; Monahan 1960).

Thus, relying on the inconsistency shown by the studies using frequency of crime rather than participation in crime, Blumstein and Grady (1982:255) claim

> that one set of factors distinguishes between those persons who become involved in crime the first time and those who do not, and that a different set of factors distinguishes those who persist in crime once involved, from those who discontinue criminality at an early stage.

The logic to Blumstein and Grady's claim is consistent with traditional positivistic analyses of crime and delinquency (see Gottfredson and

Hirschi 1990). Specifically, the first concern is to explain why a person commits crime, or, why a person becomes a criminal. This would then represent participation in crime. The second concern is to then try and explain why the person persists in committing crime. In this tradition, the world is assumed to be too complicated to fit a single behavioral explanation, and multiple theories must be used to explain the wide variety of criminal activity. In other words, Blumstein and Grady (1982) assume that the factors causing an individual to commit one crime will be different from the factors causing another individual to commit two crimes, and yet a third individual to commit five crimes, and so on (Blumstein et al. 1986; Blumstein, Cohen, and Farrington 1988a, 1988b reiterate this claim).

The position of different causes for different frequencies of offending lies in stark contrast to Gottfredson and Hirschi's (1990) claim that the causes of crime are the same, regardless of the frequency at which crime is committed. For Gottfredson and Hirschi the primary cause of criminal behavior is low self-control. Individuals with low self-control are expected to have higher probabilities of committing crime. The additional factor influencing crime commission is the social situation of the individual, which provides varying degrees of opportunity. In other words, individuals with high levels of self-control would not normally be expected to commit criminal acts, but the social situation may provide opportunities attractive even to them. Conversely, individuals with low self-control may be prevented from committing crimes if they are located in situations where it is very difficult for them to act on their impulses.

Gottfredson and Hirschi's discussion is important for the participation-frequency distinction because they assert that the individual-level causes of crime for the first and subsequent acts are the same (i.e., low self-control). What accounts for the frequency of activity is level of self-control and opportunity, or social situation. In short, the key elements to crime commission are not expected to change as individuals commit more crime. They are always self-control and opportunity. Thus, whether crime is operationalized as a dichotomy to represent participation or a count to represent frequency, the correlates of these measures will be the same, according to Gottfredson and Hirschi (1990).

In sum, the hypothesis to be tested in this chapter is the similarity of the causes of participation and frequency of illegal behavior. Proponents of the criminal career view argue that the causes are different for participation and frequency, whereas proponents of control theory relied on in this study argue that the causes are the same.

Recent Research

There have been two recent attempts to test for differences in the causes of partipation and frequency of crime. Gottfredson and Hirschi (1988), using data from the Richmond Youth Survey, show how several correlates of participation—race, smoking, drinking and dating behavior, grade-point average, and delinquency of friends—have comparable associations with delinquency operationalized as participation or frequency among active delinquents.

Paternoster and Triplett's (1988) study of participation and frequency of delinquency tested the hypothesis of different causes for these two measures of illegal activity using a multivariate model. They analyzed a sample of eleventh grade students in southeastern high schools (n=1,544), using independent variables representing four popular perspectives in criminology—social learning, social control, strain, and deterrence—to model participation and frequency of offending. Four delinquency items—marijuana use, drinking, petty theft, and vandalism—were coded as a dichotomy (0,1) to represent participation and as a count (1,2,3,...) for those individuals who had at least one commission of the act in the previous year to represent frequency.[1] Overall, Paternoster and Triplett found that the same sets of variables tended to explain both participation and frequency in each of the four delinquent acts, and concluded "there was very little difference in the effects of the exogenous variables on the two outcome measures of delinquency" (1988:614).

However, Paternoster and Triplett argued that the illegal acts they focused on were not serious offenses, and that studies focusing on more serious acts, and using different samples, might reveal a different pattern of results.[2]

Methodological Issues

The Gottfredson and Hirschi (1988) and Paternoster and Triplett (1988) studies thus provide preliminary evidence contradicting the claim of different causes for participation and frequency of offending. However, there are two important methodological issues that have not been satisfactorily resolved. First, does the operationalization of illegal behavior as a dichotomy (to measure participation) or a count of illegal acts among active offenders (to measure frequency) produce misleading results? Limiting the frequency analysis to those individuals with one or more illegal acts introduces censoring, since individuals are excluded from the sample unless the dependent variable (criminal behavior) has a value greater than zero. Censored samples, such as those created in testing multivariate models of frequency of offending among active offenders, can be analyzed with the tobit statistical model (see Judge et al. 1985; Maddala 1983). The tobit model provides unbiased and consistent regression estimates (where a regression model on the censored sample would not) by introducing controls for the individuals with zero scores on the dependent variable. The tobit model accomplishes this by first computing an individual's chances of having a value on the dependent variable greater than zero (with a probit model). This probability then represents a "hazard rate" parameter that is computed for every individual with a nonzero value on the dependent variable and included as an additional variable in a classic regression analysis on the censored sample.

The parameter estimates produced from a tobit analysis require some care in their interpretation because they represent both (1) the change in the dependent variable, weighted by the probability of having a nonzero value on the dependent variable, and (2) the change in the probability of having a nonzero value on the dependent variable, weighted by the expected value of the dependent variable, given that it is nonzero (Judge et al. 1985). For our purposes below, we will be concerned primarily with the sign and statistical significance of each parameter, rather than with a formal interpretation of each parameter's magnitude.

Also, some concern has been raised in the literature over the "cutpoint" to represent participation and frequency of offending (see, especially, Gottfredson and Hirschi 1986, 1987, and 1988). If the distinction between participation and frequency is made at 0 and 1 to represent active offenders, then researchers using self-report data will likely have some individuals coded as nonoffenders (a zero value on the dependent variable) when they have, in fact, committed some other act that was just not recorded or used in the present analysis. In short, the number of illegal acts used to distinguish active offenders from nonoffenders is arbitrary. Gottfredson and Hirschi's (1988) and Paternoster and Triplett's (1988) use of one or more offenses is consistent with concerns of the criminal career view that researchers focus on anyone with one or more criminal acts in the same time period. However, it would also be reasonable to make a cut at five, ten, or even twenty offenses to try and distinguish the so-called "serious, high-rate" offender from both low-rate and nonoffenders (see, for example, Chaiken and Chaiken 1983; Greenwood 1982). Fortunately, the tobit model discussed above can be modified to represent a different cut point. Thus, insofar as the data will permit analysis, different cut points will be compared in the analyses below.

The Current Study

To test the hypothesis of different causes for participation and frequency of illegal activity, data from the Bail Decisionmaking Study (BDS), Seattle Youth Study (SYS), and National Youth Survey (NYS) are used.[3] The models to be examined with each data set are essentially multivariate replications of Gottfredson and Hirschi's (1988) effort. A limited number of variables are taken from each data set to represent variables found to be significant predictors of participation in offending in the crime and delinquency literature.[4] The focus of each analysis below is a test of whether predictors of participation also act as predictors of frequency of offending. To further advance our understanding of the frequency distinction, two cut-points (one or more and five or more illegal acts) will also be examined to assess whether different definitions of the active offender substantially alter the pattern of statistically significant predictors in a multivariate model.[5]

Bail Decisionmaking Study

Dependent variables. To address the question of different causes of participation and frequency, the dependent variables used here are two measures of rearrest while on release status. The measure of participation is simply whether the offender was rearrested in the 120-day period following release. Frequency was measured as the number of times an offender was rearrested, given that there was at least one arrest while on release. Given the time limit on the occurrence of a rearrest in the BDS sample, this measure provides a nice way of evaluating the participation-frequency distinction, since there is an additional control (time) on acceptable values for this measure.[6]

TABLE 11.1
Bail Decisionmaking Study Means, Standard Deviations, and Ranges
for the Participation and Frequency Analyses (*n*=4,006)

Variable	Mean	Standard Deviation	Minimum	Maximum
Female	0.140	0.347	0	1
Age	29.270	11.330	14	87
White	0.328	0.470	0	1
Phone service	0.795	0.404	0	1
Prior record	0.627	0.484	0	1
Theft offense	0.268	0.443	0	1
Number of rearrests	0.246	0.836	0	8
Any rearrest	0.153	0.360	0	1

Independent variables. The literature on the rearrest of released offenders has shown that a combination of legal, community ties, and demographic characteristics provides the best predictors of the likelihood of rearrests (i.e., participation). For the following analysis, gender, age, race, phone service, prior record of arrests, and current charge will be used as the predictors of both the occurrence and the frequency of rearrest. As coded for the following analysis, all variables are expected to reduce both the chances of rearrest and the frequency of rearrest among those arrested for a new offense, except prior arrest record and theft, which are of course expected to increase the chances of rearrest and frequency of rearrest.

Findings. Table 11.1 presents the means, standard deviations, and ranges for the variables included in the following analysis of the released population at risk of committing a new crime and being rearrested (*n*=4,006).

Table 11.2 presents the probit and tobit estimates for the hypothesized model. The probit analysis tests the participation model. Age, phone service, and prior record have statistically significant effects on rearrest. As expected, individuals with prior records were more likely to be rearrested, while older individuals and people with phone service were less likely to have been rearrested.

The second column of table 11.2 displays the tobit estimates testing the hypothesized model against frequency of rearrest among all offenders with one or more arrests while on release. The pattern of statistically significant findings in the frequency model is identical to that found in the participation model. Increased age and having phone service predict lower odds of being rearrested and fewer rearrests among those offenders who were rearrested. Individuals with prior records had higher chances of rearrest and increased frequencies of rearrests.

To summarize, the BDS sample of released offenders in Philadelphia seriously questions the validity of the criminal career claim that the causes of participation and frequency of offending are substantially different. Using variables found to have significant effects on the chances of pretrial misconduct in other criminal justice literature, the results in table 11.2 show the statistically significant predictors of participation to be the same as the statistically significant predictors of frequency of rearrest. This finding is, again, contrary to predictions made by the criminal career view.

Seattle Youth Study and National Youth Survey

Dependent Variables. In analyses of the Seattle Youth Study and the National Youth Survey, participation and frequency measures of delinquency were constructed by combining two theft and two violence measures. From the SYS, the four items are:

1. Theft of an item worth $2 or less
2. Theft of an item worth $10 to $50
3. Hit a teacher
4. Fought with other students

The NYS delinquency items are similar:
1. Theft of an item worth less than $5
2. Theft of an item worth $5 to $50
3. Hit a teacher

4.   Fought with other students

TABLE 11.2
Probit and Tobit Estimates with Standard Errors for the Bail Decisionmaking
Study Participation and Frequency Analyses

Variable	Probit Estimates(s.e.)	Tobit Estimates(s.e.)
Intercept	-0.819 (0.090)	-2.515 (0.309)
Female	-0.105 (0.076)	-0.191 (0.224)
Age	-0.016 (0.002)	-0.051 (0.007)
White	0.017 (0.054)	0.142 (0.159)
Phone service	-0.154 (0.059)	-0.547 (0.173)
Prior record	0.581 (0.057)	1.814 (0.177)
Theft offense	-0.057 (0.056)	-0.142 (0.166)
Sigma		3.064 (0.104)
Likelihood function	-1635.8	-2538.2
Restricted likelihood	-1712.5	

The only substantive difference between the two measures is the value of the stolen items. However, both items represent theft of $50 or less. Participation in delinquency is measured by whether an individual has committed any one of the four delinquent acts and is coded as (0,1). Frequency of delinquency among active delinquents is represented by the total number of times the individual claims to have committed all four acts.

Independent variables. Similar to the BDS analysis, demographic characteristics—age, race, and gender—are included below to model the different mean levels of delinquency among the different groups. The

TABLE 11.3
Seattle Youth Study Means, Standard Deviations, and Ranges for the Participation and Frequency Analyses (*n*=1,471)

Variable	Mean	Standard Deviation	Minimum	Maximum
Female	0.250	0.433	0	1
Age	16.502	0.928	14	18
White	0.703	0.457	0	1
No delinquent friends	0.542	0.498	0	1
GPA	2.681	0.744	1	4
Date	1.107	0.310	0	1
Number of delinquent acts	1.862	9.031	0	215
Any delinquency	0.311	0.463	0	1

coding of these variables also follows that in the BDS analysis. Again, based on prior research on the demographic correlates of delinquent behavior, females, whites, and older individuals are expected to have both lower chances of participating in delinquency and fewer delinquent acts, if they have committed any delinquent acts.

Three other variables are included because prior research has shown them to be strongly related to delinquency. First, having delinquent friends has a positive relationship with delinquency, where those individuals claiming to have friends involved in delinquent activities are themselves more likely to be involved in delinquency (see, for example, Akers et al. 1979). In the SYS, this item was measured by whether the respondent had any friends who had been arrested. Those individuals responding yes were coded as a (0), while individuals responding no were coded as a (1) to represent the variable "No Delinquent Friends." In the NYS, "No Delinquent Friends" is represented by those individuals

TABLE 11.4
National Youth Survey Means, Standard Deviations, and Ranges for the Participation and Frequency Analyses

Wave 1:
($n=1,442$)

Variable	Mean	Standard Deviation	Minimum	Maximum
Female	0.482	0.500	0	1
Age	13.870	1.925	11	17
White	0.806	0.395	0	1
No delinquent friends	0.085	0.279	0	1
GPA	2.752	0.818	0	4
Date	0.769	0.422	0	1
Number of delinquent acts	7.992	52.940	0	1413
Any delinquency	0.539	0.499	0	1

responding that none of their friends had committed any one of ten delinquent acts.[7] Again, individuals with no delinquent friends received a (1), while individuals with friends involved in any of the ten delinquent acts received a (0). Individuals with no delinquent friends are then expected to be unlikely to participate in delinquency and to have low frequencies as well.

Second, grade point average (GPA) has also been shown to have a negative relationship with delinquent behavior. Based on prior work, it is expected that as GPA increases, the chances and frequency of delinquency will decrease.

Third, dating behavior has a positive relationship with delinquency, where those individuals who regularly date have increased chances of delinquent behavior (Hirschi 1969). In both the SYS and NYS, this item is coded as a (1) if the respondent said that he or she regularly dates (at least once a week), and (0) otherwise.

TABLE 11.4 (Continued)

Wave 2:
($n = 1,440$)

Variable	Mean	Standard Deviation	Minimum	Maximum
Female	0.478	0.500	0	1
Age	14.850	1.924	12	18
White	0.809	0.393	0	1
No delinquent friends	0.076	0.265	0	1
GPA	2.744	0.803	0	4
Date	0.819	0.385	0	1
Number of delinquent acts	4.402	18.350	0	400
Any delinquency	0.478	0.500	0	1

In sum, females, whites, older individuals, those individuals with no delinquent friends, and those persons with higher GPAs are expected to have lower chances of participation in delinquency and lower frequencies of delinquency. In contrast those individuals who regularly date are expected to have higher chances of participation and higher frequencies of delinquent behavior.

Findings. Tables 11.3 and 11.4 display the means, standard deviations, and ranges for the variables included in the SYS and NYS participation and frequency analyses below. Table 11.5 presents the probit and tobit estimates for the SYS analysis. The probit results show that increased age, having no delinquent friends, and higher GPA all have statistically significant effects that reduce the chances a person has participated in

TABLE 11.4 (Continued)

Wave 3:
($\underline{n}$ = 1,474)

Variable	Mean	Standard Deviation	Minimum	Maximum
Female	0.472	0.499	0	1
Age	15.680	1.890	13	19
White	0.807	0.394	0	1
No delinquent friends	0.068	0.252	0	1
GPA	2.714	0.822	0	1
Date	0.851	0.356	0	1
Number of delinquent acts	3.865	21.650	0	400
Any delinquency	0.398	0.490	0	1

any delinquent behavior, as expected. Dating has a significant positive relationship with participation, also as expected.

The tobit estimates for frequency operationalized as one or more delinquent acts shows the same variables have statistically significant effects as in the participation model. In other words, increased age, having no delinquent friends, and higher GPA reduce the chances of delinquency and reduce the frequency of delinquency. Similarly, dating increases the chances of delinquency and its frequency, too.

To investigate the effects of a different cutpoint for frequency of delinquent behavior, frequency was also operationalized as five or more delinquent acts. The number of statistically significant variables is reduced, with age and dating no longer having significant effects on the frequency of delinquent behavior, while having no delinquent friends and higher GPA still reduce the frequency of delinquent behavior. While these results, at first glance, appear to support the criminal career claim of

TABLE 11.4 (Continued)

Wave 4:
(n=1,301)

Variable	Mean	Standard Deviation	Minimum	Maximum
Female	0.482	0.500	0	1
Age	16.500	1.833	14	20
White	0.795	0.404	0	1
No delinquent friends	0.051	0.221	0	1
GPA	2.699	0.821	0	4
Date	0.893	0.309	0	1
Number of delinquent acts	3.402	20.775	0	502
Any delinquency	0.344	0.475	0	1

different causes of frequency of illegal behavior, the variation in all the independent variables is reduced considerably when the cutpoint is changed from one to five or more delinquent acts. The lack of variation in the independent variables make the statistical estimation more uncertain and difficult, implying that the parameter estimates and their standard errors may be unstable.

Table 11.6 presents the probit estimates for all four waves of data from the NYS. In all four years, females, older individuals, those with no delinquent friends, and those with higher GPAs were less likely to participate in any delinquent activity. In all but the second year, dating significantly increased the chances of participating in delinquency, as expected. The one statistically significant finding that provides an anomaly is that whites were significantly more likely to participate in

TABLE 11.5
Probit and Tobit Estimates with Standard Errors for the Seattle Youth Study
Participation and Frequency Analyses

Variable	Probit Estimate (s.e.)	Tobit (1+) Estimate (s.e.)	Tobit (5+) Estimate (s.e.)
Intercept	3.265 (0.642)	31.147 (10.993)	10.659 (42.890)
Female	-0.061 (0.086)	-2.198 (1.502)	-4.503 (5.841)
Age	-0.194 (0.039)	-2.023 (0.666)	-1.940 (2.477)
White	-0.100 (0.078)	-0.425 (1.348)	-2.893 (5.144)
No delinquent friends	-0.424 (0.073)	-6.225 (1.281)	-16.966 (4.995)
GPA	-0.246 (0.050)	-3.702 (0.878)	-11.628 (3.418)
Date	0.418 (0.127)	-4.192 (2.234)	-4.474 (8.556)
Sigma		18.290 (0.646)	44.207 (3.591)
Likelihood function	-849.54	-2390.6	-741.02
Restricted likelihood	-911.49		

delinquent activity in the third year. However, given the lack of this variable's statistical significance in all other analyses, this finding may be a chance result.

Table 11.7 shows the tobit estimates for frequency of delinquent behavior operationalized as one or more delinquent acts. The statistically significant parameters in table 11.7 are identical to those in table 11.6, with two exceptions. First, whites do not have statistically lower frequencies of delinquency in Wave 3, compared to the lower level of participation found in table 11.6. Second, dating significantly increased the

TABLE 11.6
Probit Estimates with Standard Errors for the National Youth Survey
Participation Analyses, Waves 1 through 4

Variable	Wave 1	Wave 2	Wave 3	Wave 4
Intercept	1.762 (0.300)	1.741 (0.310)	2.733 (0.331)	2.821 (0.382)
Female	-0.754 (0.071)	-0.805 (0.071)	-0.740 (0.072)	-0.801 (0.078)
Age	-0.061 (0.019)	-0.054 (0.019)	-0.140 (0.020)	-0.136 (0.022)
White	-0.035 (0.089)	-0.017 (0.088)	0.186 (0.090)	-0.051 (0.093)
No delinquent friends	-1.027 (0.146)	-1.014 (0.160)	-1.331 (0.200)	-1.073 (0.225)
GPA	-0.213 (0.043)	-0.242 (0.045)	-0.294 (0.044)	0.325 (0.047)
Date	0.316 (0.087)	0.149 (0.097)	0.276 (0.106)	0.347 (0.131)
Likelihood function	-872.63	-875.26	-852.78	-717.24
Restricted likelihood	-995.16	-996.80	-990.54	-837.04

chances of delinquency in Wave 4, but did not increase the frequency of delinquency in the same year.

Table 11.8 provides the tobit estimates for frequency operationalized as five or more delinquent acts. Overall, there is considerable similarity between the pattern of statistically significant parameters in tables 11.7 and 11.8 since the two tables reveal only four major differences. In Wave 1, age and no delinquent friends had significant negative effects on both participation and frequency defined as one or more delinquent acts, but these items had no effect on frequency when defined as five or more delinquent acts. In Wave 2, age again fails to reduce significantly the frequency of delinquency for the subsample of individuals with five or more delinquent acts. Lastly, in Wave 3, no delinquent friends fails to

TABLE 11.7
Tobit Estimates with Standard Errors for the National Youth Survey Frequency Analyses for One or More Delinquent Acts, Waves 1 through 4

Variable	Wave 1	Wave 2	Wave 3	Wave 4
Intercept	69.105 (20.135)	27.021 (7.560)	45.624 (10.934)	67.289 (13.354)
Female	-39.380 (4.860)	-17.214 (1.804)	-19.014 (2.494)	-19.371 (2.856)
Age	-3.924 (1.290)	-0.875 (0.481)	-3.003 (0.671)	-3.643 (0.787)
White	-1.602 (5.939)	-3.466 (2.132)	4.246 (3.038)	-0.241 (3.270)
No delinquent friends	-59.889 (11.135)	-23.385 (4.386)	-39.237 (7.463)	-33.319 (8.653)
GPA	-11.982 (2.937)	-5.171 (1.079)	-6.914 (1.436)	-10.890 (1.633)
Date	17.711 (5.964)	2.276 (2.374)	7.789 (3.543)	6.966 (4.627)
Sigma	77.490 (1.992)	27.717 (0.771)	36.642 (1.110)	37.874 (1.318)
Likelihood function	-4802.8	-3626.4	3313.6	-2584.4

significantly reduce the frequency of delinquency among the individuals with five or more delinquent acts.

To summarize, there is a great deal of similarity in both the SYS and NYS analyses comparing participation with frequency of delinquency, when the cutpoint is operationalized as one or more delinquent acts. When the cutpoint for frequency is changed to five or more delinquent acts, the pattern of results is still quite similar to the participation and one or more frequency analyses, although there is some variation. Overall, however, the results in tables 11.5 through 11.8 imply support for the idea that the causes of participation and frequency of illegal activity are indeed the same, regardless of the operationalization of frequency of illegal activity. Once again, the results call into question the validity of the criminal career view, since the significant predictors of participation also predict frequency of illegal activity, which is contrary to the predictions of this view.

TABLE 11.8
Tobit Estimates with Standard Errors for the National Youth Survey Frequency Analyses for Five or More Delinquent Acts, Waves 1 through 4

Variable	Wave 1	Wave 2	Wave 3	Wave 4
Intercept	-13.379 (54.299)	4.302 (22.460)	-15.791 (33.518)	45.461 (38.903)
Female	-94.731 (14.006)	-40.337 (5.933)	-53.695 (8.853)	-45.565 (9.271)
Age	-3.998 (3.510)	-1.453 (1.443)	-3.669 (2.063)	-5.607 (2.341)
White	-3.841 (15.850)	-3.684 (6.246)	7.279 (9.448)	10.648 (9.973)
No delinquent friends	-541.942 (1748.360)	-71.550 (23.087)	-268.825 (1049.460)	-69.314 (31.729)
GPA	-31.712 (7.929)	-12.271 (3.158)	-11.508 (4.299)	-20.292 (4.644)
Date	51.047 (17.188)	8.739 (7.176)	25.132 (11.809)	8.457 (13.301)
Sigma	151.719 (7.323)	58.788 (3.280)	79.353 (4.886)	79.279 (5.453)
Likelihood function	-1859.8	-1386.9	-1206.3	-981.77

Summary and Conclusions

The analyses in this chapter attempt to test the claim that the causes of participation in some form of illegal activity are somehow different from the causes of the frequency of that illegal behavior once it occurs. Using data from the Bail Decisionmaking Study, Seattle Youth Study, and National Youth Survey, multivariate models of participation and frequency of offending were tested with probit and tobit statistical models, respectively, to assess whether the same set of variables that predicted participation also predicted frequency of illegal behavior. Further, in the SYS and NYS analyses, two operationalizations of frequency of delinquency were compared. Specifically, "one or more" and "five or more" delinquent acts were used as two different cutpoints to see whether the different operationalizations of delinquency could substantially alter the findings.

Using the Bail Decisionmaking Study, the measure of illegal behavior was operationalized as whether any arrest occurred following an individual's release from jail (participation), and if the offender was rearrested, the number of times (frequency). Testing a model that contained variables representing background characteristics (age, race, and gender), community ties (phone service), and legal characteristics (prior record and current charge), the statistically significant effects predicting participation (analyzed with a probit statistical model) were identical to the statistically significant effects predicting frequency of rearrest (analyzed with a tobit statistical model). Although the use of rearrest as a measure of additional criminal activity among a sample of already arrested individuals could lead to statistical estimation problems due to lack of variation on the independent variables, no such problems were encountered here. But the results do pose a problem for the claim that the causes of initial participation and subsequent frequency of illegal activity are different.

The two self-report data sets revealed a similar pattern of results. In both the Seattle Youth Study and National Youth Survey, the same six items representing demographic (age, race, and gender) and social (delinquent friends, GPA, and dating behavior) characteristics were available to evaluate the proposed hypothesis. In the SYS, there was no difference in the form of the statistically significant model for participation and frequency, when the cutpoint for frequency was one or more delinquent acts. When the cutpoint was shifted to five or more delinquent acts, there was variation in the set of statistically significant parameters. However, this variation was not sufficient to undermine support for the claim that the causes of participation and frequency of delinquency are the same— because when all results are close to the borderline of statistical significance, apparent differences in outcome are simply much more likely.

In the National Youth Survey, two trivial differences in the pattern of statistically significant effects in the participation and frequency models were observed, when frequency was operationalized as one or more delinquent acts. When the cutpoint for the frequency analysis was changed to five or more delinquent acts, there was slight variation in the pattern of statistically significant effects. Again, the overall pattern was one of stability of the causes of participation and frequency of delinquency, regardless of the operationalization of frequency of illegal activity.

There is strong support for the idea that the causes of committing one illegal act are the same as the causes of committing many illegal acts. This pattern of similar effects held for all three data sets. The findings from the SYS and NYS, using relatively minor theft and violence acts, both confirm and extend the general pattern of results presented by Paternoster and Triplett (1988), namely, that delinquent behavior is predicted equally well, whether operationalized as participation or frequency of illegal activity, or whether frequency was operationalized as one or more or five or more delinquent acts. The results from the BDS extend the generality of the self-report findings by considering a sample of adults who have committed more serious crimes, and show that participation and frequency of rearrest while on release can be explained with the same model.

The claim of Blumstein et al. (1986) and Blumstein, Cohen, and Farrington (1988a) that the causes of participation and frequency of illegal activity may be different appears to be in error. While the data here have limitations—the SYS and NYS use relatively minor delinquent acts, and only two operationalizations of frequency of offending were analyzed—the three data sets, together, raise serious questions about the claim of different causes. The results in fact suggest that proponents of the claim that participation and frequency require substantively different explnations need to reevaluate this assertion, and propose an alternative that is consistent with the facts.

Notes

1. The participation model was tested with a probit statistical model, while the frequency model was tested with a tobit statistical model.
2. In light of the findings elsewhere in this volume on the generality of illegal behavior, we can anticipate that specific crimes will have very little effect on whether the causes of participation and frequency are similar or different.
3. Bail Decisionmaking Study (Goldkamp and Gottfredson 1985); Seattle Youth Study (Hindelang, Hirschi, and Weis 1981); National Youth Study (Elliott, Huizinga, and Ageton 1985).
4. While it would have been nice to test directly Gottfredson and Hirschi's (1990) substantive model of self-control and criminal behavior, none of the data sets was collected with the idea of measuring a concept such as self-control. Thus, rather than produce inaccurate findings about the validity of Gottfredson and Hirschi's (1990) substantive model of crime, simpler models, representing only a few indicators, are used to test for differences in participation and frequency of offending.

5. The BDS data would permit a test of only one cut-point due to the lack of variation on the independent variables, which caused the statistical analysis to fail and not reach a solution.
6. Of course, it is possible that a released offender may commit one or more crimes and go undetected in this 120 day period. However, the offenders who were rearrested are assumed to be similar to those individuals who committed crimes but were not arrested.
7. These delinquent acts are cheating on tests, destroying property, using marijuana, stealing something worth less than $5, hitting someone, using alcohol, breaking into a vehicle, selling hard drugs, stealing something worth more than $50, and suggesting one break the law.

References

Akers, Ronald L., Marvin D. Krohn, Lonn Lanza-Kaduce, and Marcia Radosevich. 1979. "Social Learning and Deviant Behavior: A Specific Test of a General Theory." *American Sociological Review* 44:636-55.

Ball, John, Alan Ross, and Alice Simpson. 1964. "Incidence and Estimated Prevalence of Recorded Delinquency in a Metropolitan Area." *American Sociological Review* 29:90-93.

Blumstein, Alfred, Jacqueline Cohen, and David Farrington. 1988a. "Criminal Career Research: Its Value for Criminology." *Criminology* 26:1-35.

_____. 1988b. "Longitudinal and Criminal Career Research: Further Clarifications." *Criminology* 26:57-74.

Blumstein, Alfred, Jacqueline Cohen, Jeffrey Roth, and Christy Visher, eds. 1986. *Criminal Careers and "Career Criminals," Volume 1* (Report of the Panel on Research on Criminal Careers, National Research Council). Washington, DC: National Academy Press.

Blumstein, Alfred, and Elizabeth Grady. 1982. "Prevalence and Recidivism in Index Arrests: A Feedback Model." *Law and Society Review* 16:265-90.

Chaiken, Jan M., and Marcia R. Chaiken. 1983. "Crime Rates and the Active Criminal." In *Crime and Public Policy*, ed. James Q. Wilson, 11-29. San Francisco: ICS Press.

Douglas, J.W.B., J.M. Ross, W.A. Hammond, and D.G. Mulligan. 1966. "Delinquency and Social Class." *British Journal of Criminology* 6:294-302.

Elliott, Delbert S., David S. Huizinga, and Susan Ageton. 1985. *Explaining Delinquency and Drug Use*. Beverly Hills, CA: Sage.

Goldkamp, John S., and Michael Gottfredson. 1985. *Policy Guidelines for Bail: An Experiment in Court Reform*. Philadelphia, PA: Temple University Press.

Gordon, Robert. 1976. "Prevalence: The Rare Datum in Delinquency Measurement and Its Implications for the Theory of Delinquency." In *The Juvenile Justice System*, ed. Malcolm W. Klein, 201-84. Beverly Hills, CA: Sage.

Gottfredson, Michael, and Travis Hirschi. 1986. "The True Value of Lambda Would Appear to be Zero: An Essay on Career Criminals, Criminal Careers, Selective Incapacitation, Cohort Studies, and Related Topics." *Criminology* 24:213-33.

_____. 1987. "The Methological Adequacy of Longitudinal Research on Crime." *Criminology* 25:581-614.

_____. 1988. "Science, Public Policy, and the Career Paradigm." *Criminology* 26:37-55.

_____. *A General Theory of Crime*. Stanford, CA: Stanford University Press.

Greenwood, Peter. 1982. *Selective Incapacitation*. Santa Monica, CA: The Rand Corporation.

Hindelang, Michael, Travis Hirschi, and Joseph G. Weis. 1981. *Measuring Delinquency*. Beverly Hills, CA: Sage.

Hirschi, Travis. 1969. *Causes of Delinquency*. Berkeley: University of California Press.

Judge, George G., William E. Griffiths, R. Carter Hill, Helmut Lutkephol, and Tsoung-Chao Lee. 1985. *The Theory and Practice of Econometrics*, 2nd ed. New York: John Wiley and Sons.

Little, Alan. 1965. "The Prevalence of Recorded Delinquency and Recidivism in England and Wales." *American Sociological Review* 30:260–63.

Maddala, G.S. 1983. *Limited Dependent and Qualitative Variables in Econometrics*. New York: Cambridge University Press.

Monahan, Thomas. 1960. "On the Incidence of Delinquency." *Social Forces* 39:66–72.

Paternoster, Raymond, and Ruth Triplett. 1988. "Disaggregating Self-Reported Delinquency and Its Implications for Theory." *Criminology* 26:591–625.

Reiss, Albert J., Jr. 1975. "Inappropriate Theories and Inadequate Methods as Policy Plagues: Self-Reported Delinquency and the Law." In *Social Policy and Sociology*, ed. N.J. Demerath III, Otto Larsen, and Karl F. Schuessler, 211–22. New York: Academic Press.

Wolfgang, Marvin E., Robert M. Figlio, and Thorsten Sellin. 1972. *Delinquency in a Birth Cohort*. Chicago: University of Chicago Press.

12

The Victim-Offender Relationship

Leonore M. J. Simon

Although interest in violence in general is not new, legal and mental health professionals have become increasingly interested in distinguishing between nonstranger and stranger violence. Family violence and violence between people who know each other (e.g., spouse battering, date rape, child abuse, and incest) are typically studied as separate and distinct from general criminal violence (e.g., Browne 1987; Lundsgaarde 1977; Peterson et al. 1982; Widom 1989a, 1989b), and this "intimate violence" is believed to merit and receive more lenient treatment in the legal system (e.g., Gottfredson and Gottfredson 1988; Rosen 1986; Wexler 1979, 1984, 1985).

This distinction between stranger and nonstranger offenders assumes that the two are sufficiently different to merit separate research and differential treatment. This study considers whether the two types of offenders are in fact different by looking at the relationship of the victim-offender relationship to recidivism, versatility, and specialization in a sample of prisoners incarcerated for violent crimes.

Criminal Behavior of Violent Offenders

One way to see whether stranger and nonstranger offenders are different is to examine information about their criminal behavior prior to incarceration. This study aims to increase public knowledge about offenders who commit violent crimes and how they differ from general criminal offenders. Such offenders' reports of their motives, methods, and self-perceptions can help us understand the circumstances in which crimes are committed and the probable effects of criminal justice policies on crime.

Although the existing literature supports the idea that the relationship between the victim and offender is an important determinant of the immediate outcome of the violent encounter and the legal outcome in violent offenses (Wiersema 1988), research on the victim-offender relationship is hampered by the fact that many essential characteristics of the relationship are not routinely recorded in official files. In this research, nineteen categories of relationships were devised for the commitment offense. They ranged from "spouse" to "complete stranger." For most of the analyses, the victim-offender relationship categories were collapsed into nonstranger and stranger, based on the degree of emotional distance, which is a variant of relational distance (Silverman and Kennedy 1987). Category 1 consists of relationships with the least amount of emotional distance, including spouses, ex-spouses, girlfriends (living together, living apart, and ex-girlfriends), child, parent, close friend, and casual friend. This category also consists of more casual relationships, including coworkers, schoolmates, casual acquaintances, neighbors, nonrelative acquaintances, and strangers known by sight. The second category consists of relationships with the most emotional distance, including only complete strangers.

This study first considers the connection between the victim-offender relationship and the offenders' criminal record. It is expected that offenders who victimize strangers will have longer, more extensive juvenile and adult criminal records, more motor vehicle accidents, and more serious substance abuse problems than offenders who victimize nonstrangers. This study then examines variability and patterns in committing crimes. Does the commission of one type of crime tend to be associated with the commission of others? Do stranger offenders exhibit different patterns of crime commission than do nonstranger offenders? Also considered in this study is the degree to which the respondents are (1) highly active criminals who commit many types of crimes at relatively high rates; (2) specialists who commit only one type of crime but at a high rate; or (3) marginal offenders, who have little prior involvement with the criminal justice system and who report only one or a few offenses.

Method

Subjects

The data were collected as part of a broader study examining victim-offender relationships in crimes of violence. A sample of 273 incarcerated, sentenced offenders who committed violent crimes was recruited from among all the male prison inmates admitted to the Arizona Department of Corrections over a two-year period. This population was selected because of the obvious efficiencies it provides. General population samples and even samples of offenders as a whole provide adequate numbers of violent offenders and offenses only when they are extremely large and expensive.

A crime of violence was defined as an attempt or completed attack against another, with or without a weapon, for which the inmate was convicted. The term *attack* included attempted or completed acts of homicide, sexual assault, kidnapping, assault, and robbery. Inmates in all custody levels were interviewed, including inmates in maximum and super-maximum security. They were told that the study was interested in why they committed their crime or were accused of committing it. Participation was strictly voluntary and no payment or benefit accrued to those who chose to be interviewed.

Confidential Interviews

Due to the low educational level of most prison inmates and to insure complete and high-quality data, this study relied on personal, confidential interviews instead of the self-administered questionnaires that have been used in other prisoner surveys (Peterson and Braiker 1980; Peterson et al. 1982). This allowed the interviewer to develop a personal rapport with the respondent, ensured that inmates understood the questions, and allowed interviewers to probe further when responses were vague or incomplete. Interviewers were undergraduate and graduate students at a local university who were trained to conduct the interviews and supervised on an hourly basis.

TABLE 12.1
Offender Self-Report Questionnaire

"During those 3 years before you started your present term, altogether how many times did you do each of the following--"

a. Armed robbery--threatened someone with a weapon in order to get money or something else.

b. Totally lose your temper.

c. Beat or physically hurt someone badly.

d. Hustled or conned someone.

e. Cut someone with a knife or shot someone with a gun.

f. Burglary--broke into a home or business in order to take something.

g. Got into a fist fight.

h. Forced someone to have sex with you.

i. Got drunk and hurt someone.

j. Threatened to hurt someone with a gun, knife, or other weapon.

k. Tried to kill someone.

l. Forged a check or other paper.

m. Stole a car.

n. Sold hard drugs.

Participation Rate

Of 341 inmates who were approached and asked to volunteer, 273 consented to being interviewed, and 68 (20 percent) declined. The prison provided access to the records of those who declined so that comparisons could be made between participants and nonparticipants. Except for a few variables, no significant differences were noted between the two groups. The two groups did not exhibit statistically significant differences in race, educational level, marital status, first offender status, drug and alcohol abuse, type of crime, acceptance of a plea-bargain, length of sentence, or number of disciplinary problems in prison. However, non-participants were more likely to be older, less educated, to have victimized strangers, and to have fewer solitary confinements in prison.

Survey Instrument

A structured interview was developed for the overall study that incorporated portions of the first Rand (Peterson and Braiker 1980) survey. The interview was eighteen pages long and took about an hour to administer. Among the question asked were queries about what crimes and antisocial acts they had committed during a three-year reference period prior to incarceration. In particular, inmates were asked whether they had engaged in any of a list of fourteen acts that are or might be criminal or antisocial. These questions were borrowed from the first Rand inmate survey and are shown in table 12.1.

Categorized Offense Rates

In answering questions about their crimes, inmates could endorse one of five categories (0, 1-2, 3-5, 6-10, or more than 10). Different response categories were used for drug sales (less than 10, 10-50, 50-100, more than 100). The main reason for using response categories was that there was evidence that inmates find it too difficult to remember and report on every commission of fourteen acts.[1] The difficulty that respondents had with remembering their offense rates resulted in treatment of offense rates as categorical rather than continuous variables for purposes of statistical analyses. Thus, inmates were asked to provide only an approximate number of commissions for each offense which provided information only about the general level of criminal activity. Consequently, instead of assuming that respondents who reported having committed six to ten robberies actually committed eight robberies, the numbers are intended to represent that respondents who reported six to ten robberies probably committed appreciably more robberies than those who reported one or two (Peterson and Braiker 1980). Thus, offense rate variables should distinguish among several levels of offense rates.

Another reason for using categorized offense rates was the skewed distribution of each offense rate. As in prior studies (Peterson and Braiker 1980; Greenwood and Abrahamse 1982), most respondents denied having committed the offense (a zero offense rate), and among those who

TABLE 12.2
Median and Mean Annual Offense Rates*

Offense	Total Sample		Stranger Offenders		Nonstranger Offenders	
	Median	Mean	Median	Mean	Median	Mean
Armed robbery	1.7	5.9	1.7	3.0	1.7	9.7
Cons	3.3	3.6	3.3	3.9	3.3	3.2
Burglary	3.3	4.5	3.3	4.1	3.3	5.2
Forgery	1.3	1.9	0.6	1.2	1.6	2.5
Auto theft	1.3	2.4	1.4	2.6	1.2	2.2
Drug sales	33.3	29.0	33.3	29.8	33.3	27.9
Shot/cut	1.3	2.0	1.4	1.7	1.1	2.2
Threat	1.3	2.1	2.7	2.6	1.3	1.8
Agg. assault	1.4	2.5	1.3	2.1	1.4	2.7
Att. murder	1.4	2.3	1.5	1.7	0.8	2.8
Rape	1.3	18.7	3.0	3.0	1.3	25.0
Temper	2.4	3.1	2.7	3.5	1.6	2.8
Fist fight	2.0	3.1	1.8	3.1	2.4	3.1
Drunk/hurt	1.3	2.7	1.5	2.2	0.7	3.1

* Among those who report committing the offense

reported committing an offense, most reported low rather than high offense rates. The skew characteristic of offense rates for all eleven offenses is illustrated by the example of armed robbery. The majority of respondents, 215 (78.8 percent), committed no armed robberies; 16 (6.1 percent) reported that they committed armed robberies at rates between zero and one robbery per year. A few respondents, 6 (2.4 percent) reported committing armed robbery at a rate of ten or more armed robberies per year.

One consequence of such a skewed distribution is that the mean offense rate is distorted by the few respondents with high offense rates (Peterson and Braiker 1980). Whereas the median annual rate for active robbers is 1.7 robberies per year, the mean annual robbery rate, lambda, is 5.9, over three times the median figure. In fact, very few respondents have offense rates equal to or greater than the mean rate of 5.9 armed robberies per year.

Table 12.2 indicates both the median and mean offense rates for each of the fourteen criminal or antisocial acts. As this table indicates, distributions of offense rates for each crime were substantially skewed, making it difficult to examine offense rates by standard statistical procedures.

However, the categorical transformations allowed for statistical tests of the offense rates. Following the procedure used by the first Rand survey, each of the relevant offense rates was transformed into categorical variables to obtain general levels of offense rates. First, respondents who reported no commission of an offense (zero offense rate) were placed in Category 0. Second, those respondents who reported committing the offense were divided in half on the basis of the median of their offense rate. Third, respondents who had offense rates below the median were placed in Category 1. Respondents who had offense rates above the median were placed in Category 2. As a result, these categories reflect offenders who did not commit a particular offense (Category 0), those who committed the offense only occasionally (Category 1), and those who committed the offense relatively often (Category 2).

Reference Period

Previous research shows that most incarcerated offenders have been committing crimes for long periods of time and that their criminal behavior probably is quite variable over time (Chaiken and Chaiken 1982; Peterson and Braiker 1980; Peterson et al. 1982; Petersilia et al. 1977). The present survey sampled the criminal behavior of each respondent during a limited period of time that was as near as possible to the time they completed the interview. Survey questions about crimes and correlates of crimes concentrated on a thirty-six-month period, ending with the respondent's current incarceration.[2] The thirty-six-month period was chosen to allow offenders to commit a sufficient number and variety of crimes, some of which would have come to the attention of the criminal justice system. A sequence of interview questions was intended to help each respondent identify this reference period and think about important events that occurred during it.

Procedures

The survey used a cross-sectional retrospective design. Subject recruitment began by identifying eligible inmates through the central computer system of the Arizona Department of Corrections. If the inmate was sentenced to prison for more than one violent offense, the most serious offense was selected. This hierarchy of seriousness consisted of murder, manslaughter, negligent homicide, sexual assault, kidnapping, assault, and robbery. Eligible inmates were contacted in person by the researcher and individually recruited to participate.

In addition to the completed individual interviews of inmates, official record data were obtained for each respondent. Information was obtained for over 100 variables per case, supplementing the substantive survey data and allowing evaluation of the quality of survey responses.

Reliability of Categorized Offense Rate Measures

As in the first Rand survey, two sets of questions within the survey provided alternative estimates of offense rates: (1) rates derived from the list of criminal offenses, and (2) rates obtained directly by asking the number of robberies, burglaries, and violent acts committed during a typical month.

To be reliable, answers for comparable questions must have a substantial positive correlation (Peterson and Braiker 1980). That is, respondents who reported a high offense rate on one question should tend to report high rates on a second question about the same offense. Low correlations would show that there was little consistency between answers to the two questions; respondents who reported high rates for one question might or might not report high rates for the other. This lack of consistency would indicate that self-reports were unreliable and of little use.

Of the three possible comparisons, the alternative questions about burglary, robbery, and assault were comparable and provided an opportunity to examine the reliability of the self-reports. Questions relating to each offense were:

> "In a typical month, how many burglaries did you actually do?"
> "Altogether, how many times did you do: ... Burglary—broke into someone's home or business in order to take something?
> "In a typical month, how many robberies did you actually do?"
> "Altogether, how many times did you do: ... Robbery—threatened someone with a weapon in order to get money or something else?"
> "In a typical month, about how many times did you commit a violent offense against a person such as assault, rape, murder, etc.?"
> "Altogether, how many times did you do: ... Beat or physically hurt somebody badly?"

TABLE 12.3
Sample Characteristics: Past Offenses and Behaviors

Variable	Strangers		Nonstrangers	
	N	%	N	%
Juvenile record				
Assault	15	11.7	10	8.4
Robbery	7	5.5	7	4.9
Kidnapping	1	0.8	0	0.0
Rape	0	0.0	1	0.1
Other[b]	65	50.8	49	34.3
Prison[d]	43	33.6	28	19.6
Adult record				
Homicide	3	2.4	1	0.1
Assault	17	13.3	24	16.8
Robbery[c]	15	11.7	11	7.7
Kidnapping	3	2.3	1	0.1
Rape	1	0.8	3	2.1
Other	79	61.7	83	58.0
Prison[b]	43	33.6	31	21.7
Drug abuse[b]	73	57.0	63	44.0
Alcohol abuse	65	50.8	73	51.0
Kid accidents	44	34.3	56	39.2
Adult accidents	60	46.9	76	53.1

Variable	Mean	Range	S.D.	Mean	Range	S.D.
Juvenile						
Assault	.21	0-8	.86	.11	0-4	.48
Robbery	.08	0-2	.35	.04	0-2	.24
Kidnap	.01	0-1	.09	.00	0	
Rape	.00	0-1	.00	.01	0-1	.08
Other[b]	1.61	0-13	2.54	.98	0-16	2.26
Prison[d]	.82	0-11	1.82	.28	0-4	.69
Crime*[c]	14.41	5-46	6.68	16.30	3-65	9.59
Smoke*[b]	14.76	0-42	6.02	13.20	4-26	3.74
Drive*	13.68	8-22	2.84	13.86	5-22	2.69
Sex*	14.19	7-23	2.71	13.75	4-21	3.27
Accidents	.73	0-12	1.46	.88	0-17	1.94
Adult						
Homicide	.02	0-1	.14	.01	0-1	.04
Assault	.21	0-3	.58	.26	0-3	.65
Robbery	.18	0-4	.58	.07	0-2	.28
Kidnap	.02	0-1	.15	.01	0-1	.08
Rape	.01	0-1	.09	.03	0-2	.20
Other	2.60	0-22	3.75	2.48	0-35	4.63
Incar*[c]	4.80	.25-35	5.67	3.62	.08-35	4.32
Accidents	1.78	0-33	4.54	1.52	0-20	2.94

* Age when first began specified activity. [a] Total number of years spent incarcerated. [b] $p < .04$. [c] $p < .06$. [d] $p < .002$.

TABLE 12.4

Number of Offenses/Acts Committed during the Three-Year Period, by Victim-Offender Relationship (in Percentages)[b]

	Strangers Number of Offenses					Nonstrangers Number of Offenses				
	0	1-2	3-5	6-10	10+	0	1-2	3-5	6-10	10+
Offenses										
Robbery	75.0	7.8	4.7	2.3	7.0	82.5	5.6	3.5	0.0	4.9
Cons	49.2	5.5	9.4	5.5	27.4	65.0	6.3	6.3	2.1	16.8
Burglary	64.1	7.8	5.5	5.5	14.1	77.6	7.0	2.1	0.0	9.8
Forgery	85.2	8.6	.8	0.0	1.6	84.6	4.9	0.0	2.8	4.2
Car theft	75.0	8.6	5.5	3.1	3.9	78.3	10.9	4.2	2.1	1.4
Drug sales[a]	58.6	7.0	5.5	5.5	21.1	61.5	9.8	4.2	2.1	18.2
Assault:										
Beating	50.8	21.1	7.0	7.0	11.7	58.7	14.7	9.8	2.8	10.5
Cut/shot	73.4	12.5	7.0	1.6	2.3	74.8	11.9	8.4	0.0	1.4
Threat	70.3	11.7	2.3	2.3	8.6	62.2	15.4	10.5	3.5	5.6
Rape	95.3	.8	0.0	0.0	.8	93.0	.7	2.2	0.0	.7
Att. murder	79.7	10.9	2.3	.8	2.4	81.8	9.8	1.4	2.8	.7
Other violent acts										
Lost temper	28.9	23.4	10.9	5.5	28.9	30.1	23.8	14.0	6.3	22.4
Fist fight	23.4	24.2	14.8	9.4	25.8	31.5	22.4	11.9	3.5	27.3
Drunk/hurt	69.5	9.4	4.7	3.9	9.4	65.7	16.8	2.1	4.2	7.7

[a] Categories for drug sales are: 0, 1-10, 10-50, 50-100, more than 100.
[b] Bivariate Chi-Square analyses were not significant for any of the comparisons between strangers and nonstrangers.

Results

Prior Criminal Record of Violent Offenders

The criminal records of these violent offenders revealed that the most frequent convictions for the sample were nonviolent offenses such as thefts, burglaries, and drunk driving, both as juveniles (42.5 percent) and as adults (60.2 percent). The second most frequent prior convictions were assaults, both as juveniles (10.6 percent) and as adults (14.9 percent). Robberies constituted 5.9 percent of juvenile convictions and 8.9 percent of adult convictions. Homicides were their least frequent offense, with juveniles having no prior convictions and prior adult convictions for homicide consisting of 1.4 percent. More than a quarter of the sample (27 percent) had served at least one prior prison term. In addition to sundry past convictions and incarcerations, a full one-half of the sample had been heavy drug users, and one-half had been problem drinkers or alcoholics prior to incarceration.

In terms of prior offense and behavior variables, table 12.3 shows few statistically significant differences between stranger and nonstranger offenders. Offenders who victimized strangers were more likely to have been convicted of nonviolent offenses as juveniles (p < .04), and were more likely to have had frequent incarcerations in juvenile institutions, (p < .002). Offenders who victimized strangers were also likely to have begun smoking at an earlier age than nonstranger offenders (p < .04).

In terms of adult criminal records, there are even fewer differences between the two groups. Only one variable related to the adult criminal record distinguishes stranger and nonstranger offenders, with offenders who victimized strangers more likely to have been in prison before (p < .04). In one other significant comparison, 57 percent of stranger—and 44 percent of nonstranger—offenders have drug abuse histories (p < .04).

Survey Measures of Self-Reported Crime

Table 12.4 shows the distribution of self-reported offenses during the three-year period prior to incarceration, by victim-offender relationship. Analysis did not yield significant differences in the number of offenses stranger and nonstranger offenders report committing. In the sample as a whole, confidence games and burglary were the crimes reported most frequently by respondents. Less than one-quarter of respondents reported having committed robbery or car theft. Almost half of the sample reported having committed at least one aggravated beating.

Comparison of Commitment Offenses with Self-Reports of Crime Prior to In- carceration

A majority of respondents denied having committed each of the eleven listed offenses in table 12.4. The portion of the respondents who denied committing offenses ranged from 54.9 percent for beating someone to 93.8 percent for rape. For most offenses, less than one-third of the respondents reported even one commission. The denials of criminal behavior suggest that either inmates are not being candid or that most of them were not actively committing crimes prior to their incarceration (Peterson and Braiker 1980).

Ten percent of respondents totally denied committing all listed crimes. Of these, seven had victimized strangers and eighteen had victimized

TABLE 12.5
Versatility Scale—Number of Crime Types in Which Respondent
Is Active, Total Sample

Types	Total Sample		Stranger[d] Offenders		Nonstranger Offenders	
	N[a]	Percent Reporting Crimes	N[b]	Percent Reporting Crimes	N[c]	Percent Reporting Crimes
One	54	19.8	24	18.8	27	25.9
Two	42	15.4	17	13.3	23	16.1
Three	33	12.1	12	9.4	20	14.0
Four	29	10.6	16	12.5	13	9.1
Five	9	3.3	5	3.9	5	3.5
Six	17	6.2	10	7.8	6	4.2
Seven	15	5.5	13	10.2	2	1.4
Eight	9	3.3	3	2.3	6	4.2
Nine	4	1.5	1	0.8	3	2.1
Ten	1	.4	0	0.0	1	0.7

[a] Total=213, excludes 50 respondents who denied committing all 11 crimes.
[b] Total=101, excludes 27 stranger respondents who denied committing all 11 crimes.
[c] Total=106, excludes 37 nonstranger respondents who denied committing all 11 crimes.
[d] Analysis of difference between stranger and nonstranger offenders was not significant (t=1.59, p < .11).

nonstrangers. The difference between strangers and nonstrangers in terms of completely denying committing all listed crimes approached statistical significance (p < .07) with offenders who victimized non-strangers being slightly more likely to deny commission of crimes prior to incarceration.

All twenty-six respondents who denied committing the listed crimes denied engaging in any of the antisocial acts that might or might not be criminal (acts such as completely losing their temper, getting into fistfights, and getting drunk and hurting someone). The relationship between denying commission of the listed crimes and denying engaging in these other antisocial acts was statistically significant, with those offenders denying commission of one being more likely to deny the commission of the other. Stranger and nonstranger offenders were equally likely to deny commission of these violent and antisocial acts.

Reliability of Offense Rate Measures: Results

Examination of internal consistency for comparable items in the survey produces a correlation (gamma) between the two sets of categorical variables of .96 for robbery, .96 for burglary, and .84 for violent

TABLE 12.6
Varimax Rotated Factor Loading of Eleven Offenses on "Violent Offense"
and "Property Offense" Factors

	Violent Offense Factor	Property Offense Factor
Armed robbery	.950*	-.058
Rape	.931*	-.188
Shot/cut	.884*	.286
Att. murder	.877*	.171
Beating	.625*	.500*
Burglary	.310	.298
Drug sales	.048	.723*
Cons	.065	.611*
Car theft	.138	.576*
Threat	.039	.562*
Forgery	.001	.465*
Eigenvalue[a]	4.1	1.9
Percent of variance	37.6	17.7

[a] The eigenvalues shown are after rotation.
* Indicates loadings ≥ 0.40

offenses. Among strangers, the correlation between the two methods of measurement is .93 for robbery, .93 for burglary, and .76 for violent offenses. For nonstrangers, the correlations were .99 for robbery, .97 for burglary, and .90 for violent offenses. These results indicate that respondents were highly consistent in their self-reports from question to question. Respondents categorized by one measure are highly likely to be placed in the same category by the other measure.

An examination of the offense rates derived for each question illustrates the difficulty of relying on specific numerical estimates provided by respondents, especially when comparing items with reference periods of varying lengths. For example, respondents committing burglaries reported a median number of four per month. However, when the monthly rate of burglary is derived from the total number reported for the three-year period, the median for active burglars is .28 burglaries per month. Similar results for robbery are 4 versus .14, and for violent offenses such as assault, 2 versus .11. Thus, one question produces an average that is between 14 and 28 times the other. These results are consistent with research on telescoping and with those of the first Rand survey. They suggest that the rate differences merely reflect differences

TABLE 12.7
Factor Loadings of Eleven Offenses Forced into One Factor, Total Sample

Offense	One General Factor
Armed robbery	.861*
Rape	.795*
Shot/cut	.927*
Att. murder	.878*
Beating	.766*
Burglary	.399*
Drug sales	.313
Cons	.287
Car theft	.342
Threat	.245
Forgery	.174
Eigenvalue[a]	4.1
Percent of variance	37.6

[a] The eigenvalues shown are after rotation.
* Indicates loadings $\geq$ 0.40.

in the way the two questions were asked. Such results again question reliance on self-reports for specific estimates of crime rates (see Hindelang, Hirschi, and Weis 1981).

When offense rates are categorized to reflect approximate values, the survey apparently provides reliable information about the respondents' general level of criminal activity for the eleven measured offenses. At least for robbery, burglary, and assaults (the only crimes measured in two forms), it is possible to distinguish among respondents with different levels of activity.

Patterns of Offenses

One of the most striking features of their self-reports are the wide range of criminal behavior reported by most offenders. One might expect nonstranger offenders to specialize more and to commit fewer types of crimes than stranger offenders, who would be expected to be more versatile in their criminal offending.

Table 12.5 shows the versatility of offending in terms of the victim-offender relationship. Most respondents report committing a number of

TABLE 12.8
Correlations (gamma) between Offense Rates for Specific Crimes and Summary Indices

Offenses	Property Offenses Scale	Violent Offense Scale	Total Offense Scale
Robbery	.610	.764	.751
Cons	.831	.479	.706
Burglaries	.550	.511	.572
Forgeries	.786	.282	.563
Car theft	.772	.591	.697
Drug sales	.830	.453	.679
Beating	.483	.800	.724
Shot/cut	.446	.890	.773
Threats	.303	.643	.530
Att. murder	.573	.862	.808
Rape	.166	.557	.460

different offenses. For both stranger and nonstranger offenders, 75 percent of those reporting crime reported activity in more than one crime type. Almost half (46.2 percent) of stranger offenders and one-third of nonstranger offenders report committing at least four of the eleven different types. However, there were no significant differences between stranger and nonstranger groups in terms of versatility of offending ($t = 1.59$, $p < .11$). Thus, not only were the general sample of offenders versatile in their crime commission in that they committed a variety of crimes, but offenders who victimized nonstrangers appeared to be no different from offenders who victimized strangers or from offenders in general in the heterogeneity of offenses they engaged in.

The possibility of more general patterns was explored by factor analysis (Peterson and Braiker 1980). The factor analysis of the entire sample, and that of nonstranger offenders, as well (data not shown) revealed two independent factors that seem to correspond with common descriptions of property offenses and violent offenses (see table 12.6). The violence factor accounted for 37.6 percent of the variance. It indicates associations among armed robberies, rapes, use of weapons, attempts to kill, and beatings. Other than robbery, no monetary crime was associated with this violence factor. A second factor accounted for 17.7 percent of the variance and showed strong associations among drug sales, frauds, car thefts, threats, beatings, and forgeries. "Beatings" loaded on both factors, and burglary was only weakly associated with either of these factors.

To test the idea that a one-factor solution, general criminality (Gottfredson and Hirschi 1990), might better represent the underlying structure of the eleven offenses, an analysis was conducted forcing the offenses into one factor. The results are displayed in table 12.7.

For the entire sample, this factor accounted for 37.6 percent of the variance and indicated an association among committing armed robberies, rape, use of weapons, attempts to kill, beatings, and burglary. This one factor accounted for the same amount of variance as the violent offense factor in the two-factor solution but, with the exception of the burglary item, did not include property type offense items. The finding that multiple orthogonal factors cannot be derived from the data is consistent with the general theory of crime.

Multioffense Scales

The results of the factor analyses were used to inform construction of violence and property offense scales (Peterson and Braiker 1980). As in the first Rand survey, the property scale was constructed by taking the mean of the categorical rating (i.e., 0, 1, or 2) of offense rates for cons, forgeries, drug sales, and car thefts. The violent scale was derived by taking the mean of the categorical rating of offense rates for armed robberies, beatings, use of weapons, threats with weapons, and attempted murder. Burglary was not included in either scale because it did not have an appreciable loading on either factor derived from the factor analysis.

As with the single offenses, each multioffense scale ranges from 0 to 2. Respondents who report a high commission rate across related offenses will have scores that approach 2. Those who commit no property crimes or no violent crimes will have a score of zero on the appropriate multioffense scale.

Three scales were also developed to indicate the extent of criminal activity across eleven listed offenses (Peterson and Braiker 1980). The first of these, the versatility scale, indicates how many different types of crimes respondents reported committing during the three-year period. Respondents were given one point on this scale for each of the eleven listed offenses in which they reported at least one or two commissions. Consequently, scores on this scale ranged from one to eleven. The distribution for this scale was shown earlier in table 12.5. The table indicates that almost one-third of respondents report having committed four or more different types of crimes during the three-year period, and almost one-sixth report having committed at least six different types.

The second scale, the intensity scale, summarizes the relative frequency with which offenders commit their active crimes. For each crime in which an offender is active (i.e., categorized offense rate is not zero), the intensity measure averages the respondents' likelihood of committing that crime at low rates (a category rating of 1) or at high rates (a category rating of 2). Thus, an intensity score of 2 indicates that an offender committed all of his active crimes at high rates. An intensity score of 1 indicates that he committed all of his active crimes at low rates.

The third scale, total offenses, measures both the breadth of respondents' criminal activity (number of different types of crimes) and level of activity (intensity) for each offense. This scale was derived by averaging the three category ratings across all eleven listed offenses. Respondents who reported little activity (i.e., Category 1) for only one or two offenses have low scores on this scale. Respondents who reported substantial activity (i.e., Category 2) for only one or two offenses have low scores on this scale. Respondents who reported substantial activity (i.e., Category 2) for a large number of offenses have high scores. Intermediate scores on the scale could indicate either heavy activity for a few offenses or relatively little activity across a broad range of offenses.

Since it represents both the extent and level of criminal activity, the total offense scale serves as the most general measure of criminal activity. In fact, the scale has a substantial correlation with every specific offense rate (table 12.8).

Criminal Specialists

Criminal specialists are offenders who become proficient at one crime, which they commit exclusively and at a high rate (Peterson and Braiker 1980). Some suggest that a substantial number of offenders may be principally involved in one specialized, monetary offense (e.g., Peterson and Braiker 1980, citing Irwin 1970)—burglary, robbery, car theft. Since over one-third of respondents report committing only one or two offenses, this sample could potentially include a substantial number of such specialists. A procedure similar to the one followed by the first Rand survey to assess the number of specialists was used in this study.

Analysis of the data indicates that relatively few respondents can be considered specialists who commit only one crime at a high rate. The number of specialists was examined by plotting the uncategorized offense rates for each offense against the total offense scale. These plots showed that respondents who reported extreme commission rates for any one crime usually had high total offense scale scores. Respondents with extreme commission rates for a particular offense were also committing a number of other crimes at high rates. Only four (1 percent) respondents who had lower than average total offense scores report extreme commission rates for any offense. This is evidence that most respondents with extreme commission rates are not specialists.

Discussion

Respondents' self-reports about their criminal activities for eleven different offenses and three other antisocial acts were obtained for a thirty-six-month period immediately preceding their most recent incarceration. Self-reports indicate substantial variability among prisoners in the amounts and types of crimes they commit. Over one-third of respondents reported only one or two different types of crimes during the three years prior to their incarceration. Almost one-third reported four or more types of crime. Respondents who report a high rate of activity for one crime tend to report high rates for others.

The reliability of self-reports of offending was also examined. For three offenses, a second self-report measure was obtained, indicating activity for a typical month. Comparisons of these alternative measures suggest that the survey provides reliable data about the general level of criminal activity. Thus, offenders who reported having committed an offense at a high rate on one measure tended to report having committed the offense at a high rate on the second measure. Examination of the actual offense rates derived for each question demonstrates that one method produced an average offense rate that is between fourteen and twenty-eight times the other. These results are consistent with those of the first Rand survey and suggest that the differences might reflect methodological differences in the way the two questions were asked. More importantly, such results raise questions about relying on self-reports for specific estimates of crime rates. To permit analyses of relationships between offender characteristics and self-reported crimes, several summary scales were derived from the self-reports for specific offenses. These findings in the main call into question the distinction between offenses based on the relationship between the victim and the offender.

Notes

1. Initially, following the procedure of the Rand surveys, respondents who indicated more than ten commissions of an act were also asked to supply the precise number. However, in our experience, inmates who indicated committing more than ten offenses were unable to remember and provide estimates of the total number. Due to this difficulty, the effort to obtain precise numerical estimates was eventually abandoned.
2. Within the three-year period, the amount of time respondents were on the street and able to commit crimes varied. About half the respondents were incarcerated, hospitalized, or otherwise restrained during a portion of the period, ranging in duration from one to thirty-six months. The median length of such institutionalization was six months. For example, two respondents may have reported the same total number of offenses although they were on the street for substantially different lengths of time. Of course, the crime commission rates for the respondents with less street time would be higher.

   To permit comparisons among respondents who were on the street for substantially different periods of time, the total number of offenses was converted into a monthly offense rate, which was simply the total number of commissions for a particular crime, divided by the months the respondent was free of constraints, that is, thirty-six months minus the total number of months in jail, prison, or hospital. The midpoint of each category was used to provide the total number of commissions. Thus, the monthly rate provided a standardized index of criminal activity.

References

Browne, Angela. 1987. *When Battered Women Kill.* New York: The Free Press.

Chaiken, Jan M., and Marcia R. Chaiken. 1982. "Varieties of Criminal Behavior." Santa Monica, CA: The Rand Corporation.

Gottfredson, Michael R., and Don M. Gottfredson. 1988. *Decision Making in Criminal Justice: Toward the Rational Exercise of Discretion,* 2nd ed. New York: Plenum Press.

Gottfredson, Michael R., and Travis Hirschi. 1990. *A General Theory of Crime.* Stanford, CA: Stanford University Press.

Greenwood, Peter W., and Allan Abrahamse. 1982. *Selective Incapacitation.* Santa Monica, CA: The Rand Corporation.

Hindelang, Michael J., Travis Hirschi, and Joseph G. Weis. 1981. *Measuring Delinquency.* Beverly Hills, CA: Sage.

Irwin, J. 1970. *The Felon.* Englewood Cliffs, NJ: Prentice-Hall.

Lundsgaarde, Henry P. 1977. *Murder in Space City: A Cultural Analysis of Houston Homicide Patterns.* New York: Oxford University Press.

Peterson, Mark A., and Harriet B. Braiker. 1980. *Doing Crime: A Survey of Prison Inmates.* Santa Monica, CA: The Rand Corporation.

Peterson, Mark, Jan Chaiken, Patricia Ebener, and Paul Honig. 1982. *Survey of Prison and Jail Inmates: Background and Method.* Santa Monica, CA: The Rand Corporation.

Rosen, Cathryn J. 1986. "The Excuse of Self-Defense: Correcting a Historical Accident on Behalf of Battered Women Who Kill." *The American University Law Review* 36:11–56.

Silverman, Robert A., and Leslie W. Kennedy. 1987. "Relational Distance and Homicide: The Role of the Stranger." *Journal of Criminal Law and Criminology* 78:272–308.

Wexler, David. 1979. "Patients, Therapists, and Third Parties: The Victimological Virtues of Tarasoff." *International Journal of Law and Psychiatry* 2:1–28.

———. 1984. "An Offense-Victim Approach to Insanity Defense Reform." *Arizona Law Review* 26:17–25.

———. "Redefining the Insanity Problem." *The George Washington Law Review* 53:528–61.

Widom, Cathy S. 1989a. "The Cycle of Violence." *Science* 244:160–66.

———. 1989b. "Does Violence Beget Violence? A Critical Examination of the Literature." *Psychological Bulletin* 106:3–28.

Wiersma, Brian. 1988. "Complexities of Homicide Classification: The Status Relationship Between Victim and Offender." Paper presented at the Annual Meeting of the Law and Society Association, June 9–12, Vail, Colorado.

13

Unemployment, Marital Discord, and Deviant Behavior: The Long-Term Correlates of Childhood Misbehavior

John H. Laub and Robert J. Sampson

This chapter explores the linkage between childhood misbehavior and later adult behavior in a variety of life domains. Surprisingly, this substantive area has been ignored by most criminologists, especially sociological criminologists. We believe this neglect is unfortunate because childhood behaviors may have important ramifications in later adult life. For example, Huesmann et al. (1984), in a study of the aggressiveness of 600 subjects, their parents, and their children over a twenty-two-year period, found that early aggressiveness predicted later antisocial behavior, including criminal behavior, spouse abuse, traffic violations, and self-reported physical aggression. In addition, Olweus (1979) reviewed over sixteen studies on aggressive behavior and found "substantial" stability. More precisely, the correlation between early aggressive behavior and later criminality averaged .68 for the studies reviewed (1979: 854–55). Loeber (1982) completed a similar review of the extant literature in many disciplines and concluded that a "consensus" has been reached in favor of the stability hypothesis: "Children who initially display high rates of antisocial behavior are more likely to persist in this behavior than children who initially show lower rates of antisocial behavior" (1982: 1433).

These findings are not necessarily new. Over sixty years ago the Gluecks found that virtually all of the 510 reformatory inmates in their study of criminal careers "had experience in serious antisocial conduct" (1930: 142). Their data also confirmed "the early genesis of antisocial careers" (1930: 143). Findings regarding behavioral continuity are thus supported by a rich body of empirical research (see also Robins 1966; 1978; West and Farrington 1977; Wolfgang, Thornberry, and Figlio 1987, and Gottfredson and Hirschi 1990). Nonetheless, criminologists still focus primarily on the teenage years in their studies of offending, apparently disregarding the connections between childhood delinquency and later adult crime.

Perhaps most interesting is the fact that the linkage between childhood misbehavior and behavior as an adult is evidenced across several non-crime domains. For instance, Caspi (1987) has argued that personality characteristics in childhood (e.g., ill-tempered behavior) will not only appear across time but will manifest itself in a number of diverse situations. Specifically, Caspi found that "the tendency toward explosive, under-controlled behavior in late childhood was re-created across the age-graded life course, especially in problems with subordination (e.g., in education, military, and work settings) and in situations that required negotiating interpersonal conflicts (e.g., in marriage and parenting)" (1987: 1211). In *Deviant Children Grown Up*, Lee Robins also found strong relations between childhood antisocial behavior and adult employment status, occupational status, job stability, income, and mobility (1966: 95–102). In fact, Robins concluded that "antisocial behavior [in childhood] predicts class status more efficiently than class status predicts antisocial behavior" (1966: 305).

Drawing on Caspi (1987) and Robins (1966), it is our thesis in this chapter that antisocial behavior in children (e.g., juvenile delinquency, childhood misbehavior) is linked to later adult behavior across a variety of domains of life including behavior in the military, general deviance and criminality, economic dependency, educational attainment, employ-ment history, and marital experiences. Furthermore, we argue that these outcomes occur independent of traditional sociological variables such as social class and race/ethnicity. As such we seek to establish the impor-tance of studying crime and deviance over the full life course. We also discuss the implications of our findings for general theories of crime and deviance (e.g., see Gottfredson and Hirschi 1990). Finally, we identify promising areas for future research consideration.

Description of the Glueck Data

The authors are currently engaged in a long-term project analyzing data derived from Sheldon and Eleanor Glueck's *Unraveling Juvenile Delinquency* (1950) plus subsequent follow-up studies (see Glueck and Glueck 1968). The Gluecks' original study utilized a matched-sample longitudinal research design. One component was a delinquent sample consisting of 500 white males, from Boston, ages ten to seventeen, who, because of their persistent delinquency, were committed to correctional schools in Massachusetts. The second component was a nondelinquent sample made up of 500 nondelinquents, also white males ages ten to seventeen, from the Boston public schools. Nondelinquent status was determined on the basis of official record checks and interviews with parents, teachers, local police, social workers, recreational leaders, as well as the boys themselves. The sample procedure was designed to maximize differences in delinquency and by all accounts appears to be successful; for instance, the average number of convictions among the delinquent sample is 3.5 (Glueck and Glueck 1950: 27).

Another unique aspect of the Gluecks' design was that the boys were matched on a case-by-case basis according to age (e.g., mean = 14.8 for delinquent subjects and 14.6 for nondelinquent subjects); race/ethnicity (e.g., 26 percent were English, 25 percent were Italian, and 19 percent were of Irish origin); general intelligence (e.g., mean = 92 for the delinquent subjects and 94 for the nondelinquent subjects); and neighborhood socioeconomic status (Glueck and Glueck 1950: 35–38). All of these matching variables were classic criminological variables thought to influence both delinquency and official reaction (see Sampson 1986). Thus, both sets of boys grew up in high risk environments with respect to poverty and exposure to delinquency and antisocial conduct.

For a twenty-five-year period (1940 to 1965), the Gluecks' research team collected data on these subjects. The men were originally interviewed at an average age of fourteen and then again at age twenty-five and again at age thirty-two. Data are available at all three time periods for 438 of the original 500 delinquent subjects (88 percent) and for 442 of the original 500 nondelinquent subjects (88 percent). The follow-up success is 92 percent when adjusted for mortality—very high by current standards (see Wolfgang, Thornberry, and Figlio 1987).

The Gluecks collected the most extensive information during the first wave of data collection. For instance, information was gathered on a wide range of biological, psychological, and social factors for all 1,000 subjects age ten to seventeen. In the follow-up interviews at age twenty-five and thirty-two, the Gluecks collected data primarily on social factors including criminal history information. Overall, data are available with regard to the following items: social, psychological, and biological factors relating to crime—parental criminality, family mobility, economic status, family structure, patterns of parental supervision and discipline, peer relationships, school, work, and leisure time activities, companionship, participation in civic affairs; the initiation of criminal/deviant behavior as measured by official records, self-reports, parental, and teacher reports, including information on both delinquent and early conduct disorder; official criminal justice interventions (e.g., all arrests, convictions, and dispositions including actual time served) from the first official criminal justice contact to age thirty-two for all 880 subjects who were followed up.

These data were gathered through detailed investigations by the Gluecks' research team that included interviews with the subjects themselves and their families, employers, schoolteachers, neighbors, and criminal justice/social welfare officials. This research team also conducted a field investigation by meticulously culling information from records of both public and private agencies that had any involvement with the family. Therefore, the Gluecks' strategy of data collection focused on multiple sources of information that were independently derived. The basic Glueck data represent the comparison, reconciliation, and integration of these multiple sources of data (see Vaillant 1983: 245–46).

Overall, data collections for the follow-up periods were conducted between 1949 and 1965. On average, the original subjects were followed for eighteen years—from age fourteen to age thirty-two. In the first follow-up of the original subjects in the *UJD* study, field investigations were initiated as each subject approached his twenty-fifth birthday. The second wave interview covered the period from age seventeen to twenty-five and the Gluecks' research team utilized on average twelve sources of information for the original delinquents and nine sources for the original controls (Glueck and Glueck 1968: 47). It is not surprising that additional sources of information were available for the delinquent subjects given that these subjects and their families were more likely to have more contact with various social agencies in comparison with the original control group subjects. Similarly, in the second follow-up, field investigations were initiated as each subject approached their thirty-second birthday. The third wave interview covered the period from age twenty-five to thirty-two. For this interview, the Gluecks' research team utilized an average of nine sources of information for the original delinquents and seven sources for the original controls (Glueck and Glueck 1968: 47).

Despite this rich body of longitudinal data, the Gluecks' main analyses were cross-sectional (1950). Indeed, their attention to the follow-up data was sparse and the resulting book (Glueck and Glueck 1968) was only a descriptive overview of the delinquent and nondelinquent samples. Fortunately, the Gluecks' coded data and complete raw interview records were stored in the basement of the Harvard Law School Library. A major aspect of our project has been devoted to coding and computerizing the full longitudinal data set. Our reconstruction and validation of these data involve numerous steps that we report in detail elsewhere (Laub, Sampson, and Kiger 1990; Sampson and Laub 1990, 1993).

Construction of Key Variables

Measures of Childhood Antisocial Behavior

In the analysis that follows we use three measures of antisocial behavior during childhood and adolescence. The first is official delinquency status as determined by the sampling design of the Glueck study. As mentioned above, the Gluecks selected 500 white males who were incarcerated in juvenile correctional facilities because of persistent delinquency at the time of the study, and a control group of 500 nondelinquents who were students in the Boston public schools. The nondelinquents had no official record of involvement in crime and delinquency at the time they were selected for the study.[1]

The second measure is a composite measure of self, parent, and teacher reports of delinquency and other misconduct (ranging from zero to thirty acts) for each subject in the study. The total report variable used in the cross-tabular analysis is a summary measure which we trichotomized into three groupings of involvement in delinquency. This measure captures both unofficial delinquency as well as incidents known to the police (for more details see Laub, Sampson, and Kiger 1990).

The third measure—temper tantrums—is a specific item taken from our composite measure of self, parent, and teacher reports of delinquency and other antisocial behavior. This measure reflects the extent to which a child engaged in violent temper tantrums on a frequent basis while growing up. The Gluecks collected data on habitual tantrums, namely, when tantrums were "the predominant mode of response" by the child to difficult situations growing up (Glueck and Glueck 1950: 152). We selected this measure because it has been used in prior research on continuity in behavior over the life course (see Caspi, Elder, and Bem 1987).

Measures of Adult Behavior

In our analysis of childhood effects on adult behavior outcomes, we use several indicators of adult crime, deviance, and problematic adjustment to work, military, and family relations.[2]

Crime and deviance. From the detailed criminal history information collected by the Gluecks' research team, we created a variable assessing whether or not the subject had an official arrest during the follow-up periods (seventeen to twenty-five and twenty-five to thirty-two). Using information derived from interviews conducted by the Gluecks' research team at each wave, we also created a measure of specific deviance focusing on excessive use of alcohol and/or drugs as well as a composite measure of general deviance including frequent involvement in gambling and engaging in illicit sexual behavior (e.g., use of prostitutes).

Military service. Given the time period during which the Glueck study was conducted, a majority of the Glueck men served in some branch of the military (67 percent overall). Data were collected on the military experience for each of these subjects during the Wave 2 investigation (age twenty-five). The sources of information that were used included records from the specific branch of military service in question (e.g., army or navy), Selective Service, State Adjutant General, Veterans Administration, and Red Cross, in conjunction with interviews with the subject himself.

In this context, we are especially interested in the criminal/deviant behavior (e.g., desertion, AWOL, theft, etc.) of the men while serving in the military. Our dichotomous measure charge captures illegal conduct that came to the attention of military authorities during military service.

We also have available a measure of *frequent offending* (more than one official charge) and *serious offending* (felonies) while serving in the military. In addition, we were also able to assess other important outcomes with respect to military service, namely, rank achieved and type of discharge.

School, work, and family Life. These measures cover a variety of dimensions of school, work, and family life and range from single objective indicators (e.g., divorce) to composite measures of qualitative experiences (e.g., attachment to spouse).

1. *Educational Attainment and Commitment.* Our measure of educational attainment was collected during the Wave 2 interview and was derived from home interviews as well as record checks. From this information we created a variable that allowed us to assess the proportion of high school graduates among the Glueck men.

The measures we are calling "commitment" are available at both Waves 2 and 3. At Time 2, commitment is a composite variable combining three different measures—work, educational, and economic ambitions. Work ambitions assess the desire for professional advancement (e.g., to become a professional man) by the subject. Educational ambition measures the extent of educational aspirations (either professional or vocational) while the measure of economic ambitions focuses on material aspirations among the men (e.g., a more adequate income). Those subjects with low commitment expressed no particular work, educational, or economic ambition. Moreover, these individuals had not thought about further schooling or had vague educational ambitions. In sharp contrast, subjects with high commitment expressed strong desire for further schooling, either academic, vocational, or professional. These individuals were also eager to better themselves and their families (e.g., to become a professional, gain more income, etc.).

At Time 3, commitment is a composite variable combining two different measures—work ambitions and ambitions generally. Work ambition captures efforts to improve occupational status over the seven year follow-up period (age twenty-five to thirty-two). These efforts focus on behaviors beyond those generally associated with working hard or joining a union, such as obtaining additional on-the-job training, registering for courses, or taking civil service exams. Note that this measure of work ambitions is different from the measure used at Time 2 and is in fact a better indicator of work ambition. The second component of

TABLE 13.1
Relationships between Delinquent and Antisocial Behavior in Childhood (up to mean age of 14) and Later Adult Crime and Deviance (ages 17–32)*

	Childhood Antisocial Behavior:						
	Official Delinquency[a]		Self-Parent-Teacher-Reported Delinquency			Early Tantrums	
	No	Yes	Low (0-3)	Medium (4-13)	High (14-30)	No	Yes
Adult Crime and Deviance:							
% Arrested 17-25	20	76	15	48	80	41	72
% Arrested 25-32	14	61	10	36	66	32	58
% Excessive alcohol/ drug use 17-25	11	41	7	23	47	22	37
% Excessive alcohol/ drug use 25-32	9	35	6	19	40	19	31
% General deviance 17-25	5	25	5	15	24	11	29
% General deviance 25-32	6	30	5	18	30	14	33

Note: All relationships are significant at $p < .05$.
[a] Official delinquency status matched case-by-case on age, IQ, ethnicity, and neighborhood SES.
*Reprinted from Sampson and Laub (1993) by permission of Harvard University Press.

commitment at Time 3 is a measure of the subject's ambitiousness generally. The Gluecks did not collect information with respect to specific ambitions (e.g., educational, economic) at the Time 3 interview.

2. *Economic Dependency and Job Stability.* The variable economic dependency measures the extent to which the subject was dependent on outside economic aid (e.g., welfare). The data for economic dependency at Wave 2 cover the last five years—age twenty to twenty-five and at Wave 3 cover the last seven years—age twenty-five to thirty-two.

Job stability is a composite scale of three separate measures—employment status, length of job, and work habits—collected at Time 2 and Time 3. Specifically, using interview data on employment patterns, we created a variable that measures whether or not the subject was employed at the

TABLE 13.2
Relationships between Delinquent and Antisocial Behavior in Childhood (up to mean age of 14) and Later Adult Behavior in the Military (ages 18–25)*

	Childhood Antisocial Behavior						
	Official Delinquency[a]		Self-Parent-Teacher-Reported Delinquency			Early Tantrums	
	No	Yes	Low (0-3)	Medium (4-13)	High (14-30)	No	Yes
Adult Military Behavior:							
% Charged	20	64	18	35	70	33	62
% Frequent offender	4	29	3	12	33	12	25
% Serious offender	4	32	3	12	38	13	30
% Dishonorable discharge	4	30	2	12	34	12	29
% Rank of corporal or higher	64	36	67	46	37	54	41

Note: All relationships are significant at p < .05.
[a] Official delinquency status matched case-by-case on age, IQ, ethnicity, and neighborhood SES.
* Reprinted from Sampson and Laub (1993) by permission of Harvard University Press.

time of the interview. We were also able to assess the stability of the employment patterns of the Glueck men by examining data collected on the length of time employed on present or most recent job. This variable is measured as an eight-point scale ranging from less than three months to forty-eight months or more. Finally, we included a variable that measured work habits on a three-point scale. Individuals were classified as having poor work habits if they were unreliable in the work setting or if they lacked a work ambition or failed to give any effort on the job. Fair work habits were characterized by a generally good job performance except for periodic absences from work or periods of unemployment as chosen by the subject. Finally, good work habits were evidenced by reliable performance on the job that was noted by the employer as well as instances in which the subject was considered an asset to the organization. The data for job stability at Wave 2 cover the last five years—age twenty to twenty-five—and at Wave 3 cover the last seven years—age twenty-five to thirty-two. For the cross-tabular analysis, we trichotomized job stability into three equal proportionate groupings—low, medium, and high job stability.

3. *Divorce and Attachment to Spouse.* The subject's civil condition on the date of inquiry was also assessed and from this information we created a measure that allowed us to determine those men divorced/separated from their wives at each interview.

We also constructed a measure of attachment to spouse. At Time 2, this variable is a composite measure derived from interview data describing the general conjugal relationship between the subject and his spouse during the follow-up period, plus the subject's attitude toward marital responsibility. Those subjects who were weakly attached to their spouse displayed some signs of incompatibility as evidenced by a brief period of separation or were already divorced, separated, or had deserted the marriage. Moreover, these individuals were also neglectful of marital responsibilities (financial as well as emotional responsibilities). In contrast, those subjects who were strongly attached displayed close, warm feelings toward their wife or were compatible on the whole in a generally constructive relationship. In addition, these individuals assumed marital responsibilities toward their spouse as well as their children.

At Time 3, attachment to spouse is a composite measure derived from interview data describing the general conjugal relationship between the subject and his spouse during the follow-up period plus a measure of cohesiveness of the family unit. Conjugal relations at Time 3 is measured identically to the Time 2 measure described above. Family cohesiveness assesses the extent to which the family unit was characterized by an integration of interests, cooperativeness, and overall affection for each other. Unfortunately, this measure was not available at the Time 2 interview, so as a substitute we used marital responsibility which to some extent captures an aspect of family cohesiveness. For the cross-tabular analysis, we dichotomized attachment to spouse into two equal groupings—weak and strong attachments.

Results

The data in table 13.1 display the results of our examination of the continuity between delinquency and antisocial behavior in childhood and later adult crime and deviance. The pattern is quite remarkable—all relationships are statistically significant ($p < .05$)[3] in the direction

TABLE 13.3
Relationships between Delinquent and Antisocial Behavior in Childhood (up to mean age of 14) and Later Adult Outcomes Relating to School, Work, and Family (ages 17–32)*

| | Childhood Antisocial Behavior | | | | | |
| | Official Delinquency[a] | | Self-Parent-Teacher- Reported Delinquency | | | Early Tantrums |
	No	Yes	Low (0-3)	Medium (4-13)	High (14-30)	No	Yes
Adult School, Work, and Family Outcomes:							
% High school graduate	34	2	39	13	2	22	3
% Weak occupational commitment 17-25	39	74	35	55	77	51	71
% Weak occupational commitment 25-32	25	59	20	40	64	36	61
% Economically dependent 17-25	6	29	5	17	31	14	29
% Economically dependent 25-32	11	39	8	21	44	19	43
% Low job stability 17-25	19	47	16	32	51	27	50
% Low job stability 25-32	16	50	12	29	56	27	51
% Divorced/separated 17-25	5	22	5	9	26	12	21
% Divorced/separated 25-32	12	27	10	15	33	16	32
% Weak attachment to spouse 17-25	14	49	12	26	56	26	54
% Weak attachment to spouse 25-32	22	52	18	35	57	31	56

Note: All relationships are significant at $p < .05$.
[a] Official delinquency status matched case-by-case on age, IQ, ethnicity, and neighborhood SES.
* Reprinted from Sampson and Laub (1993) by permission of Harvard University Press.

predicted, and substantively large. Arrests as an adult during both periods are three to four times greater among those delinquent in childhood. Thus, continuity in official criminal behavior is found over an eighteen-year period. Furthermore, similar patterns appear for reports of excessive drinking and general deviance—on average, delinquents were four times more likely than nondelinquents to later abuse alcohol and engage in deviance.

These results are also replicated with the unofficial (i.e., parent, teacher, self) reports of delinquency and early temper tantrums. In all cases, the relationships are monotonic across categories of unofficial delinquency and in some cases even stronger. Youth reported to have high rates of delinquency in adolescence were more than five times as likely to be arrested at seventeen to twenty-five than those with low reported rates of juvenile misbehavior, and almost seven times more likely to be arrested in young adulthood (twenty-five to thirty-two). Even temper tantrums in childhood exhibit strong relationships with adult criminality, although to a lesser extent than official and unofficial delinquency. The same basic findings hold for reports of excessive drinking/drug use and for our measure of general deviance. In any event, regardless of which measure of delinquent/antisocial behavior in childhood is used, childhood misbehavior has a substantively powerful relationship with adult crime and deviance.

Table 13.2 presents data on the behavior of the Glueck men while in the military. We believe the military is a particularly important area because it represents a relatively homogeneous social environment in which to explore differences in behavior. Also, World War II provided full employment for delinquents and nondelinquents alike and thus represents "a natural experiment" of the unemployment-crime hypothesis (Gottfredson and Hirschi, 1990: 164). With respect to criminal behavior, over 60 percent of the official delinquents were subsequently charged while in the military compared to only 20 percent of the controls. The pattern emerges even more strongly when we examine frequency and seriousness of offending in the military—delinquent youth faced a sevenfold greater risk of frequent/serious offending compared to nondelinquents. This general pattern is also confirmed when unofficial delinquency is used as the measure of childhood misbehavior. For instance, 70 percent of those with reports of high unofficial offending in childhood were charged in the military, while only 18 percent of those with low unofficial offending reports were so charged. Finally, those subjects that engaged in severe temper tantrums as a child were more than twice as likely to be charged in the military.

Overall, those who had been delinquent in childhood were more likely to desert or be absent without leave compared with their nondelinquent counterparts. As the Gluecks themselves noted, "the nature of the offenses with which the men were charged suggests that the same difficulty in adjusting satisfactorily to the discipline of parents and teachers and the demands of behavioral codes ... persisted in the former juvenile delinquents when they were faced with the demands of adult life" (Glueck and Glueck 1968: 136–37).

Not surprisingly, the original delinquents were more likely to have dishonorable discharges from the military than those originally nondelinquent (30 percent vs. 4 percent, respectively). Relatedly, those with delinquency in their childhood were far less likely to achieve the rank of corporal or higher in the army (or the equivalent rank of seaman first class or higher while in the navy) compared with their nondelinquent counterparts (36 percent vs. 64 percent, respectively). Notably, both of these patterns held for unofficial delinquency as well as temper tantrums. In sum, those subjects with delinquency in their background did not fare as well in the military as their nondelinquent counterparts. Again, regardless of the particular measure of childhood misbehavior used, the continuity of childhood misbehavior to adulthood emerges even while under military service.

The most intriguing long-term consequences of child misbehavior are found in a wide range of later adult domains not typically considered by criminologists. Indeed, table 13.3 displays data for several adult behaviors spanning educational, economic employment, and family domains in an effort to illustrate the generality of the link between childhood delinquency and adult behavior. The Glueck data show that delinquents (official *and* unofficial) were much less likely than nondelinquents to finish high school by age twenty-five. The same is true for those that engaged in temper tantrums as a child. With respect to ambitions and aspirations (i.e., commitment), we find that the vast majority of the boys who were delinquent in childhood were more likely to display weak educational, economic, and professional aspirations in their attitudes and behavior. In contrast, 39 percent of the official nondelinquents expressed weak commitment at seventeen to twenty-five and 25 percent indicated the same at twenty-five to thirty-two.

Similarly, delinquency in childhood is related to economic dependency (e.g., welfare) in young adulthood (seventeen to twenty-five) and later adulthood (twenty-five to thirty-two). Furthermore, across all three measures of childhood misbehavior, delinquent boys were far more likely than nondelinquents to have a history of unstable employment in later adulthood. For instance, for those delinquent in childhood, about half at each wave experienced job instability as an adult.

In terms of family life as an adult, delinquents were more than three to five times more likely to get divorced or separated from their spouses. A similar pattern emerges when using measures of total reported misbehavior as well as early tantrums. We find that more than half of those delinquent (official and unofficial) in childhood had weak attachment to their spouses. Even early tantrums in childhood was related to weak attachment to spouse as an adult (54 percent versus 26 percent at Time 2 and 56 percent versus 31 percent at Time 3).

Conclusions

Overall, we have found that delinquent behavior in childhood has significant and very substantial relationships with a wide range of adult criminal and deviant behaviors, including charges initiated by military personnel, interview-based reports of involvement in deviance and excessive drinking, and arrest by police. Perhaps more important, the same childhood antisocial behaviors are predictive of educational, economic, employment, and family status up to *eighteen* years later. These results hold regardless of the particular measure of delinquency used, and because of the matched design of the Gluecks' study cannot be explained away in terms of the original differences between delinquents and nondelinquents in age, IQ, neighborhood SES, and ethnicity—variables often associated with stratification outcomes. Therefore, the original delinquents and nondelinquents in the Gluecks' study may be said to exhibit behavioral consistency well into adulthood (see also Glueck and Glueck 1968).

As alluded to above, our findings confirm other research (e.g., Robins 1966; Farrington 1989; Patterson, DeBaryshe, and Ramsey 1989) and suggest the existence of an underlying theoretical construct that reflects a general tendency toward criminality and other troublesome behavior. Robins and Ratcliff, for example, have argued that "there exists a single syndrome made up of a broad variety of antisocial behaviors arising in childhood and continuing into adulthood" (1980: 248). Similarly, Caspi, Elder, and Bem have contended that maladaptive behaviors are "found in interactional styles that are sustained both by the progressive accumulation of their own consequences (cumulative continuity) and by evoking maintaining responses from others during reciprocal social interaction (interactional continuity)" (1987: 313).

Such findings undergird a general theory of crime recently developed by Gottfredson and Hirschi. Specifically, Gottfredson and Hirschi (1990) suggest that "low self-control" can account for the positive correlations within specific crime types as well as the relationships between crime and noncriminal acts (e.g., accidents, alcohol use). They argue that the theory "implies that no specific act, type of crime, or form of deviance is uniquely required by the absence of self-control" (1990: 91). Gottfredson and Hirschi further contend that "Because both crime and analogous behaviors stem from low self-control (that is, both are manifestations of low self-control), they will all be engaged in at a relatively high rate by people with low self-control" (1990: 91). Although the specific ideas of the Gottfredson and Hirschi theory await empirical testing, our results in this chapter are highly supportive of the generality of crime, deviance, and other troublesome behaviors.

At the same time, others have argued that the continuity in behavior may be partially "illusory" (Farrington 1986: 373) and the result of a labeling process that begins early in childhood (Hagan and Palloni 1990). Becker in particular has developed the idea of a *deviant career*—a stable pattern of deviant behavior that is an outcome of the labeling process (Orcutt 1983: 22). Although an interesting idea, our measures of childhood misbehavior are derived from both official *and* unofficial sources (i.e., parent, teacher, and self-reports) and yet show the same results. The labeling hypothesis thus seems unlikely to be a persuasive explanation for our findings.

Using the analyses presented in this chapter as a springboard, we have identified three substantive areas as promising for future research consideration. The first concerns empirical testing of the fundamental ideas underlying a general theory of crime or deviance (e.g., the generality of deviance, low self-control, antisocial personality) with a variety of data sets from different historical periods (see Osgood et al. 1988 for a recent example of such a study).

The second area addresses the question of what accounts for differences in childhood behavior. It is commonplace to view stability of behavior patterns as indicative of biological and/or psychological processes (see especially Wilson and Herrnstein 1985). However, we believe that sociological variables (e.g., family variables) provide important insight in the area of childhood differences (see also Laub and Sampson 1988; Gottfredson and Hirschi 1990).

The third research area concerns the factors in adulthood that may modify the continuities in behavior over the life course. In other words, what are the escape routes that can overcome the effects of childhood misbehavior? Several areas have been suggested as important (e.g., marital attachment, job stability) in modifying life course pathways (Sampson and Laub 1993). The flip side of stability is change, and issues concerning change in behavior as an adult demand research attention.

In sum, it is clear that those who study crime can no longer ignore the connections between early childhood behavior and later behavior as an adult. Indeed, the finding that childhood delinquency is substantially related to criminal outcomes as an adult should give pause even to the most ardent "situational" crime theorist. Moreover, the ramifications of childhood behavior across a variety of adult noncrime domains suggests that we broaden our focus to include a range of troublesome behaviors in adulthood.

The data utilized in this study are derived from the Sheldon and Eleanor Glueck study materials of the Harvard Law School Library, which are currently on long-term loan to the Henry A. Murray Research Center of Radcliffe College. This project was supported in part by a grant from the National Institute of Justice (89–IJ–CX–0036). The support of the Henry A. Murray Research Center and Erin Phelps is also gratefully acknowledged, as is the research assistance of Kenna Davis and Sandra Gauvreau.

Notes

1. As Long and Vaillant (1984) state, "the bias resulting from selection for nondelin-quency at age 14 is ... difficult to evaluate. Certainly the men were different from the Boston youth remanded to reform school, but compared with national averages the men in this study did *not* represent a particularly law-abiding group" (345). In fact, although clearly not a random selection, the samples appear to be representative of the populations of persistent official delinquents and generally nondelinquent youth in Boston schools at the time. For more details see Vaillant (1983: 245–47) who has utilized the control group sample of the Gluecks' study in his highly regarded study of alcoholism.
2. Descriptive information on the following measures is available in Glueck and Glueck (1968: 71–141).
3. Tests of statistical significance are not technically appropriate given the Gluecks' research design. Therefore, throughout our discussion, we place greater emphasis on the magnitude of the relationships (see also Laub and Sampson 1988: 361).

References

Caspi, Avshalom. 1987. "Personality in the Life Course." *Journal of Personality and Social Psychology* 53: 1203–13.

Caspi, Avshalom, Glen H. Elder, Jr., and Daryl J. Bem. 1987. "Moving Against the World: Life-Course Patterns of Explosive Children." *Developmental Psychology* 23, 308-13.

Farrington, David P. 1986. "Stepping Stones to Adult Criminal Careers." In *Development of Antisocial and Prosocial Behavior*, ed. Dan Olweus, Jack Block, and Marian Radke-Yarrow, 359-84. New York: Academic Press.

_____. 1989. "Later Adult Outcomes of Offenders and Nonoffenders." In *Children at Risk: Assessment, Longitudinal Research, and Intervention*, ed. Michael Brambring, Friedrich Losel, and Helmut Skowronek, 220-44. New York: Walter de Gruyter.

Glueck, Sheldon, and Eleanor Glueck. 1930. *Five Hundred Criminal Careers*. New York: Alfred A. Knopf.

_____. 1950. *Unraveling Juvenile Delinquency*. New York: Commonwealth Fund.

_____. 1968. *Delinquents and Nondelinquents in Perspective*. Cambridge: Harvard University Press.

Gottfredson, Michael R., and Travis Hirschi. 1990. *A General Theory of Crime*. Stanford, CA: Stanford University Press.

Hagan, John, and Alberto Palloni. 1990. "The Social Reproduction of a Criminal Class in Working-Class London, circa 1950-1980." *American Journal of Sociology* 96: 265-99.

Huesmann, L. Rowell, Leonard D. Eron, Monroe M. Lefkowitz, and Leopold O. Walder. 1984. "Stability of Aggression Over Time and Generations." *Developmental Psychology* 20: 1120-34.

Laub, John J., and Robert J. Sampson. 1988. "Unraveling Families and Delinquency: A Reanalysis of the Gluecks' Data." *Criminology* 26: 355-80.

Laub, John H., Robert J. Sampson, and Kenna Kiger. 1990. "Assessing the Potential of Secondary Data Analysis: A New Look at the Gluecks' *Unraveling Juvenile Delinquency* Data." In *Measurement Issues in Criminology*, ed. Kimberly Kempf, 241-57. New York: Springer-Verlag.

Loeber, Rolf. 1982. "The Stability of Antisocial Child Behavior: A Review." *Child Development* 53: 1431-46.

Long, Jancis V.F., and George E. Vaillant. 1984. "Natural History of Male Psychological Health, XI: Escape from the Underclass." *American Journal of Psychiatry* 141: 341-46.

Olweus, Dan. 1979. "Stability of Aggressive Reaction Patterns in Males: A Review." *Psychological Bulletin* 86: 852-75.

Orcutt, James D. 1983. *Analyzing Deviance*. Chicago, IL: The Dorsey Press.

Osgood, D. Wayne, Lloyd D. Johnston, Patrick M. O'Malley, and Jerald G. Bachman. 1988. "The Generality of Deviance in Late Adolescence and Early Adulthood." *American Sociological Review* 53: 81-93.

Patterson, Gerald, Barbara D. DeBaryshe, and Elizabeth Ramsey. 1989. "A Developmental Perspective on Antisocial Behavior." *American Psychologist* 44: 329-35.

Robins, Lee. 1966. *Deviant Children Grown Up*. Baltimore: Williams and Wilkins.

_____. 1978. "Sturdy Childhood Predictors of Adult Antisocial Behavior: Replications from Longitudinal Studies." *Psychological Medicine* 8:611-22.

Robins, Lee and Kathryn Strother Ratcliff. 1980. "Childhood Conduct Disorders and Later Arrest." In *The Social Consequences of Psychiatric Illness*, ed. Lee Robins, Paula J. Clayton, and John K. Wing, 248-63. New York: Brunner/Mazel.

Sampson, Robert J. 1986. "Effects of Socioeconomic Context on Official Reaction to Juvenile Delinquency." *American Sociological Review* 51: 876-85.

Sampson, Robert J., and John H. Laub. 1990. "Crime and Deviance Over the Life Course: The Salience of Adult Social Bonds." *American Sociological Review* 55: 609-27.

_____. 1993. *Crime In The Making: Pathways and Turning Points Through Life.* Cambridge, MA: Harvard University Press.

Vaillant, George E. 1983. *The Natural History of Alcoholism.* Cambridge, MA: Harvard University Press.

West, Donald, and David Farrington. 1977. *The Delinquent Way of Life.* London: Heinemann.

Wilson, James Q., and Richard Herrnstein. 1985. *Crime and Human Nature.* New York: Simon and Schuster.

Wolfgang, Marvin, Terence Thornberry, and Robert Figlio. 1987. *From Boy to Man: From Delinquency to Crime.* Chicago: University of Chicago Press.

14

Substantive Positivism and the Idea of Crime

Travis Hirschi and Michael R. Gottfredson

When the idea of science prevailed over the tradition of rationalism in the nineteenth century, those espousing the new scientific outlook took destruction of prevailing conceptual schemes as one of their first tasks. Emile Durkheim said "all preconceptions must be eradicated" (1895: 31), and the famous proponent of positivistic criminology Enrico Ferri was equally explicit in his disdain for a priori conceptualization: "For us, the experimental (i.e., inductive) method is the key to all knowledge; for them everything derives from logical deductions and traditional opinion. For them, facts should give place to syllogisms; for us, the fact governs and no reasoning can occur without starting with facts" (Sellin 1973:79).

The inductivism that characterized early positivism was a self-conscious effort to avoid entrapment by the rationalist schemes that had dominated social thought. The positivists' emphasis on causation can be seen in the same light. Causes, they believed, operate at the level of measurable variables. Therefore, as long as one remained interested in causation, one could avoid the sterile terminological disputes that previously marked the study of human behavior. To be scientific, then, was to avoid abstract ideas and deductive explanatory schemes.

Early positivists thus faced the myriad phenomena of nature without ideas to tie them together or reduce their complexity, but were at the same time opposed to the invention of ideas for this purpose. The solution to this otherwise impossible situation was to assume that nature has its own categories, and that phenomena within them can be assumed to respond

From *Rationality and Society*, 4 (1990): 412–28. Copyright 1990, Sage Publications. Reprinted by permission.

to the same causal forces. Thus nature has social facts that can be explained by social causes; biological facts that can be explained by biological causes; and economic facts that can be explained by economic causes.

The idea of natural categories governed by distinct causal laws led to the idea of disciplines. At the same time, it gave these disciplines the status of "natural" sciences, sciences with a clear domain and unique modes of research and explanation.

Although the positivists thought they were starting from scratch, the two organizing principles they adopted turned out to contain significant implications for the substantive conceptual schemes they would develop. The principle of analytic induction, apparently nothing more than a reasonable attempt to identify causally homogeneous clusters of phenomena, turned out to deny the generality of the restraint theories of earlier periods. And the principle of causation, apparently nothing more than the reasonable assumption that phenomena are produced or determined by antecedent conditions, turned out to deny the choice or free will element in restraint theories. From the beginning, then, and contrary to its own program of inductive open-mindedness, positivism aligned itself with theories of crime marked by the assumption of positive and specific causation of particular criminal acts.[1]

Now that the idea of causal homogeneity has directed research for almost a hundred years, it seems to us time to assess its consistency with the findings it has produced. We argue here that modern disciplinary positivism cannot account for generally accepted facts about crime produced by its own methods; that, on the contrary, concepts and explanatory principles abandoned by substantive positivism provide a better description and explanation of crime than any model consistent with the conceptual paradigms of the disciplines. We begin by sketching briefly an outline of a discipline-free, choice or restraint theory of crime. Using examples from each of the disciplines, we assess the comparative adequacy of these rival perspectives.

The Idea of Crime

In practice, substantive positivism focuses on the causes of phenomena, on independent variables, and has little or nothing to say directly about the nature of its dependent variables. The reason for this silence is that in positivism the connection between independent and dependent variables is statistical, unmediated by human purpose. Or, as

Coleman has noted, "statistical association between variables has largely replaced meaningful connection between events as the basic tool of description and analysis. The 'meaningful connection' was ordinarily provided by the intentions or purposes of an actor or combination of actors" (Coleman 1986:1327–28). Thus, many sociologists are concerned with "social class," a concern that leads them to interest in the correlation between crime and status, income, success, culture, and other class-related social variables. Biologists are concerned with genetics. They are thus interested in inherited predispositions to antisocial behavior, which leads to concern for the effects of temperament, body build, hormones, conditionability, or some other presumably heritable characteristic on crime. Psychologists concerned with individual differences ask whether criminals differ from noncriminals on such personality dimensions as aggressiveness, psychopathy, and neuroticism.

Restraint theories (e.g., Hirschi 1969; Gottfredson and Hirschi 1990; Cohen and Felson 1979; Cornish and Clarke 1986; Cook 1986; Reuter 1983), in contrast, start with the dependent variable, with the phenomenon they wish to explain. They therefore look directly at crime, at its costs and benefits for people, making distant antecedents (e.g., class, heritable traits, personality) and distant consequences (e.g., prison) equal and equally problematic as potential causes. This strategy puts at risk the causal variables central to the major disciplines, which may after all turn out to be irrelevant to the judgments of the actor.

In restraint theory, human action is oriented to the pursuit of pleasure and the avoidance of pain. In some situations, it is faster or easier (more efficient) to gain pleasure or avoid pain by employing force or fraud. Because force and fraud by definition conflict with the interests of others, their uses are opposed by "society" and denoted "crimes." In other situations, efficient pursuit of short-term pleasure entails potential long-term physical or social sanctions that are not necessarily supported by the state. Such acts include rudeness to others, sexual promiscuity, driving too fast, skiing with abandon, eating rich food, consuming drugs, and skipping school. In restraint or choice theory, crimes and analogous pleasure-producing activities are distinguished among themselves only by the source of the long-term sanctions they evoke (Bentham 1789). In restraint theory, crimes and other deviant activities follow not from a base or antisocial human nature, but from the natural tendency to use efficient means in pursuit of one's own interests.

Such an analysis of crime focuses attention directly on the mechanisms producing restraint. It allows inferences about personal and situational characteristics conducive to crime. A full restraint theory of crime would outline the mechanisms causing individuals to differ in the restraints on their behavior (whether they be antecedent or consequent to crime). Our own version (Gottfredson and Hirschi 1990), focuses on individual differences in self-control produced early in life by family child-rearing practices. It notes that such differences are relatively stable over the life course, and that once established, self-control is highly resistant to change. Those lacking self-control are not oriented toward status, success, income, or culture. They are likely to pursue short-term gratification in a direct way without concern for long-term consequences such as the disapproval of family or friends, the loss of educational possibilities or occupational prospects, or the penalties of the criminal justice system. Restraint theories like ours are thus extremely general, predicting differential involvement in a wide variety of activities connected only by their provision of immediate benefits and potential long-term costs. In other words, those with a tendency to commit criminal or analogous acts are less likely to feel the restraining influence of the social and legal consequences of their behavior.

Given this conceptualization of the actor, restraint or choice theories are able to describe properties of the environment or situation that affect the likelihood of crime because they limit or enable the pursuit of short-term pleasures. (Given the short-term orientation of the actor, almost any obstacle will reduce the likelihood of crime.) Thus restraint theories have two parts: On the one hand, they describe the characteristics of people that make crime more likely or unlikely—for example, level of self-control; on the other hand, they describe the characteristics of situations that restrain those not restrained by prior training.

The differences between such perspectives and the perspectives of substantive positivism can now be provisionally identified: (1) The restraint perspective does not start from the presuppositions of any discipline about the causes of behavior; (2) the restraint perspective does not accept the notion that the causes of a phenomenon require that it occur—that is, it rejects the notion that persons committing criminal acts are compelled to do so by prior events and forces over which they have little or no control; (3) the restraint perspective assumes that characteristics of acts are relevant to their causation; (4) the restraint perspective assumes that all criminal acts and many noncriminal acts may be homogeneous with respect to causation and explanation (that there is not one explanation for drug use and a different explanation for homicide); (5) the restraint perspective assumes that motivation to crime is given in the nature of criminal acts themselves, and therefore need not enter a theory of crime causation.

All of these principles are contrary to the observed practices of disciplinary positivism. They thus allow systematic comparison of the empirical adequacy of the two paradigms.

1. *The disciplinary frame of reference*. The organizational principle of substantive positivism is the discipline, a collection of possible causes of behavior around a particular unit or level of analysis. All disciplines share the view that their causal variables are in the absence of specific evidence to the contrary important and relevant to all topics. Given that disciplines are not substantive theories, their typical strategy is to claim substantive areas by default, proceeding first to show that other disciplines are inadequate to the task.

For example, sociology begins with the idea that crime is a social phenomenon. Sellin summarizes the argument: "Everything the criminal law of any state prohibits today it will not prohibit at a given future time....The variability in the definition of crime...is too familiar to the social scientist to require any demonstration" (1938:23, cited by Kornhauser 1978: 182). Put another way: given the social nature of crime, it cannot be a general phenomenon, and nonsocial explanations are impossible; social phenomena must have social causes (Durkheim, 1895:104). Or, as Sutherland and Cressey (1978:118) disdainfully note: "Although crime and criminality are by definition social phenomena, people have for centuries entertained the notion that they are products of nonsocial causes."

The restraint perspective is contrary to the assumptions of sociological positivism on these points. According to the restraint perspective, the use of force and fraud in the pursuit of self-interest is everywhere condemned. What varies from society to society, at least to a small degree, is what is regarded as self-interest. (Agreeing with one's competitor about prices is a crime in some systems and not in others; entrepreneurialism is a crime in some systems and not others.) Criminal behavior is in fact asocial or even antisocial behavior. The restraint perspective accepts the possibility of social causes of crime, but cannot give such causes logical priority because it does not judge causes in terms of the discipline that owns them. Thus, for example, social institutions can obviously affect the constellation of restraints facing individuals, restraints that may influence the development of the propensity to commit criminal acts, or the opportunity to do so. Indeed, considerable evidence suggests that this is so (Hirschi 1969). Thus, for example, although individuals may on occasion use force and fraud to gain the esteem of others, such acts are by definition destructive of social life (and cannot therefore be encouraged by larger or more encompassing units) or they are by definition not crimes at all (e.g., heroic acts in battle). Indeed, to suggest as some social theories do that force and fraud are used only to gain the esteem of others is to deny the possibility of crime.

As another example, biology begins with the assumption that behavior is the product of the "interaction" of inherited tendencies and environmental influences. Given the broad acceptance within substantive positivism of the notion that crime is a social or environmentally caused phenomenon, modern biological positivism has been reluctant to go beyond the claim that biology is relevant to crime. To this end, biologists collect statistics on crimes committed by parents and their children (Mednick, Gabrielli, and Hutchings 1984). Were the correlation between the convictions of adopted children and those of their biological parents greater than the same correlation for their adoptive parents, the biologist would conclude that convictions may be inherited (see also Eysenck and Gudjonsson 1989; Wilson and Herrnstein 1985). Obviously, if this were the case, the sociologist's conclusion that such findings are impossible—given the social nature of crime—would require modification.

Another tendency of biological positivism is important in understanding its ultimate contribution to the study of crime. Researchers in this tradition move from one concrete dependent variable to another in serial fashion (a practice that stems from substantive positivism's emphasis on measurable variables). Thus the sample used by Mednick and his colleagues to study crime was originally collected to allow study of the genetic transmission of schizophrenia (Kety et al. 1968). It has also been used to study the genetic transmission of alcoholism (Goodwin 1977), and could be (if it has not been) used to study the genetic transmission of truancy, obesity, smoking, and accidents.

What escapes notice is that such samples could also document the "genetic transmission" of illegitimate parenthood, unstable job performance, broken marriages, poor child-rearing practices, and being late for school. Biological positivism shares with the behavioral sciences the view that the study of concrete acts is scientific whereas the study of abstract concepts is not. The tenet of positivism that acts have causes is translated via research practice into the idea that specific acts have specific causes. Because research identifies correlations of varying magnitude between specific causes and specific acts, and because disciplinary positivism has no way of accounting for such variety, it necessarily assumes that it is dealing with different phenomena.[2]

The restraint perspective would not a priori deny the possibility of biological causes of the tendency to commit criminal or equivalent acts. Nor would it a priori deny the possibility of multiple causal structures for various aspects of human behavior. However, in its terms, what must be inherited or acquired is differential susceptibility to the influence of antecedents or restraints. One cannot inherit a tendency to commit specific criminal acts, any more than one can inherit a tendency to wreck Oldsmobiles.[3]

2. *The thesis of determinism.* From the beginning, positivistic disciplines insisted on a particular, narrow interpretation of the thesis of determinism—the idea that human behavior is the product of causal forces over which individuals or collectivities have little control. The concept of restraint or choice was considered antipositivistic or antiscientific (e.g., Ferri 1897). Consequently, it was easy to reject restraint theories on the obvious ground that they were remnants of a prescientific era. (Restraints follow the behavior in question, and it was argued therefore cannot be its causes. Such naïveté was more common in the past than it is today.) Although this debate has moved to the background of scientific discourse (with rare exceptions, see e.g., Matza 1964), it has done so to the disadvantage of restraint theories.

There is no incompatibility between science and restraint, between causation and choice. The illusion of incompatibility is in fact a major device used by substantive positivism to foster the view that it alone travels under the banner of science. Consider the working definition of causation employed by social scientists as embodied in the controlled experiment: Causation is inferred when the treatment variable is correlated with the outcome and plausible alternative explanations have been ruled out in the design. Nothing more is required. The more theoretically sophisticated social sciences sometimes ask that the observed association be deducible from abstract theory before it is accepted as causal, but most sciences cannot afford a definition of causation that involves theory. Most, in other words, must be content with causes defined strictly at the level at which the relevant variables are measured.

Given a definition of causation restricted to the level of measurement, there is no way that causation can be said to be inconsistent with something like "restraint" or "choice," concepts remarkably more abstract than any possible measure of causes or effects. (The experimental decision-making literature shows in fact the easy compatibility of the idea that choices are determined.)

The idea that causation contradicts restraint or choice must therefore be part of the legacy of *substantive* positivism, with its emphasis on measurement, or of philosophical traditions interested in doing battle with certain conceptions of science. No restraint or choice theory of crime disputes the idea of causation. All grant that at one level it is possible to identify factors necessary and collectively sufficient for particular criminal acts; all grant that at another level it is possible to find factors reliably related to the decision to choose crime rather than some alternative behavior.

The alternative conceptualization of the causation-restraint issue adopted by substantive positivism is clearly contrary to the practice of science and to the results of research. According to this conceptualization, people in the clutches of the causes of crime must commit criminal acts consistent with the gravity of the causes operating on them, regardless of their own assessment of the consequences. No credible evidence supports this view. Offenders, even the most active offenders, are not offending most of the time. All offenders are easily dissuaded from crime—by a locked door, by an alternative opportunity for fun or amusement, by the threat of immediate sanction. And most offenders eventually desist from crime of their own accord (Hirschi and Gottfredson 1983; Gottfredson and Hirschi 1988).

As would be expected, theories crafted to be consistent with substantive views of causation suffer most at the hands of positivistic research. Perhaps the most egregious example is found in the psychologist's concept of "aggression," a term favored for its consistency with the idea that crime is positively caused behavior. On examination, operational definitions of aggression cannot be distinguished from operational definitions of crime and delinquency. As a result, aggression predicts such nonaggressive acts as truancy and drug use as well as it predicts violence (Gottfredson and Hirschi 1990; see also chap. 2 in this volume).

In sociology, it is traditional to "explain" the relation between aggression and crime by introducing a distinction between passivity and activity, or between attack and withdrawal. By this device Merton (1938) separated innovators (criminals) from retreatists (drug users); by the same device Parsons (1957) doubled his several "directions of deviant orientations." In economics, the same problem leads to a distinction between risk preferrers and risk avoiders (e.g., Ehrlich 1974). These solutions share a common problem: They are not consistent with the evidence. Offenders do not specialize or even tend to specialize in aggressive or nonaggressive ("retreatist") behavior. In fact, they do not tend to specialize in any particular type of crime.

Substantive disciplines create distinctions that embody their major premises. They then go about measuring and explaining them without regard to the fact that they also exist in other disciplines. It is hard to see what is gained by this practice.

3. *The idea that causes take explanatory precedence over effects.* In substantive positivism, the characteristics of acts are determined by their causes. Thus, positivists infer the nature of crime from the theory that explains it. If crime is caused by frustrated aspirations for material success, then crime must somehow reflect this goal and its frustration. Restraint theories, in contrast, begin with the dependent variable, seeking causes from an understanding of the nature of their effects. The contrast in result could not be more dramatic. While positive theories equate crime with success, status, high aspiration, altruistic motivation, exposure to pornography, or severe internal conflict, restraint theories see crime as producing immediate and ephemeral benefits and long-term costs. These two conceptions generate altogether different predictions about the character of criminal acts and the causes of crime. Two facts derived from contemporary research are particularly instructive in this regard: Throughout the twentieth century, evidence has accumulated that people who tend to lie, cheat, and steal also tend to hit other people; that the same people tend to drink, smoke, use drugs, wreck cars, desert their spouses, quit their jobs, and come late to class. At the same time, evidence has accumulated that differences in such tendencies across people are reasonably stable over the course of life (Glueck and Glueck 1950, 1968; Robins 1966; Wolfgang, Figlio, and Sellin 1972; Klein 1984; Farrington

1973; West and Farrington 1977; Olweus 1979; Hindelang, Hirschi, and Weis 1981; Loeber 1982; Osgood et al. 1988).

No credible evidence of specialization, escalation, or even patterning in criminal events exists, beyond that explicable through notions of opportunity. A stable "latent trait" of the individual must be implicated in the causation of all of these behaviors. Identification of this trait would require conceptualization of the commonalities in its many behavioral manifestations. But even without substantive identification, the stability and generality of the trait call into question disciplinary theories built on the idea that personality is irrelevant to crime (e.g., social learning, subcultural, and economic theories). Another example: It is easy to explain differences in the age distributions of specific crimes without resorting to separate etiological theories for each of them (Hirschi and Gottfredson 1983). The fact that some sociologists regard minor unexplained variation in these distributions as evidence for the importance of sociology (Greenberg 1985; Steffensmeier et al. 1989) is evidence that disciplinary positivism has difficulty facing the "findings" it produces.

The findings of *general differences* between people that are *stable over time* have, after all, been produced by positivistic social science, using its standard methods of data collection and analysis. Expressed in these very abstract terms, such findings appear perfectly compatible with the assumptions of substantive positivism. However, substantive positivism, it will be recalled, is interested in independent variables, while the facts described are features of a dependent variable. In the case of crime, generality by definition transcends disciplines and therefore has no one to recognize it, while stability contradicts the radical environmentalism of the favored disciplinary (sociological and economic) explanations of crime. Thus, substantive positivists continue to ignore or deny evidence of the redundancy of acts and the stability of differences and argue to continue the search for unique and temporary explanations for each item of deviant or criminal behavior. Researchers therefore study violence, smoking, drug use, and theft as though they had nothing in common. Theorists therefore explain crime as though it had no connection to such problems as accidents, teenage pregnancy, or unemployment. And of course all this is supported by public policies that target specific problems without regard to the connections among them (e.g., the current war on drugs).

A science that cannot deal with the basic facts it produces would normally be said to face a paradigm crisis. Indeed, when seen in this light, positivism turns out to be something it has pretended from the beginning not to be, *a substantive perspective* as well as a method of knowing. As a substantive perspective, positivism can make no claims to special privilege because of its historic connection to the methods of science. On the contrary, once understood as a substantive perspective, positive theory must be treated like other theories and compared with them in terms of explanatory power and consistency with empirical evidence.

4. *The principle of multiple effects.* Substantive positivism creates distinctions among phenomena in order to produce the homogeneity thought to be prerequisite to explanation. If criminal acts appear diverse, substantive positivism divides them into person and property crimes. If these crimes are too heterogeneous, one focuses more narrowly on, say, white-collar crimes, and so on until the topic is embezzlement among bank tellers in a small city (with the usual caveat that the results may not be generalizable to bank tellers in medium-sized cities). Having divided the world into myriad discrete acts, substantive positivism suggests that the number of explanations must be consistent with the number of discrete acts. If events can be distinguished, so too can their explanations. In fact, if events can be distinguished, there must certainly be a tendency for them to be mutually exclusive—after all, they take time and energy (especially in positivistic theory). Clearly if this is so, individuals must specialize in particular offenses and different people must engage in different offenses, and we are immediately led to multiple causation, a solution equal in complexity to the dependent variable. The only problem with this solution is that it begs the issue, treating as discrete, independent events acts that are, as described above, conceptually identical and empirically strongly correlated with one another.

Nowhere is this clearer than in the drug-crime connection. Despite a considerable body of evidence to the contrary, positivism continues to suggest that drug use and crime (1) are causally linked (Blumstein et al. 1986); (2) are mutually exclusive (e.g., Merton 1938; Cloward and Ohlin 1960); or (3) that they are simply manifestations of learning processes operating in common environments (Akers 1977). The contrary evidence says that drug use and other deviant acts are likely to be found together in the same people because they are manifestations of a single latent trait. In our view, this evidence falsifies theories that deny it.

5. Causal theories must be motivational theories. Substantive positivism confuses motivation and causation, assuming that a complete explanation identifies the motives that cause particular acts. Thus, substantive positivism automatically finds unsatisfactory accounts of the motivation to crime that assume it is given in human nature and the nature of criminal acts. Because in substantive positivism the motive *is* the explanation, the statement "I rob banks because that's where the money is" is seen as incomplete, shallow, and insufficiently rich in detail to serve as an adequate account of the motivation for bank robbery. In substantive positivism, an adequate explanation invokes an indirect, complex, strong, and nonobvious motive for behavioral events (thus the disdain for "trivial" phenomena). In positivism, the motive is also only indirectly connected to the behavior it explains (i.e., bank robbery provides thrills, status, or display of power; drug use provides escape, status, peer approval; rape provides revenge, control, power) because a motive directly connected to the behavior (e.g., money, a high, sex) would imply choice. In restraint theories, direct motives are unproblematic, and the availability of a target is itself a cause of crime. This issue is easily resolved by straightforward evidence: Individual offenders commit every kind of crime; they are easily dissuaded from any one of them; the invocation of strong, specific motives for criminal acts is thus inconsistent with the evidence.

Substantive positivism is attracted to phenomena whose complexity corresponds to the complexity of its explanatory apparatus. Because its analyses tend to be elaborate, complex, or sophisticated (at least statistically), there is a tendency to impute sophistication to the actor or to the act itself. For example, it appears that variation in auto theft rates by type of vehicle (e.g., Cameros, Oldsmobile station wagons) are largely a function of the number of such vehicles on the road, the age of their owners, and their relative attractiveness to young males. Positivistic explanations focus nonetheless on the satisfactions derived from particular vehicles and on the peculiar needs they satisfy. While such explanations may be more satisfying within the perspective of substantive positivism, they are not as good at predicting auto theft rates as explanations based on opportunity or obvious motives.

Conclusions

The restraint or choice perspective seems to us to qualify as a theory of crime and a theory of the tendency to commit crime. Yet it is on all points contradicted by the tenets of substantive positivism. How, one might ask, did it come to pass that a theory of human behavior could be rejected a priori on the grounds that it is contrary to established scientific principles. Presumably, the purpose of science is to arbitrate disputes among theories of behavior, not to be a theory of behavior.

The influence of substantive positivism on the study of behavior is so far-reaching that opposition to it is often dismissed as antiscientific negativism. We believe automatic acceptance of "positivism" and automatic rejection of its critics is equally unjustified. In our view, science involves basic assumptions about nature (e.g., cause and effect, reproducibility of results) and agreed-upon rules of procedure (e.g., public statement of methods), but does not fix the concepts to be used in explanations of phenomena, and guarantees success to none of its constituent disciplines. As noted, the positivistic disciplines require more than this.

Disciplinary positivism resists general conceptual schemes or theories. Its tendency is to proliferate concepts without concern for their distinctiveness or significance. This tendency extends to the invention of statistical categories whose substantive content, if any, must be supplied by subsequent research. Thus, for example, much recent work in criminology divides the offender population into frequent and infrequent offenders (Blumstein et al. 1986), even though it has not been established that the causes of crime differ between these categories (Gottfredson and Hirschi 1988). More commonly, of course, offenders are separated on the grounds that their offenses have different names, or differ in seriousness (Wilson and Herrnstein 1985). This tendency eventually produces endless distinctions among behavioral categories and generates apparent interest in the countless permutations and combinations of units and their properties.

One way to produce *apparent* order out of such chaos is to divide the conceptual domain among "disciplines," giving each primary responsibility for the variables within its area. But disciplinary organization does not solve the problem. On the contrary, by tending to grant proprietary rights to concepts, it creates petty jealousies and territorial disputes that restrict the growth and sharing of knowledge.

A way to produce true order out of such conceptual chaos is to focus on acts or behaviors of interest and ask what they might have in common. If commonality is discerned, this may lead to conclusions about causal mechanisms rather different from those generated by adherence to the notion that each item of behavior has unique causes to be found within the realm of the discipline owning it. In our view, examination of the acts that cluster together around crime and deviance reveals that they share a common structure and therefore the possibility of a common causation. In all cases, the behavior produces immediate, short-term pleasure or benefit to the actor; in all cases, the behavior tends to entail long-term cost. As Bentham long ago (1789) pointed out, these costs may be physical, political, religious, or social, but they are costs nonetheless, and those pursuing such behavior must weigh current benefits against them. It follows that those pursuing such behaviors may therefore tend to have something in common, something that causes them to choose short-term advantage over long-term cost (see also Piliavin et al. 1986).

Many social scientists who regard themselves as scientists reject a priori the idea that consequences can cause human behavior. They presumably do so because they find "restraint" incompatible with or in fact contrary to the scientific notion of determinism. In psychology, this position surfaces in the conclusion that the principles of operant conditioning (according to which behavior is determined by its consequences) contradict the position of positivistic science that causes must precede their effects. In biology, it is encountered in the conclusion that the principles of evolution (according to which selection of traits is affected by their survival value) contradict the position of positivistic science according to which causes must precede their effects. In sociology, antirestraint sentiment favors the argument that to be fully social a theory must account for behavior without resort to decision-making properties of individuals or to a theory of action (Coleman 1986).

Obviously, the mechanism of causation is fair game for all disciplines and cannot reasonably be claimed to be the sole province of any of them. For example, family socialization practices may produce variation in concern for the costs of short-term hedonistic behavior (Hirschi 1969). By the same token, biological differences in physical size could influence the costs of deviant behavior, thus affecting the probability that the actor will choose to engage in it. It is important to stress that the disciplinary source of such causes is irrelevant to the explanatory scheme and that it does not distinguish between restraint theories and theories that rely on scientific notions of causal analysis. Indeed, the methods of positivism are fully applicable to such theories. All that is missing is the misguided notion that science favors particular substantive theories of human behavior and the notion that specific causes belong to specific disciplines.

Notes

1. In our terminology, methodological positivism, which we accept, was thus turned into substantive positivism—the view that "science" favors or even requires particular theories or modes of explanation. The discussion here assumes that the social and behavioral sciences were initially successful in eradicating the preconceptions of earlier theories, and that their eventual opposition to restraint theories was a by-product of widely accepted, if misunderstood, methodological principles. An equally plausible if less charitable history argues that modern theories were constructed in explicit opposition to restraint theories, and methodological principles were misconstrued in the service of this enterprise (see Hirschi 1986; Gottfredson and Hirschi 1987, chap. 1).

2. The tendency to examine concrete variables is not required by the logic of biological causation. It appears to be a consequence of faulty conceptualization and misinterpretation of research findings. Individual differences in the general tendency to delay gratification may well be, in part, inherited. There is thus no necessary inconsistency between biology and restraint theory. However, biological positivists do not approach the problem in this way. Instead, as indicated, they frequently assert inheritance of specific criminal acts: "Due to different transmission patterns for crimes against persons and crimes against property [three references, including Mednick et al. 1984], it is important to distinguish between violent offenses and nonviolent property offenses (Baker et al. 1989:359):

   > This suggests that different patterns of ... criminal offenses have distinct genetic determination.... The data presented here indicate that the etiologies of prepubertal delinquency, adult property crime, adult crime against persons, and alcoholism are relatively distinct qualitatively from one another in terms of their genetic antecedents. (Cloninger and Gottesman 1987:96,105)

   (The discussion here suggests that the issue is largely interpretation of otherwise noncontroversial results of biological research. Actually, we believe that the scientific adequacy of this research is also problematic; see Gottfredson and Hirschi 1990: chap. 3.)

3. With respect to crime, the major presupposition of psychology appears to be the apparently nonproblematic notion that crime is learned behavior. The fact of the matter is that the efficiencies of crime are so obvious that they are not learned in any meaningful sense of the term.

References

Akers, Ronald K. 1977. *Deviant Behavior: A Social Learning Approach.* Belmont, CA: Wadsworth.

Baker, Laura A., Wendy Mack, Terrie E. Moffitt, and Sarnoff Mednick. 1989. "Sex Differences in Property Crimes in a Danish Adoption Cohort." *Behavior Genetics* 19:355-70.

Bentham, Jeremy. [1789] 1970. *An Introduction to the Principles of Morals and Legislation.* London: The Athlone Press.

Blumstein, Alfred, Jacqueline Cohen, Jeffery Roth, and Christy Visher. 1986. *Criminal Careers and "Career Criminals."* Washington, DC: National Academy Press.

Cloninger, C.R., and I.I. Gottesman. 1987. "Genetic and Environmental Factors in Antisocial Behavior Disorders." In *The Causes of Crime: New Biological Approaches,* ed. Sarnoff A. Mednick, Terrie E. Moffitt, and Susan Stack, 92-109. Cambridge: Cambridge University Press.

Cloward, Richard, and Lloyd Ohlin. 1960. *Delinquency and Opportunity.* New York: The Free Press.

Cohen, Lawrence, and Marcus Felson. 1979. "Social Change and Crime Rate Trends: A Routine Activity Approach. *American Sociological Review* 44:588-608.

Coleman, James. 1986. "Social Theory, Social Research, and a Theory of Action. *American Journal of Sociology* 91:1309-35.

Cook, Philip. 1986. "The Demand and Supply of Criminal Opportunities." In *Crime and Justice: An Annual Review of Research,* vol 7, 1-27, ed. Michael Tonry and Norval Morris. Chicago: University of Chicago Press.

Cornish, Derek, and Ronald Clarke. 1986. *The Reasoning Criminal.* New York: Springer-Verlag.

Durkheim, Emile. [1895] 1938. *The Rules of Sociological Method.* Glencoe, IL: The Free Press.

Erlich, Isaac. 1974. "Participation in Illegitimate Activities: An Economic Analysis." In *Essays in the Economics of Crime and Punishment,* ed. Gary Becker and William Landes, 68-134. New York: Columbia University Press.

Eysenck, Hans, and Gisli Gudjonsson. 1989. *The Causes and Cures of Criminality.* New York: Plenum.

Farrington, David. 1973. "Self Reports of Deviant Behavior: Predictive and Stable?" *Journal of Criminal Law and Criminology* 64:99-110.

Ferri, Enrico. 1897. *Criminal Sociology.* New York: Appleton & Co.

Glueck, Sheldon, and Eleanor Glueck. 1950. *Unraveling Juvenile Delinquency.* Cambridge: Harvard University Press.

_____. 1968. *Delinquents and Nondelinquents in Perspective.* Cambridge, MA: Harvard University Press.

Goodwin, Donald. 1977. "Family and Adoption Studies of Alcoholism." In *Biosocial Bases of Criminal Behavior,* ed. Sarnoff Mednick and Karl Christiansen, 143-57. New York: Gardner Press.

Gottfredson, Michael R., and Travis Hirschi. 1987. *Positive Criminology.* Newbury Park, CA: Sage Publications.

_____. 1988. "Science, Public Policy, and the Career Paradigm." *Criminology* 26:37-55.

_____. 1990. *A General Theory of Crime.* Stanford: Stanford University Press.

Greenberg, David F. 1985. "Age, Crime, and Social Explanation." *American Journal of Sociology* 91:1-21.

Hindelang, Michael, Travis Hirschi, and Joseph Weis. 1981. *Measuring Delinquency.* Beverly Hills, CA: Sage.

Hirschi, Travis. 1969. *Causes of Delinquency.* Berkeley: University of California Press.

_____. 1986. "On the Compatibility of Rational Choice and Social Control Theories of Crime." In *The Reasoning Criminal,* ed. Ronald Clarke and Derek Cornish, 105-18. New York: Springer-Verlag.

Hirschi, Travis, and Michael Gottfredson. 1983. "Age and the Explanation of Crime. *American Journal of Sociology* 89:552-84.

Kety, Seymour, David Rosenthal, Paul Wender, and Fini Schulsinger. 1968. "The Types and Prevalence of Mental Illness in the Biological and Adoptive Families of Adopted Schizophrenics." In *The Transmission of Schizophrenia,* ed. David Rosenthal and Seymour Kety, 345-62. Oxford: Pergamon.

Klein, Malcolm. 1984. "Offense Specialization and Versatility among Juveniles." *British Journal of Criminology* 24:185-94.

Kornhauser, Ruth. 1978. *Social Sources of Delinquency.* Chicago: University of Chicago Press.

Loeber, Rolf. 1982. "The Stability of Antisocial and Delinquent Child Behavior: A Review." *Child Development* 53:1431-46.

Matza, David. 1964. *Delinquency and Drift.* New York: Wiley.

Mednick, Sarnoff, William Gabrielli, and Barry Hutchings. 1984. "Genetic Influences in Criminal Convictions: Evidence from an Adoption Cohort." *Science* 224:891-94.

Merton, Robert. 1938. "Social Structure and 'Anomie.'" *American Sociological Review* 3:672-82.

Olweus, Dan. 1979. "Stability of Aggressive Reaction Patterns in Males: A Review." *Psychological Bulletin* 86:852-75.

Osgood, D. Wayne, Lloyd Johnston, Patrick O'Malley, and Jerald Bachman. 1988. "The Generality of Deviance in Late Adolescence and Early Adulthood." *American Sociological Review* 53:81-93.

Parsons, Talcott. 1957. *The Social System.* New York: Macmillan.

Piliavin, Irving, Rosemary Gartner, Craig Thornton, and Ross Matsueda. 1986. "Crime, Deterrence, and Rational Choice." *American Sociological Review* 51:101-19.

Reuter, Peter. 1983. *Disorganized Crime: The Economics of the Visible Hand.* Cambridge, MA: MIT Press.

Robins, Lee. 1966. *Deviant Children Grown Up.* Baltimore: Williams & Wilkins.

Sellin, Thorsten. 1938. *Culture Conflict and Crime.* New York: Social Science Research Council.

_____. 1973. "Enrico Ferri." In *Pioneers in Criminology,* ed. Herman Mannheim, 277-300. Montclair, NJ: Patterson Smith.

Steffensmeier, Darrell, Emilie Allan, Miles Harer, and Cathy Streifel. 1989. "Age and the Distribution of Crime." *American Journal of Sociology* 94:803-31.

Sutherland, Edwin H., and Donald Cressey. 1978. *Principles of Criminology,* 10th ed. Philadelphia: Lippincott.

West, Donald, and David Farrington. 1977. *The Delinquent Way of Life.* London: Heinemann.

Wilson, James Q., and Richard Herrnstein. 1985. *Crime and Human Nature.* New York: Simon and Schuster.

Wolfgang, Marvin, Robert Figlio, and Thorsten Sellin. 1972. *Delinquency in a Birth Cohort.* Chicago: University of Chicago Press.

Contributors

CHESTER L. BRITT is assistant professor in the Department of Sociology at the University of Illinois at Urbana. His research focuses on the sociodemographics of crime, testing the criminal career perspective, and the relationship between drug use and pretrial misconduct among criminal defendants.

MICHAEL S. GARR is associate professor of sociology and health administration at Wilkes University. He is also co-director of the Wilkes University Survey Research Center. His current research examines sobriety checkpoints as a deterrent to drinking and driving and the effects of rituals in different locations on drinking and drinking-related behaviors.

MICHAEL R. GOTTFREDSON is professor of management and policy, law, and psychology, at the University of Arizona. In addition to *A General Theory of Crime* (Stanford, 1990), his books include *Decision Making in Criminal Justice* (with Don Gottfredson, Plenum, 1988), and *Victims of Personal Crime* (with Michael Hindelang and James Garofalo, Ballinger, 1978).

TRAVIS HIRSCHI is Regents Professor and professor of sociology at the University of Arizona. He has served as president of the American Society of Criminology, and has received that society's Edwin H. Sutherland Award. Hirschi's books include *Delinquency Research* (with Hanan Selvin, Free Press, 1967), *Causes of Delinquency* (University of California Press, 1969), and *A General Theory of Crime*.

MARIANNE JUNGER works at the Netherlands Institute for the Study of Criminality and Law Enforcement. She has published in the field of juvenile delinquency and the etiology of crime, victims of crime, fear of crime, the measurement of crime, restitution within the judicial system, selection processes within the judicial system, and crime prevention. Her current research interests include the generality of deviance, correlates of crime, and the relation between crime and accidents.

VICTOR LARRAGOITE is a graduate student in the Department of Sociology at the University of Arizona. His current work centers on the police sting that netted several Arizona legislators (AZSCAM).

JOHN H. LAUB is professor in the College of Criminal Justice at Northeastern University and a visiting scholar at the Murray Research Center of Radcliffe College. His areas of interest include crime and deviance over the life course, juvenile justice, and the history of criminology. His recent publications include *Crime in the Making: Pathways and Turning Points Through Life*, with Robert J. Sampson, Harvard University Press.

ROBERT J. SAMPSON is professor of sociology at the University of Chicago and research associate at the Ogburn-Stouffer Center, NORC. With John Laub he recently completed *Crime in the Making: Pathways and Turning Points Through Life*. He continues his research interests in crime, the life course, and community social disorganization.

LEONORE M. J. SIMON is an assistant professor of criminal justice at Temple University. She practiced criminal law for six years, and presently focuses her research on mental health-criminal justice interactions.

DAVID W. M. SORENSEN is a graduate fellow at the School of Criminal Justice, Rutgers University.

GEORGE C. STRAND, Jr. is a Ph.D. candidate in the Department of Sociology at the State University of New York at Albany. He is interested in rational choice theories of crime, social psychological perspectives on deviance, and a social interactionist approach to coercive actions.

CAROLYN UIHLEIN is a Ph.D. candidate in the Department of Sociology at the University of Arizona. In addition to crime, she is also interested in the study of gender, and is currently involved in research examining the relation between these two areas.

MARY ANN ZAGER is an assistant professor in the College of Criminal Justice at Northeastern University. She is interested in criminology, particularly juvenile delinquency, and in statistics and research methods.

Index

Academic achievement: and accidents, 118; and driving under the influence, 139; and frequency of offending, 203. *See also* Intelligence

Accidents: and age, 118-119, 121, 122; and age of mother, 89; and aggression, 102; and alcohol, 123, 132; bias in literature, 86; as cause of death, 83; common, 83; correlates of, 86; and crime theory, 106; distinguished from crimes, 83; and education of mother, 88; and family factors, 87; and gender, 98, 100, 101, 102, 119; and home environment, 90, 118; and hyperactivity, 95; and mobility, 90; and mother's employment, 89; and parental supervision, 91; and physical acuity, 123; prediction of, 125; as problem behaviors, 81; and psychological problems, 94; and single-parent family, 90; and self-control, 94, 107; and socialization, 91. *See also* Accident proneness, driving under the influence, Motor vehicle accidents

Accident proneness, 84, 113; and academic achievement, 118; and childhood, 118; clinical approach, 115; and crime, 115, 118, 119; defined, 114; and occupation, 119; origin of term, 114-116; and smoking, 119

Acquiescence, 43. *See also* Aggression

Active-passive distinction, 261.

Acts: legal and illegal, 10; serious and trivial, 19

Adult behavior: as crime and deviance, 240.

Age: and accidents, 119, 121, 122; and crime, 51; and frequency of offending, 203; and invariance hypothesis, 12; and offenses analogous to crime, 51; and rape, 169; and versatility, 176-183.

Age invariance hypothesis: implications of, 12-13; and incapacitation, 13; and organized crime, 13; and rehabilitation, 13; rigidity of defense, 20n.1; and variation in age curves, 13

Aggression, 23-43; and accidents, 102; as acquiescence, 29; challenge to control theory, 23; compatibility with causation, 24; convergent validity of, 26; and criminal behavior, 27; in field studies, 34; frustration-aggression hypothesis, 23, 42; inconsistent with versatility, 25; laboratory measures, 27-31; as a latent trait, 41; measured in field studies, 26; and moral outrage, 30; and obedience to authority, 29; operational definitions of, 26; not personality trait, 40; and policy oriented research, 26; as retribution, 29; and social-control 24, 39-41; stability of, 26; and television violence, 35; as unprovoked violence, 28; validity of field measures, 36; and violence, 24. *See also* Self-control

Akers, Ronald, 7-9

Alcohol: and accidents, 123; and driver performance, 132; and driving under the influence, 139; and violence, 224. *See also* Drugs

Alwash, Rafi, 99

Anderson, Craig, 28

Antisocial behavior in children. *See* Childhood misbehavior, Delinquency

Attachment: to parents, 57; to spouse, 244

Attachment to parents: and family size, 65; scale, 157

Attachment to peers: scale, 157

Baker, Laura, 267

Bearing children: as analogous to crime, 66

Beautrais, A., 92, 93

Bentham, Jeremy, 133, 255, 266
Berkowitz, Leonard, 28
Bijur, Polly, 86
Biology: and crime as social behavior, 258; focus on concrete acts, 259; focus on specific crimes, 258; and inheritance of crime, 267; and the restraint perspective, 259
Blake, Judith, 58, 67
Blumstein, Alfred, 173, 177, 193, 211
Britt, Chester, 14, 19
Brown, George, 87, 92
Brown, Roger, 28
Brownmiller, Susan, 160

Career paradigm: and participation and frequency of offending, 115. *See also* Criminal career, Frequency of offending
Caspi, Avshalom, 236
Causation: and aggression, 260; and choice, 259; at level of measurement, 260; and motivation, 264; working definition, 259
Childhood misbehavior: and adult behavior, 235-36; and attachment to spouse, 248; measures of, 239
Child-rearing model, 53-54
Choice theory. *See* General theory, Restraint theory, Self-control
Cloninger, C., 267
Cohen, Jacqueline, 174-75
Coleman, James, 255
Commitment: and ambition, 241
Continuity of behavior. *See* Stability
Costs of crime. *See* Sanctions
Crime: and accidents, 83, 104; costs and benefits, 266; as force and fraud, 255; and human nature, 255; and hyperactivity, 95; as noneconomic activity, 61; prevalence and incidence, 14; and single-parent family, 90; and socialization, 91. *See also* Frequency of offending
Crimes: and analogous acts, 49; distinguished from noncrimes, 49; motives for, 50
Criminal career: and frequency of offending, 194, 199; invalidity of concept, 208; and versatility, 173

Criminals, 49-50
Criticisms: of general theory, 6-8

Delinquency: and accidents, 103; and commitment, 247; and economic dependency, 247; and drugs and alcohol, 149-55; and family factors, 87-88; index of, 77; measures in National Youth Survey, 74
Determinism. *See* Causation
Deviant careers. *See* Stability
DiFranza, J. R., 119
Divorce, 244
Dornbusch, S., 59
Driving under the influence: correlates of, 139; and drugs, 138-39; general theory of, 131-33, 142; prevalence of, 131; psychology of, 132; and risk-taking, 133, 142; and self-control, 131, 135, 140-43; and smoking, 142; and versatility, 143. *See also* Accidents
Drugs, 149-55; and age, 150; and crime, 263; and driving under the influence, 138; and general theory of crime, 149; and violence, 224. *See also* Alcohol
Drunk driving. *See* Driving under the influence
Durkheim, Emile, 253

Economic dependency, 242
Economic status, 61
Economics: as radical environmentalism, 262
Elliott, Delbert, 74. *See also* National Youth Survey
Eron, Leonard, 34-35
Exposure to risk: and accidents, 123. *See also* Opportunity

Family: as advocate for child, 58; and age, 53; child-rearing practices, 256; guarding the home, 57; protection of members, 57-58; and socialization, 53; and stability, 52; and versatility, 52. *See also* Child-rearing model
Family size: and delinquency, 62; and guarding the home, 67; as indicator of self-control, 66; and intelligence, 64; and self-control, 64; and single-

parent family, 63-64; and supervision, 64-65; trends in, 67; and verbal ability, 64-65
Family structure: and crime, 47-48. *See also* Family size, Single-parent family
Farrington, David, 82, 176
Ferri, Enrico, 253
Frequency of offending: correlates of, 203; methodological issues in study of, 195; and self-control, 194. *See also* Career paradigm, Criminal career
Friedman, Debra, 134
Frustration-aggression hypothesis. *See* Aggression
Fuller, E. 84, 94

Gambling: and versatility, 183
Garr, Michael, 11
Gender: and accidents, 119; as challenge to self-control theory, 77; and crime, 71-77; and opportunity, 72-74; as opportunity variable, 73, 77; and self-control, 72-74; and specialization, 184
General theory of crime: and accidents, 119, 126; and driving under the influence, 131-33, 142; and identity of events, 7; and motor vehicle accidents, 119, 126; and rape, 166; source of self-control theory, 1; and victim-offender relationship, 230. *See also* Self-control
Generality: of trait underlying crime, 262
Genetics: and biology, 255
Glueck, Sheldon and Eleanor, 87, 89, 90-91, 237; and child-rearing model, 53; data and sample, 238-39
Gould, L., 143
Greenwood, M., 114

Harrington, D., 118
Hechter, Michael, 134
Herrnstein, Richard, 54-55, 145
Huesmann, Rowell, 27, 35, 235

Immediacy: of benefits of crime, 50-51
Incidence: defined, 14. *See also* Frequency of offending

Intelligence: and time orientation, 61. *See also* Academic achievement

Jessor, Richard, 81
Job stability, 242-43
Johnson, V., 133
Junger, Marianne, 11, 99

Kulik, James, 28
Kurokawa, Minako, 91, 99

Labeling hypothesis: and stability, 249
LaFree, Gary, 161
Langley, John, 95, 102
Larragoite, Victor, 17
Larson, Charles, 87, 91
Larson, J., 119
Latent trait: and career paradigm, 15; as problem behavior, 105; as syndrome, 81
Laub, John, 14, 94
Learning theory: and rape, 162
Loeber, Rolf, 88, 235
Long, Jancis, 250

McFarland, R., 117, 125
McGuire, F., 115
Male to female crime ratios. *See* Gender
Manheimer, Dean, 94
Marcusson, H., 98
Marital discord: and deviant behavior, 235
Matheny, Adam, 87, 90, 93, 94
Mednick, Sarnoff, 258
Merton, Robert, 23, 261
Messerschmidt, J., 160, 161
Milgram, Stanley: obedience experiments, 29; and validity of obedience, 42
Military service: and criminal behavior, 240; and stability of delinquency, 246-47
Mother's employment: and accidents, 89; and crime, 89
Motivation, 264
Motor vehicle accidents: and age, 121-22; causes of, 113, 132; and driver error, 120; and exposure, 123; and gender, 114; and general theory of crime, 119; and self-control, 121; and

stability, 125. *See also* Accidents, Accident proneness

National Crime Survey: and measurement of rape, 168
National Health Examination Survey: and effects of family structure, 59-60
National Youth Survey, 74, 149
Natural sanctions, 3; and alcohol, 4; and efficiency of self-control, 4; and extinction, 3; as source of norms, 4. *See also* State sanctions
Newbold, E., 114

Occupation: and accidents, 119
Offenders: not driven by need, 61
Offense seriousness, 18; and effort or difficulty, 17; and homicide, 17; and public policy, 19; and punishment, 19; and rape, 17; and strong motives, 17; victim vs. offender point of view, 16
Olweus, Dan, 235
Opportunity, 194; objective, 73; offense specific, 74; measurement of, 73
Oregon Social Learning Center. *See* Patterson, Gerald
Osgood, Wayne, 82, 88, 89, 106

Parent training model. *See* Child rearing model
Parental supervision: and delinquency, 55-56; and indicators of self-control, 55
Parsons, Talcott, 261
Paternoster, Raymond, 195
Patterson, Gerald, 53-54
Pless, Barry, 91, 93
Positivism: and causation, 253; and complexity of nature, 253; and the disciplines, 254; and the idea of crime, 254; and induction, 253; and restraint theory, 254; substantive, 253-54
Prevalence, 14. *See also* Frequency of offending
Problem behavior: defined, 81
Psychology, 267. *See also* Aggression

Race: and accidents, 99, 101; and crime, 102
Rand Survey of Inmates, 219, 221, 232

Rape: and age, 169; extent of, 168; and feminist theory, 159-61; and frustration, 164; and learning theory, 162; logical structure of, 167; masculinity hypothesis, 163; and patriarchy, 159-60; and police, 162; and pornography, 164; and power, 165; and race, 170; regional variation in, 162; and self-control, 159, 166; subcultural deviance theory of, 163
Rapists: characteristics of, 168
Rational choice: and driving under the influence, 133, 134.
Restraint theory: basic approach, 255; and causation, 260; mechanisms, 256; and definition of crime, 257. *See also* General theory of crime, Self-control
Richmond Youth Study, 41, 59
Robins, Lee, 82, 236, 248
Roshier, Bob, 7
Ross, H. Lawrence, 131
Routledge, D., 101
Rutter, M., 104

Sampson, Robert J., 14, 54, 94
Sanctions. *See* Natural sanctions, State sanctions
Science: basic assumptions, 265; as substantive perspective, 263
Seattle Youth Study, 41
Self-control: and accidents, 107, 121, 126; and age effect, 5; and aggression, 52; attitudinal measures of, 72, 76, 78-79; behavioral measures of, 76-78; and career criminal, 5; and conscience, 52; consequences of low, 256; as continuum, 53; and criminality, 52; criticisms of, 5-6; defined, 3; and driving under the influence, 131, 135, 140, 143; and the family, 5; favored by institutions, 53; and frequency of offending, 194; and generality of crime, 249; indicators of, 9, 72; as latent trait, 2; and long -term costs, 53; measured, 75; and opportunity, 5, 71-72, 194; and organized crime, 5; and rape, 159, 166; the theory of, 1, 72; and use of tobacco and alcohol, 10; and versatility, 174, 190; and white collar crime, 5. *See also* General theory of crime

Self-report surveys: and official data, 227; and versatility, 186
Sellin, Thorsten, 257
Sex. *See* Gender
Shaw, L., 125
Sheehy, N., 101
Simon, Leonore, 16
Single-parent family: and academic achievement, 61; as advocate for child, 59; and difficulties in child-rearing, 58-59; and economic disadvantage, 61; and intelligence, 61; and supervision, 60
Smoking: and accidents, 119; and driving under the influence, 142. *See also* Drugs
Social class: and accidents, 96; and crime, 97-98; and sociology, 255
Socialization: as education, 4
Sociology: antirestraint sentiment, 266; crime as social behavior, 257; as radical environmentalism, 262
Sorensen, David, 11, 14
Specialization: and age, 176, 179, 180, 183; in deviant acts, 3; faulty claims for, 177; and gender, 184; and race, 186, 188; rigor of research about, 178; and victim-offender relationship, 231. *See also* Versatility
Stability: and accidents, 125; of criminal behavior, 244-246; of differences, 2, 51; of drug use, 151-52; in Gluecks' data, 248; and positive theory, 261-62; and situational theory, 250; as test-retest reliability, 3
State sanctions: irrelevancy of, 19
Steffensmeier, Darrell, 182
Strain theory, 24. *See also* Aggression
Strand, George, 11
Substantive positivism: defined, 267; and distinctions among offenses and offenders, 265; and explanatory complexity, 264; vs. restraint perspective, 256; and search for homogeneity, 263
Suchman, Edward, 107
Sutherland, Edwin, 257

Tautology: as criticism of general theory, 8; as definitional consistency, 8. *See also* Akers, Ronald

Tedeschi, James, 42
Temper tantrums: and adult criminality, 246; and continuity of behavior, 240
Tillmann, W., 116
Tittle, Charles, 7
Toby, Jackson, 19
Truancy: and accidents, 118

Uihlein, Carolyn, 14
Unemployment: and deviant behavior, 235
Unraveling Juvenile Delinquency. See Glueck, Sheldon and Eleanor

Vaillant, George, 250
Validity: convergent, of aggression, 26, 36-37; criteria of, 36; discriminant, of aggression, 26, 37-39; and laboratory measures of aggression, 34
Versatility: and acts analogous to crime, 50; among children, 82; and control theory, 174, 180; and driving under the influence, 143; and drug use, 153; and internal consistency, 3; of offenders, 2; and positive theory, 261-62; and race, 186, 188; and self-report data, 50, 186; variation among offenders, 12; and victim-offender relationship, 226-228; and violence, 178; and white-collar crime, 12. *See also* Specialization
Victim-offender relationship: defined, 216; prior record, 225; and versatility, 226-231
Violent offenders: and alcohol use, 224; prior records of, 224

Werner, E., 88, 89
White-collar crime: characteristics of, 18
White-collar workers: and self-control, 12
Wicklund, Kristine, 101
Wilson, James Q., 54-55, 144
Wolfgang, Marvin, 175
World War II: as natural experiment, 246

Yeager, Catherine, 103

Zager, Mary Ann, 14
Zylman, R., 124